# THE
# COMMON
# BOND

# THE COMMON BOND

*Maintaining Constancy of Purpose*
*Throughout Your*
*Health Care Organization*

———

## Francis L. Ulschak

Jossey-Bass Publishers • San Francisco

Substantial discounts on bulk quantities of Jossey-Bass books are available to corporations, professional associations, and other organizations. For details and discount information, contact the special sales department at Jossey-Bass Inc., Publishers. (415) 433-1740; Fax (415) 433-0499.

For sales outside the United States, contact Maxwell Macmillan International Publishing Group, 866 Third Avenue, New York, New York 10022.

Manufactured in the United States of America. Nearly all Jossey-Bass books and jackets are printed on recycled paper containing at least 10 percent postconsumer waste, and many are printed with either soy- or vegetable-based ink, which emits fewer volatile organic compounds during the printing process than petroleum-based ink.

Credits are on p. 329.

### Library of Congress Cataloging-in-Publication Data

Ulschak, Francis L., date.
 The common bond : maintaining constancy of purpose throughout your health care organization / Francis L. Ulschak. — 1st ed.
  p.  cm. — (The Jossey-Bass health series)
 Includes bibliographical references and index.
 ISBN 1-55542-614-X (acid-free paper)
 1. Health services administration.  2. Health services administration—Philosophy.  I. Title.  II. Series.
RA971.U39 1994
362.1′1′068—dc20                                                          93-33143
                                                                          CIP

FIRST EDITION
*HB Printing*    10  9  8  7  6  5  4  3  2  1                    *Code 9409*

The
Jossey-Bass
Health Series

# Contents

# Tables, Figures, and Exhibits

# Preface

THE CORE OF ANY health care organization is purpose: What is the purpose of the organization? How does this purpose benefit society? How does it add value to society? Whom does it serve? The answers to these questions vary with the particular organization. Put yourself in the following situations:

- You are a for-profit health care organization. You have investors to please.
- You are a not-for-profit health care organization established as a specialty hospital to serve a particular area.
- You are a health care organization that is academically based. Your role is to be a teaching center as well as a health care provider.
- You are a health care organization oriented toward wellness; your mission is to keep the beds filled by finding new cases earlier.
- You are a health care organization committed to wellness and are trying to find ways to keep people from accessing acute care settings by early identification and management of illness.
- You are . . .

As you move from setting to setting, the core of the organization—its purpose—changes. This book is about creating *constancy of purpose*. Why is this important? Health care organizations live in a sea of complexity. They have multitudes of audiences to respond to. Each brings its own goals and agendas. Without a sense of purpose, health care organizations are like boats without rudders.

Vaill (1989) points out that management preparation in today's world is predicated on the wrong set of assumptions. His point is that most management theories were developed based on a view of organizations as stable systems. Sure, there was some change but, for the most part, the systems remained stable. However, in the past few years, organizations have become increasingly unstable. In fact, they have become downright turbulent. The metaphor that Vaill uses is that of white water rafting. In the past, most organizations functioned like a calm river that had occasional moments of white water. For the most part, they were predictable and stable. There were moments of panic, but following them were long periods of calm. However, in today's world, the opposite is the case. The norm is that of the white water ride. Over the years, I have frequently used the "white water" metaphor in groups of health care professionals and have found the response to be immediate—the crowd identifies with it instantly!

Frequently, it is in the midst of chaos (white water) that new approaches and ways of understanding organizations emerge. For us as health care professionals, the challenge is to learn how to survive and prosper in the midst of the white water and to use the learnings from chaos to guide us toward new structures. Constancy of purpose can be the rudder keeping us on course.

This book argues that constancy of purpose can be achieved by creating an *on-purpose organization* (OPO). An OPO is an organization that has defined and communicated its mission and purpose and that is acting in accordance with them. The concept is simple: all the parts of the organization know their purpose and act on purpose. This model is based on the premise that organizational strength and survival derive from being purposeful.

Building this kind of organization is not easy, however. *The Common Bond* provides helpful guidelines for this task. It is both a road map offering a framework for understanding where you need to go and a toolbox filled with tools that will help you get there.

The goal of health care OPOs is to maximize both their potential and the potential of employees. OPOs bring into alignment organizational work units and individual purpose. They also satisfy certain community needs.

Ultimately, health care organizations are there to serve the community. Since community has both an external and an internal aspect, they serve in two ways. First, health care organizations can help individuals lead healthy and productive lives by giving the community the services and products it demands. When they meet these needs, health care practitioners know that they have contributed to the larger community. This is their *external* role.

The second role is *internal*. In today's world, health care organizations—like other organizations—play a special role in their employees' search for meaning. Organizations have become communities akin to the neighborhoods of the past. A century ago, a community consisted of friends and family living in immediate proximity. It provided a structure around which organizations and families worked and lived. Since then, much of the traditional neighborhood has broken down. Today's health care organizations provide a partial substitute for those earlier kinds of communities. The employee of today is looking for more than economic security from the organization. The workplace is a meeting ground where friendships are established. Reisman (1979) clearly articulates the types of friendships available. The workplace is also a place to find fulfillment—personal meaning. Moore (1992) suggests that the workplace has a vital impact on an individual's sense of "soul."

This book is ultimately about meaning—meaning for individuals, for work units, and for the organization. The on-purpose health care organization strives to harmonize employees' sense of purpose and meaning with that of the work unit and the organization. The result of this merger is an energized organization and dedicated and productive employees.

## The Condition of Health Care

The purpose of this section is to discuss where health care is moving in the next few years. Some of the key issues that I find important are:

- Rising costs
- Changing reimbursements
- Changing environments
- Inability of health care organizations to meet health care needs
- Public dissatisfaction with health care
- Shortages of professionals

- Ethics in decision making
- Insurance coverage
- Health care reform

The list is long and by no means inclusive. However, while useful to a degree, it does not answer the question What do we need to be doing? One of the best studies that does get us to one answer is a project entitled *Bridging the Leadership Gap* (Healthcare Forum, 1992, p.48ff) produced by the Healthcare Forum, the Institute for Alternative Futures, Health Forecasting Group, and the Geo Group. It involves research on health care leadership and what is needed for health care leadership to survive in the year 2000. A survey was sent out to over twenty-five hundred opinion leaders in the health care industry. Four hundred responses were received. The survey involved two basic questions: What will twenty-first century health care look like? and What competencies are needed for twenty-first century health care?

To get at the question of what twenty-first century health care will look like, three scenarios were developed, and the participants in the study were asked to discuss their responses to those scenarios and to the probability of their coming to fruition. Following are the scenarios.

*Scenario 1: Continued growth.* Nothing much has changed. Health care is doing business as usual, and growth continues to be very rapid. Health care grows to consume 12 percent of the GNP.

*Scenario 2: Hard times and government leadership.* A frugal approach is taken to health care. The government institutes a health care reform plan. Services are rationed. Government takes an active role.

*Scenario 3: The new civilization.* The health care paradigm is shifted. There are dramatic changes in science, technology, and society. Health care reform takes an active role in building a stronger community and society.

The respondents to the scenarios said that the most likely scenario is "Hard Times and Government Leadership," but the preferred scenario is "The New Civilization." The challenge, then, for health care leaders is how to create the preferred future. One starting place is a shift in health care paradigms. Three paradigm shifts were identified. The first is "globalization." Globalization involves the following shifts:

- From business planning to a shared vision
- From minimizing risks to mastering change
- From repairing body parts to redefining health care
- From maximum short-term profits to serving public and community
- From linear learning to systems thinking
- From business boundaries to a global approach
- From homogeneous culture to managing diversity

The second paradigm shift is "empowerment of health care workers." Empowerment involves the following:

- From technology as a tool to technology as a pathway to learning
- From protecting self-interest to continuous quality improvement
- From individual learning to team learning
- From "they" approach to "we" approach
- From managing hierarchically to managing cross functionally

- From incentive-based performance to the fostering of enrollment
- From marketing technique to managed customer relations

The third and last paradigm shift is "orchestration of technology." Orchestration of technology involves the following:

- From invasive medical technology to noninvasive therapies
- From capital budgeting for technology to strategic technology assessment
- From maximizing existing technology to building information capacity
- From employing tech specialists to user-friendly applications

These three paradigm shifts need to happen for health care to prepare itself for the next century. The OPO model provides an integrated framework for health care leaders to make the move toward that desired future.

## Merits of This Book

This book makes two major contributions. First, the model it outlines provides a road map for building and maintaining a health care organization that is

- Purposeful
- Purpose centered
- Purpose driven

The model is the result of my years of experience in health care organizations and is based on extensive familiarity with the

organizational development and organizational behavior literature. It is a practical model for viewing organizational behavior
that combines process and results. Resource A (at the back of
the book) describes how the model has been developed.

Second, the book offers practical tools for building an OPO.
In the pages ahead, I discuss concrete methods of building and
maintaining constancy of purpose in an organization. This approach provides a solid foundation for developing an OPO. Today's health care organizations need to be resilient; they must
be able not only to survive but also to grow in times that are
tough. The measures outlined in this book will help you and
your organization meet these challenges.

## Audience

The intended audience for this book includes health care executives, physicians, administrators, board members, and other
health care professionals. Administrators and executives will
find the book useful in making decisions regarding the organization and the strategic directions it needs to be taking. It will
provide senior management with tools for building and maintaining an OPO. Physicians moving into administrative roles
and taking on administrative functions will find the following
chapters helpful in understanding how to be more effective at
those tasks. Directors and managers will find the book a good
resource as they work with their specific departments and areas
of responsibility. It has obvious implications for team building
within departments and between departments. And, most important, it has implications for keeping employees focused and
empowered. Physicians will find it a practical and useful tool
to better understand what is happening in their health care

organizations and how to influence those organizations. In short, the book is practical and useful for those who have the responsibility for running successful health care organizations.

It can meet the needs of others as well. For human resource professionals, this book provides a model for viewing policies and procedures, recruitment and selection practices, employee benefits, and so on. Training and education specialists will also find the model useful, since it provides a core around which most training interventions can be built. Internal consultants can draw on the model in working with clients within the organizational environment. Another target audience is the academic world: public health schools, nursing schools, medical schools, and so on.

## Overview of the Contents

The first four chapters discuss the OPO model in detail. Chapter One provides an overview of the model and its implications, and then the next three chapters apply the model to the organization, work unit, and individual, respectively.

Chapter Two focuses on the organization. This chapter also looks at organizational culture as the context in which the OPO exists.

Chapter Three applies the OPO to the work unit. The work unit is defined as a team of people working together to get a set of tasks done. A work unit may be a department or it may be a component of a department.

Chapter Four takes the OPO one step further—to the individual level. The individual is the basic building block of the organization. This chapter is concerned with how the individual's sense of purpose and mission interfaces with the work unit and the organization.

The last four chapters focus on the support systems an OPO needs in order to survive. Chapter Five discusses leadership. Leadership drives the OPO by making OPO behaviors and actions the norm. Without appropriate leadership, an OPO cannot flourish.

Chapter Six is about conflict. Conflict is a given in any organization, and it is certainly present in the OPO. The chapter provides a model for viewing and responding to conflict in the OPO.

Chapter Seven discusses change management. There is probably no one in health care today who does not feel the impact of change. This chapter looks at change management and suggests ways to more effectively manage change in the health care environment.

Chapter Eight provides a model for problem solving. The high degree of change in the health care field generates conflict. This creates a need for problem-solving tools.

Finally, I have included three resources at the end of the book. Resource A traces the development of the OPO model and provides a short sketch of theories of organizational behavior. Resource B is an OPO toolkit; it contains workbook exercises that will help you apply the OPO model to your own organization, work unit, and individual situation. Resource C is a workbook that can be used in the problem-solving process.

## The Quest

There is one final image I leave you with. The image is that of a quest. The quest for the on-purpose organization is similar to the quest for the Holy Grail, in which Parsifal, a young man, searches and searches for the chalice of the Last Supper in order to heal the wounded king and restore his blighted kingdom. In the story, Parsifal is in the presence of the Grail at a feast but does not recognize it. He fails to ask the proper question that would redeem the kingdom. We go through a constant searching process in health care organizations. The Holy Grail is that which will take care of the organizational problems. In our quest for the ultimate solution, we fail to recognize that we are in the presence of the Grail and all we need to do is to ask the right questions. As in the original search for the Holy Grail, the quest for one right answer is elusive. Building an on-purpose organization is an ongoing quest. And some organizations have come close to the goal. This book is a map of how we might come closer in our search.

## Acknowledgments

Many individuals have influenced the writing of this book. Some have made more direct contributions. This work is greatly indebted to the contributions of Sharon SnowAntle. She has provided me with much support and encouragement in this project. Many of the themes of the book began to come together in the joint workshops and writing projects we have done. Others offered useful feedback on earlier drafts. M. Brandy Melton, Helen Harte, and Judith Pins are three examples.

Others have provided indirect support. Nicholas Porter is one such individual. He gave me opportunities to meet with others and discuss ideas and concepts in the book. John Jones continues to challenge my thinking and provide me with new ways to think about organizations and teams. Another person who has committed a significant amount of time is Cody Northrup, my administrative assistant. She did a great deal of work editing and typing the manuscript early on. Others too numerous to mention furnished assistance as well.

As is the case with all book projects, choices had to be made about how time was spent. That means there have been times that Michael, Heather, Summer, and Glennys did not see much of me. They deserve a special note of thanks.

Finally, this book has a special dedication. It is dedicated to Gustave Rath. He introduced me to systems theories, onion skin models, and organizational development, and he instilled in me a basic love of learning and teaching. He also introduced me to the concept of lifelong learning. He emphasized that getting a doctorate was not an end in itself but was a key to getting into organizations that would allow for lifelong learning. Gus, you could not have been more right.

*Brandon, Florida*                                    Francis L. Ulschak
*January 1994*

# The Author

FRANCIS L. ULSCHAK is a principal with the health care consulting firm of Ulschak/SnowAntle and Associates. Formerly, he
was vice president for organizational development at the H. Lee
Moffitt Cancer Center & Research Institute in Tampa, Florida.
He received his B.S. degree (1966) in education and mathematics
from Dickinson State College, his M.Div. degree (1970) from
Garrett Theological Seminary, his Ph.D. degree (1975) in organizational development from Northwestern University, and his
M.H.R.D. degree (1982) in organizational development and small
group process from University Associates.

Ulschak has worked extensively in the area of training and
development in health care organizations. His major area of
interest is team development and organizational development.
He received the American Society for Healthcare Education
and Training's Distinguished Service Award in 1989 and the
Distinguished Achievement Award in 1986. Ulschak's other
books include *Small Group Problem Solving: An Aid to Organizational Effectiveness* (1981, with L. Nathanson & P. Gillan),
*Human Resource Development: The Theory and Practice of Needs
Assessment* (1983), *Creating the Future of Health Care Education
and Training* (1988), *Team Building in the Operating Room* (1989,

with J. Pins), *Consultation Skills for Health Care Professionals* (1990, with S. SnowAntle), and *Leavers and Stayers: A Guide for Health Care Executives in Managing Turnover* (1992, with S. SnowAntle).

# THE
# COMMON
# BOND

CHAPTER ONE

# The On-Purpose Organization

The essence of an organization is its purpose. Without the organizing force of purpose, there is no organization, there are merely people and things in random arrangement. The integrity of an organization, therefore, lies in the extent to which it operates "on purpose." With full integrity, an organization acts with total commitment, precisely toward its purpose. With decreasing integrity, actions are off-purpose, nonsupportive, or even destructive of progress.

—James Farr of Farr
Associates, Greensboro,
North Carolina

IMAGINE TWO ORGANIZATIONS. The first—an off-purpose organization—is represented in Figure 1.1. The diagram shows the confusion of the organization. The individuals and teams represented by the arrows are moving in many different directions, and some are actually going contrary to the organization. The impact is a little bit like trying to herd cats—it is next to impossible! The result is confusion, chaos, and a waste of the organization's resources, which are not being used effectively.

*Think for a moment about organizations you know. Picture an off-purpose organization you have known. What is working in that*

1

Figure 1.1. Off-Purpose Organization.

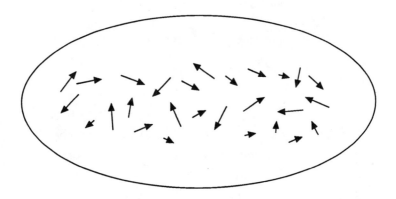

*type of organization like? What is the impact on work units? On individuals? How does the larger community perceive the organization?*

A friend once asked me about the advantages of the off-purpose organization. Initially, I was taken aback by the question. But his point was simple: since there are many examples of them around, they must have some advantages. We came up with several points:

1. There is little or no accountability. That means no one can be blamed for problems. To a degree, this means freedom.
2. The second point follows from the first. Since individuals and teams do not have to worry about accountability, they just do what they want to do. Chaos provides an opportunity to drift.
3. Developing and maintaining an on-purpose organization takes determination, time, and energy. Running an off-purpose organization is less demanding.

As an alternative, consider the on-purpose organization (OPO) represented in Figure 1.2. While perfect alignment does not exist, individuals and teams are moving in the same general direction. The force of their effort is felt, and the organization's resources are more effectively aligned. This organization has constancy of purpose.

*Think of an OPO you have been part of. What was it like for you? What was the impact on work units? On individuals? How was the organization perceived in the community?*

OPOs do have disadvantages. Some have a high degree of conflict. Once people join forces, they can fight battles with extra intensity. Thus, a lack of conflict would not be a reason for choosing an OPO. Probably the single most important advantage of an OPO is this: It gets the results the organization is after in the most cost-effective way, and it is also a dynamic, alive organization. It is a learning organization as well (Senge,

Figure 1.2. On-Purpose Organization.

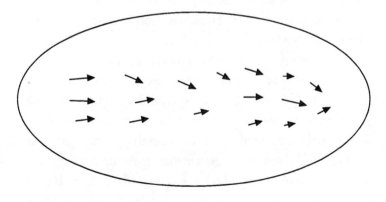

1990). Instead of moving blindly along the road, it moves intentionally. It is fun to work within and even more fun to lead.

By now it should be clear that I believe the primary responsibility of senior management in today's health care organizations is to keep the organization on purpose—that is, focused on the direction that it needs to be going in. As Farr indicates in the opening quotation, this is a question of organizational integrity. It involves more than simply telling the "troops" what the direction is and what we are doing to get there. It involves enrolling the employees in that purpose. It entails communication that goes beyond the simple "Here is what we are about . . . " to helping employees understand how it is that they contribute to that purpose. It begins with defining purpose in a way that it becomes the "plumb line" during employee recruitment and continues through to the decisions of who gets rewarded and who does not (and who gets fired). The job description for the CEO has only one line—build an on-purpose organization.

One useful metaphor comes from the experience of building a home. I began the project as an amateur carpenter. However, with the guidance and assistance of a close friend, I ended the project with a wonderful home and more wisdom. One of my reflections arising from that project concerns the variety of nails used. A multitude of nails went into building the house, each nail with a special purpose. The nails that went into the skeleton structure of the $2 \times 6$'s were big and long. These were the twenty-pound nails that served the purpose of keeping the core structure together. Next there were the framing nails that were used to put the exterior cedar panels on. These were not as large as the structural nails, yet it was their number and the way they held the $2 \times 6$'s together that made them special and added strength to the building. It was only when the nails were

4

in place that we breathed a sigh of relief that we no longer needed to be concerned about the structure's caving in. Then there were the shingle nails. These were short, fat, galvanized nails. They had a specific role, too—to keep the shingles from coming off of the roof. Finally, we can talk about the finishing nails, which were small and almost invisible. Though small, they served the vital purpose of maintaining the beauty of the room by keeping the trim in place.

What does all of this mean? When we think of the organization in which we live and work, we need a variety of employees doing their part to keep the organization together. We need them all contributing to the overall purpose of the organization. If we lose sight of that, or, if we use individuals inappropriately, we do not have the same strength. Each individual brings a specific strength to the organization that contributes to keeping the organization together.

Think for a moment about a time when you felt you were not used appropriately by the organization. How did that impact your work and the work of your work unit? When I ask individuals these questions, we quickly agree with the nail analogy—the employee is the most vital resource.

The OPO is dependent on one major resource to keep its integrity. That one resource is the human resource. It is the human resource that ultimately solves the organizational problems and creates breakthroughs. It is the human resource that creates a resilient, learning organization.

## Managing Human Capital

The premise underlying this book is simple: the key to effective organizations is the management of human capital—that is, the effective use of the employees within the organization to do the organization's work. In his insightful book on human capital, Carnevale (1983, p. 51) states that "the long view of economic history teaches us that people are the master economic resource. They are the master resource because they use their acquired skills and abilities as the agents that combine tangible elements and intangible ideas to make machinery and usable goods and services. In spite of that fact, there is a great temptation for employers to ignore the long term value of human investment. This is especially true when investment capital is short and unemployment lines are long. . . . In the short term, individual employers are faced with the prospect of losing their investment in people. Employees are mobile, machinery is not."

People are mobile, machinery is not. That is a critical point for us in health care. Human resources will be the source of solutions to both current and future health care problems.

Carnevale notes that, with the exception of human capital, the traditional forms of capital have run their course. He points to the tendency to waste anything that seems abundant. At the moment, people seem to be abundant, while machinery, financial capital, and natural resources are scarce. His major points are the following:

1. Human resources are the master economic resource. While people are apt to be the source of problems, they also provide the solutions to them. People are the ultimate problem solvers. If a new technology is needed, human beings use the existing technology to create the new technology. It is the human resources of today that will be solving the problems of tomorrow.

2. Educated, healthy, trained, and spirited people are the ultimate source of economic growth. Think about that for your organization. Something happens when people know what to do and how to do it and are excited about it. The Total Quality Management approach that permeates much of our industry today is focused on continuous quality improvement; the basis for the continuous improvement is an educated, trained, and spirited workforce.

3. Human resources are unlimited—they guarantee there are no permanent limits to economic growth. The key is that we have not reached the limits of our human potential. We have much ground yet to uncover—if, in fact, we will ever reach our full potential.

4. People, not machines, are the wellspring of productivity. Think about our experience with computers. People are constantly coming up with the questions that push the technology to a new level. People are developing software to create new applications. And people are using the technology to make improvements in many areas of society.

5. In the future, workers, not natural resources, will be scarce. Within health care organizations, this has been discussed for some time. Workers are becoming a scarce commodity.

6. But the historical dominance of the human factor in economic growth and productivity will persist and grow.

Carnevale's major point is that human resources are the key to economic growth and productivity. Translated for us in health care, the message is that human resources will meet the challenges that face us in the future. Human resources will come up with the edge allowing one health care organization to survive and grow, while another will not. Health care organizations will need to be rich in human capital.

*Take a moment and ask yourself whether you agree with Carnevale's premise that human resources are the master economic resource. What are the key implications that you see for health care organizations?*

The concept of human capital has special importance for the health care professional for several reasons. First, health care organizations are labor intensive. Think about your organization for a moment. There are simply a lot of people in that organization. Nurses provide the primary care to patients. Doctors work with the health care professional staff to arrive at quality patient care outcomes. The admissions clerk takes information from an inpatient or outpatient. And the list goes on. While we often think of health care organizations as high tech, they are also high-touch (people-intensive) organizations.

Second, health care organizations are composed of highly trained professionals who have strong professional identities. The professional tie may be stronger than the organizational tie. We frequently describe health care organizations as consisting of a multitude of fiefdoms—like medieval estates jealously guarded by their lords. If you walk into a lab area, there are unique ways of doing things, and you are certain you have just walked into one kind of fiefdom. One of the ultimate fiefdoms is the operating room, which has its own dress, language, and very secure area—"Only Authorized Persons May Enter." Administrators occupy another fiefdom.

One fiefdom has significantly more ability to impact the other fiefdoms. A unique characteristic of health care organizations is the relationship of the physician to others in the organization. Ultimately, in acute care, the physician is the person who brings in the "customer"—that is, the patient. All the other professionals involved are dependent on the physician to do this. This creates a special relationship with regard to organizational behavior.

The point: health care organizations are composed of a variety of highly technical professionals who require significant training and licensing before they are allowed to practice. In developing those professional identities, they take on special ways of doing things, different languages, and so on. That can create special difficulties for building an OPO.

Third, health care organizations require interdependence if quality patient care is to be the outcome. The various highly trained professionals are dependent on one another to get the work of the health care organization done. Think about this for a moment. The whole health care team has to work together to achieve the desired outcomes. Admissions needs to have the appropriate admissions. Nursing has to be ready to provide the care the patient requires. Radiologists have to provide physicians with accurate information. The laboratory personnel need to obtain the correct test results in a timely way. Environmental services are there to keep the physical facility clean. And then there is billing and how the business office manages the patient bill. One study reported that patients see an average of more than forty professionals over the course of a hospital stay. No wonder having a common understanding of purpose is vital. It all boils down to working together to produce the quality outcome.

Fourth, health care organizations are human value organizations. They strike at the core of the human instinct for survival. The essence of health care is to promote longevity and quality of life. Remember A. Maslow (1954) and the hierarchy of needs? The fundamental need is survival. The health care organization deals with this need. Where else do you voluntarily walk into an office, take off your clothes, and let another person poke your body? Where else (other than in prison) do you have your clothes changed, lose control over what is happening to you, and end up highly dependent on others? Health care organizations see all of life—and death. Health care organizations deal with the privacy and integrity of the human body.

What is the primary lesson of these reflections on human capital? We need to develop strategies that will enhance the human capital for which we are responsible. The OPO model allows us to do exactly that.

## The OPO Model

An OPO is an organization in which there is horizontal and vertical agreement as to why the organization exists, as to its mission and purpose, and as to how each employee contributes to that mission and purpose. What do we see as we walk through an OPO? We see people who know what the organization is about. And they share its sense of purpose. They know what their role is in the organization and how that role dovetails with those of others. When asked how they are doing, they are quick to reply, since they get regular feedback about their performance. And the rewards they receive are based on what they are doing to keep the organization on target. In the midst of a results-oriented organization, they also have a sense of contribution and accomplishment. What they do matters and adds to the value of the organization. They know it and the organization knows it. And that makes work exciting!

An OPO gets results. The results allow the organization to survive and grow. That means that the results are seen on the bottom line, in the behavior of top management, and in the organizational culture. In the following pages, my goal is to demonstrate how the OPO model is useful for health care management professionals attempting to stay afloat—and to prosper—in today's world.

According to the OPO model, the organization, work units, and individual employees are aligned (Figure 1.3). As Figure

Figure 1.3. OPO Model.

1.3 shows, an OPO has four main components—purpose, roles, feedback, and commitment. The organization also rests on four pillars—truth telling, choice, regard, and renewal. In the next two sections, I discuss these components and pillars in detail.

*Four Components of the OPO*

The components of an OPO contribute its essential core.

*Purpose.* The starting point of the OPO model is the idea of purpose. The dictionary definition of purpose has to do with something one intends to get or do. "Purposeful" is having a purpose that is full of meaning. As Marks (1989, p. 60) says, "At the heart of living with vision is purpose. Purpose is what compels us to take a stand, to act with such conviction that we may surprise ourselves, and ultimately it is what fulfills us. We live from purpose at times, without even knowing it. Without purpose, life is at best incomplete, at worst, futile. Our sense of purpose is what connects us to ourselves and to all life."

Purpose defines the direction we take. Purpose is what gives meaning to what we are about. With a sense of purpose, all things are possible. Without a sense of purpose, we wander all over the landscape. And without purpose, we have no sense of accomplishment. Being without purpose is like being in a boat without a rudder—it does not matter which way the wind is blowing or where you want to go; you will go wherever the tide takes you.

*Think for a moment about your organization. When you think of the concept of being on purpose, where would you rank your organization on a ten-point scale?*

12

| 1 | 2 | 3 | 4 | 5 | 6 | 7 | 8 | 9 | 10 |
|---|---|---|---|---|---|---|---|---|---|
| Low | | | | | | | | | High |

*What would be the reason for your choice?*

Pascarella and Frohman (1989) provide another view of purpose. They introduce the concept of the *purpose-driven organization*, arguing that this type of organization unleashes the power of direction and commitment. Their basic message is that the purpose-driven organization uses purpose as the core around which the rest of the organization's behavior revolves. Like the on-purpose organization, the purpose-driven organization uses the purpose as the standard against which all else is measured.

Another useful concept is that of the *purpose-full organization*. In this kind of organization, every nook and cranny is filled with purpose. If you were to ask individuals within the organization what its purpose is, they would be able to tell you immediately. Purpose is seen in the symbols and the written communications of the organization. The organizational behavior is congruent with its statement of purpose. Strategic business decisions are made based on purpose.

A number of ideas cluster around purpose: values, vision, mission, and goals and objectives. Values are the things that really matter to us. It may be the mobility that a job brings. It may be a sense of contribution that comes from doing a job. It may be family. Purpose only makes sense when it is consistent with our core values.

Purpose is the ground for the next step: vision. Vision is where we want to be at some future time. It is the desired future of the organization. Vision says, "In an ideal world, here is what we would be doing, how we would be doing it, and why."

Mission is next. Mission is defined by the broad goals of the organization. Mission typically has purpose molded into it, but it focuses on what the business is and who the customers are.

How do we bring about the mission that supports our vision and purpose? Here is where goals and objectives come into play. Goals and objectives become the way the mission is supported and the vision and purpose are lived out.

What does a sense of purpose do for the organization? So far, the discussion has been quite general. Jones and Becker (n.d.) identify the following as some of the key benefits of purpose:

1. *Purpose generates vision.* Purpose defines the why of what we are about. If people ask the question, "What is the purpose of your organization?", they are really asking why your organization exists. Why does it do what it does? Vision indicates what the organization is moving toward. It is a desired future. It should encompass the organization's role in serving society.

2. *Purpose frames choices.* The organization raises the question, "Should we go into a home health business?" Purpose helps frame the choice so that we can raise the question, "How would this reflect our purpose?" The standard assumption is that purpose needs to influence all the significant internal and external business decisions which the organization has to make. In this way, purpose is like riverbanks that keep the water focused and flowing. Without the banks, the water simply spreads out over the landscape and loses its force and direction.

3. *Purpose brings about alignment.* Remember the opening comments about the fiefdoms in health care organizations? We have many different kingdoms pulling in a multitude of directions. What is the mechanism for bringing those differing groups

together? Agreement (or alignment) with common purpose allows us to cross the barriers between those different fiefdoms and work together. That is why purpose is especially important in health care organizations.

A recent off-site management meeting drove this home to me. We were working with the executive team and department directors on defining integrated goals and objectives and discussing those within the management group. Each department presented its purpose and vision. It was an exciting time. And it became clear that there were some areas of common agreement and other areas where there was little agreement. The next step was to affirm the areas of agreement and negotiate the more troublesome areas. What was the foundation for the discussion of what was appropriate and what was not? Purpose.

4. *Purpose enables work.* Purpose allows us to focus on what is important and get the crucial work of the organization done. How do we know when we are leaving undone the things we ought to be doing? The answer is simple. When we are not clear on purpose, it is easy to become unproductive.

5. *Purpose empowers.* Finally, purpose empowers self and others to get the work done. Think of the world of time management. If we boil away all the trimmings, the essence of time management is knowing what purpose is. Without that core piece of information, the rest of time management becomes useless. Frankl (1963, p. 164) identifies this clearly when he states, "There is nothing in the world, I venture to say, that would so effectively help one to survive even the worst conditions, as the knowledge that there is meaning in one's life. There is much wisdom in the words of Nietzsche: 'He who has a why to live for can bear almost any how.'"

Tremendous energy is unleashed when the individuals within an organization understand the organizational purpose and how that purpose aligns with their own values and purpose. How do employees and others learn of the organization's purpose? Partly from the behavior of the executive team. Whatever the executive team lives out in their day-to-day functioning is probably what the organization begins to model as purpose. Actions speak, and they speak loudly.

Another place is the written purpose statement. The process of developing a purpose statement is critical to alignment. Without an articulated purpose statement, it becomes difficult to get people committed to a work unit or organization. Pascarella and Frohman (1989, pp. 33–36) identify some of the benefits of a written, published statement of purpose:

1. *Direction.* A purpose statement provides definition and direction.
2. *Focus.* A well-formulated purpose statement allows the organization to focus on the activities that distinguish it from other organizations.
3. *Policy.* Purpose statements allow the organization to formulate policy that is consistent with what needs to happen within the organization.
4. *Meaning.* Purpose statements give the members of the organization a sense of meaning—they can name what is unique and important about the organization.

As was mentioned earlier, the core of purpose is a value statement. Whether that value statement is articulated or not, values are the unspoken or spoken message behind a statement of purpose. The goal is for the spoken values (espoused values) and the behaviors (values in action) to be congruent. Espoused values are the values that we talk about in the organization. These are the things that we say are important to us. These are the statements in the employee handbook and in other publications, in frames on our walls, and so on. These statements say what we believe to be true about our organization. Values in action are those values that we actually live out. It does not take long to determine what values are talked about and what values are acted on. The latter are the values in action. This is where the concept of "walking the talk" comes into play. Getting espoused values and values in action congruent is difficult for most organizations but must be done.

So far, we have emphasized the advantages of purpose. However, there are disadvantages as well. If purpose is tightly defined, it can become a calcified structure that does not allow for change or growth. Purpose alone, without other components of this model informing it, can become rigid and outdated. We often see that in business structures. Many organizations have failed to shift their purpose and have become outdated—as well as out of business.

To summarize, the core component of an OPO is purpose.

*Roles.* The next component of the model is roles. Roles provide us with the security of knowing our niche. Without that role definition, we may become alienated. In an organizational context, roles are the expected set of behaviors that the organization has for us and we have for the organization. Roles include work activities as well as interpersonal activities. Think about the number of hats you wear at work. One hat might be as a manager. Another hat might be as a member of a profes-

17

sional review committee. Another hat might be as the chair of the United Way committee. Another as a subordinate. Another as a colleague. Another as a friend.

After the concept of purpose, there is no more pressing issue in most organizations than role clarity.

*Think for a moment about your organization. When you think of the concept of role clarity, where would you rank your organization on a ten-point scale?*

| 1 | 2 | 3 | 4 | 5 | 6 | 7 | 8 | 9 | 10 |
|---|---|---|---|---|---|---|---|---|---|
| *Low* | | | | | | | | | *High* |

*What would be the reason for your choice?*

Remember a time of role clarity in your organization. This was a time when you knew exactly what was expected of you and how your contribution fit in with the work of others. What was that like? How did it impact your work? How did it impact your productivity? What did it feel like for you?

Now think about a time when you lacked role clarity. This was a time when you did not know what was expected of you and you were confused about how your work fit in with others. What was that like? How did it impact your work? How did it impact your productivity? What did it feel like for you?

Phillips and Elledge (1989) discuss a number of factors that are important in defining role. First are *role expectations*. This has to do with what others think individuals are responsible for doing and how they should go about doing it. Second is *role conception*. This is what individuals think their role is and how they have been taught to do it. Third is *role acceptance*. This is the willingness of the individuals involved to accept

18

the roles that have been defined. Fourth is *role behavior*. This is where the "tire hits the pavement." What are the actual behaviors? What does the person actually do? Fifth, there is *role efficacy*. This is the degree to which the role is effective.

Egan (1988), in a slightly different vein, talks about roles from four different perspectives. First, roles are a *set of responsibilities*. Roles define responsibilities. Second, roles are a *set of tasks*. Third, roles are a *set of expectations*—both the employee's and the supervisor's. Fourth, a role is a *set of performance outcomes* or accomplishments.

These discussions make it clear that roles involve both formal and informal responsibilities, tasks, expectations, behaviors, expected outcomes, and so on. Two points of view are involved: There are the expectations I have for myself and the organization, as well as those the organization has for me. There is also the organization's perception of what I want. It is in this mix of expectations that role confusion and ambiguity begin to grow.

Change is omnipresent—especially in health care organizations. That means that roles are constantly shifting. About the time we have worked out agreements on what needs to happen, the situation changes and something new appears on the scene. A friend of mine refers to this as the cosmic joke—about the time I am ready for a relationship, the other person is ready to be a hermit, and vice versa. If there is one thing that we are, it is dynamic and changing.

Formal roles are descriptions of what an organization expects from employees: "You will have the responsibility for this function . . . " "Your reporting relationship and informing relationships will be with . . . " In the best organizations, the formal roles are defined early in the recruitment process. This pro-

19

vides the newcomer with good information on which to make a decision.

Informal roles can be more complex. These are the preconscious roles that each of us brings to an organization. Perhaps we want to be friendly. Or it may be that we want to be the rebel without a cause. If you examine groups and teams you are part of, you will quickly identify various roles. Informal roles grow out of our past family roles, life scripts, and so forth. The informal roles are frequently the most powerful influences on behavior in the organization. Why? Because they are typically preconscious (sitting on the edge of conscious behavior), and they are powerfully rooted in our past experiences and beliefs about the world. Understanding this is important, because typically these roles will drive behavior.

One exercise that I find useful in illustrating informal roles in health care organizations is the *headband exercise*. I ask for volunteers from the group and have them sit in a circle. Each member of the group is given a headband to wear with a label that the other members of the group can see but they cannot. Some of the labels on the headbands are "Angry Person," "Ignore me," "Clear Thinker," "Expert," and so on. The members of the group then carry on a discussion, responding to one another according to the headbands the others are wearing. Within a short time, the dynamics of the group begin to build. At the end of the exercise, I first ask the members to guess at the labels on their headbands. Then we talk about the role of informal dynamics. (P.S. What headbands do you think you are wearing in your organization?)

It is critical to focus on how well roles are defined, communicated, agreed to, and updated. Human nature dictates that we constantly assign roles to ourselves and others based on our organization's way of doing things. But to what degree are the assigned roles communicated? And to what degree do the people given these roles buy into them? These questions pertain to role clarity and agreement, respectively.

First, there is the question of clarity of roles. Having clarity of roles is critical for an organization or an individual. Purpose provides direction, and roles define how I fit in with that direction. Will I have 100 percent role clarity at all times? I doubt it. However, I can and need to have a "critical mass" of role clarity. A "critical mass" of clarity is vital for me to know how to spend my time "on purpose." The organization has brought my role into existence because it plays an important part in getting the organizational work done. Roles define boundaries. We have all been in organizations where that has not happened, and individuals are tripping over each other because each sees a role as his or her own. One feature of a changing environment is that roles continually change. As a result, the importance of role negotiation increases significantly.

Roles define:
1. How I do what I do
2. How what I do relates to what you do
3. How you relate to me and I to you
4. How I relate to the team or organization
5. How the organization or team relates to me

Without role clarification, I will not know when I am stepping on others' toes. I may know what purpose is and still be unclear about what I need to do to achieve purpose while remaining in harmony with others. This is true at the individual level, the departmental level, and the organizational level.

Second is the question of role agreement. You and I can

understand perfectly what is wanted but disagree about it. The distinction is important because it is not unusual to have someone say "I do not understand what my role is" but really be saying "I understand my role, but I disagree with the definition of that role." The level of disagreement can be low, medium, or high. It is important to ascertain the level of disagreement on roles that the organization can tolerate. In some cases, the disagreement is minor and can be within the organization's tolerance level. In other settings, the disagreement cannot be tolerated and significant negotiation is needed.

What is the importance of role clarity and agreement? Clear role expectations are the foundation for a successful employee-employer relationship. A high degree of role clarity means that choices are clear-cut. If roles are poorly defined, I may not realize until later that I do not want to conform to what is expected of me. I may not meet expectations and will probably be dissatisfied. This is why realistic expectations are set in the early phases of recruitment and selection. Role confusion can also mean unproductive conflict. This conflict can build to anger and even organizational sabotage. And the ultimate cost to the organization can be a high turnover rate (Ulschak & SnowAntle, 1992).

The negative side of role clarification is similar to that of purpose. If roles are overly defined, the organization can become overly compulsive. Any and all change will be handled in bureaucratic ways. The roles no longer reflect what really is happening. The formal structures are no longer flexible and responsive, and the informal structures take over. This will gradually erode the organization. Can too much time and energy be spent on role clarification? Yes, and the organization can lose sight of what it is really in business for.

One last comment. Roles take on meaning only when the purpose is defined. As Whyte, Wilson, and Wilson (1969, p. 219) state: "It's a bit like the umpires discussing their efforts. The first one said with some satisfaction, 'Balls and strikes, I call them as I see them.' The second, a little more arrogant, said, 'Balls and strikes, I call them as they are.' The third one, of greater experience and wisdom, said, 'Balls and strikes, they ain't nothing until I call them.'"

Until the purpose has been defined, that is, someone is umpiring the game, roles are apt to be very unclear and confused (the ball means nothing without the umpire).

*Feedback.* Young (1988, p. 94) states that "the first strategic choice for any person or any society is between that which should belong to reason of a reflective kind and that which should belong to habit." Feedback is reason of a reflective kind based on what we want to accomplish. It is intentional—not the product of habit.

How do we make that strategic decision? The answer is found in purpose. What does our purpose dictate to us in this setting? And how do we know if we are on purpose or not? Those are the questions that shape feedback.

*Think for a moment about your organization. When you think of feedback, where would you rank your organization on a ten-point scale?*

| 1 | 2 | 3 | 4 | 5 | 6 | 7 | 8 | 9 | 10 |
|---|---|---|---|---|---|---|---|---|---|
| *Low* | | | | | | | | | *High* |

*What would be the reason for your choice?*

Think back to an organization you have been part of where you felt there was excellent feedback. What was that like? How did it impact your work? How did it impact your feelings about working in that facility?

Now, think about a setting where there was a lack of feedback. How did that impact your job? How did it impact your work satisfaction?

Feedback is the next component in the OPO model. Whether I am dealing with an individual, department, or organization, feedback is vital to understanding whether I am being "purposeful" or not. What is feedback? And where do I get it?

Feedback involves directed communications. It is the impact of my behavior. The term *feedback* is used rather than *communication* because feedback implies getting responses back on the consequences of behavior or attitudes. Unlike random communication, feedback is purposeful communication. Feedback is there to let me know how I am doing in relation to the target or goal.

Feedback systems are all around us. Think about going for a drive in your car. As you drive down the road, you are getting feedback continually from the gauges on the dashboard. The speedometer lets you know how fast you are going. The fuel gauge lets you know how much fuel you have. The temperature gauge lets you know if the engine is heating up. The important point is that the gauges provide feedback in relation to some standard. And as long as the gauges are working, the feedback is valuable and useful for you.

Feedback systems are of two types. The first entails midcourse corrections. The feedback systems just mentioned are examples of this type. If I note that I am going too fast, I can slow down. Midcourse corrections allow me to make corrections in a timely manner. If we find that our infection rate is increasing, we take corrective action.

24

The second is end-point feedback. Frequently, we think of the annual performance review as a time for end-point feedback. Like taking a final test, there is a certain finality about that end point. This feedback occurs at end points. It is not useful for the current condition but may be useful for some future condition.

In the OPO model, feedback provides information to the rest of the components. Feedback allows us to know if we are on target or how far off target we are. Feedback provides the opportunity for midcourse corrections on the strategies we have implemented. Feedback lets us know if the treatment plan for the patient is working or not. Feedback gives us information to base decisions on. And, in so doing, it is motivating. Hearing the "score of the game" keeps us listening. Even when the feedback is negative, it is motivating because it lets us know where we stand.

We are constantly bombarded by feedback. The key is what feedback we decide to pay attention to—that is, what feedback is useful. There are a number of important considerations. One is our degree of openness to feedback. Can we accept negative feedback with equanimity? Another issue is the reliability of the feedback. I think of a friend who drives with a broken oil gauge in her car. The feedback from that broken gauge is not useful! When the feedback from the organization is not honest and straightforward, it can be misleading. This is why truth telling has become a critical element of the OPO model. One last function of feedback is renewal. Feedback allows us to become and remain a vital organization. It enables us to be a learning organization or a knowledge-generating organization.

As with the other components of the OPO model, there is a negative side to feedback: extensive feedback can overload an organization. The result can be "paralysis by analysis." Feedback needs to be guided by what is important—purpose! If purpose provides our organization with a rudder to keep us going in the right direction, feedback is the compass that lets us know when we get off course.

*Commitment.* The fourth component of the model is commitment. Pfeiffer (1981, p. 293) says that "commitment involves the binding of an individual to a decision so that consistent beliefs develop and similar decisions are taken in the future. The interesting thing about commitment is that it causes individuals, because they are bound to a course of action and set of beliefs, to persist even when evidence suggests that action and decisions should change. The first necessary condition for commitment to occur is choice. The second condition for commitment is that the chosen behavior is made public. A third cause of commitment is when the publicly chosen behavior is irrevocable."

To what degree is the individual, department, or organization committed to the purpose? Roles? Feedback? Commitment is vital in getting the purpose carried out. It is the passion element of the model. You need the elements that purpose brings to the model, but you also need the elements that passion (commitment) brings to it. A strong marriage of purpose and passion is critical.

*Take a moment and think back to a time you were highly committed to an organization. What was happening around you? What was it like? How did it impact your productivity?*

*Now think about a time you lacked commitment. What was happening around you? What was it like? How did it impact your productivity?*

*Think for a moment about your current organization. When you think of commitment, where would you rank your organization on a ten-point scale?*

| 1 | 2 | 3 | 4 | 5 | 6 | 7 | 8 | 9 | 10 |
|---|---|---|---|---|---|---|---|---|---|
| Low | | | | | | | | | High |

*What would be the reason for your choice?*

A few years ago, I had the privilege of being part of the start-up of a new cancer center. I came in on the ground floor with the start-up senior management team. What I remember about that time was energy and commitment. We worked around the clock, six and seven days a week. We talked continuously about how we were going to build this organization into the best facility possible. We were going to avoid all the mistakes of the other organizations we had been part of. We talked to others about their start-up experiences. We were going to make a difference in the fight against cancer. It was a very special time—a time I am pleased to have been part of.

And today, some of those dreams continue. Instead of a group of thirty to forty people continuously working and dreaming, the cancer center has become an organization with a life of its own. Things have settled down. New people have come on board who were not part of the early group—in fact, only a few remnants of that early group are left.

The start-up team needed that level of commitment and energy to get the organization moving. Now a different type of energy is needed. It is the energy of building the day-to-day operations to see that the early dreaming continues.

Jones and Bearley (1986, p. 10) note that commitment grows

27

when you feel you are doing something meaningful and can make your influence felt. Commitment is a sense of being empowered. It is a sense of being in alignment with what is being asked of you.

How does an organization build commitment? Jones and Bearley suggest that meaningful participation leads to a sense of involvement. This in turn evokes a feeling of influence that generates psychological ownership. The result is commitment. Each of these points is worth elaborating on.

*Meaningful* participation—not just participation—is the foundation of commitment. Meaningful participation needs to be defined by employees, not management. The individuals involved have to believe that their work is personally meaningful. This implies a potential "enrolling" in the organization or department.

Individuals, departments, and organizations should also believe they are *involved* in the decisions surrounding the work they do. Involvement implies a set of choices that can be made in the work setting. When I am involved in what is happening, I am less likely to view myself as passive or marginal and more likely to see myself as a significant part of the work process.

Individuals, departments, and organizations also need to feel they have *influence*. A sense of influence is empowering.

Those who have been empowered tend to develop feelings of *psychological ownership* of their project or program. They accept responsibility for the project or program because they have a sense of involvement, a feeling of influence.

The result is commitment.

Most organizations realize the problems associated with low commitment—minimal investment in work, high turnover, and so on. But as with the other three components or pillars of the OPO model that we have discussed, the opposite extreme can also be problematic. As Figure 1.4 suggests, high commitment may exact a heavy price. Schael and Fassel (1988) identify the costs of overcommitment to work as costs associated with burn-out, high incidents of accidents, other addictive behavior, family breakups, and so on. As individuals become overly committed to the organization, they tend to stop using their critical faculties. Workaholics often lack the necessary distance from an organization to be able to exercise wise judgment; after all, they are getting their fix from the organization. Their blind spot is the inability to read the organization correctly; they may also be unwilling to let go.

Commitment is the dependent variable in the OPO model.

Figure 1.4. High Versus Low Commitment in Relation to Productivity.

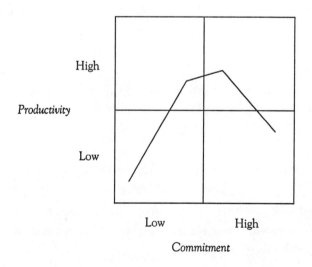

It cannot be built unless clarity of purpose, clarity of roles, and feedback are in place. This point is crucial for health care executives and others to grasp. Commitment does not come about because there is a program on commitment. It is a by-product of the other components and pillars of the model. Getting physicians committed to working for your organization means there is a common understanding of purpose, role, feedback, and trust.

Not only is commitment the dependent variable, it is also the one that can be most readily changed. Commitment can change from minute to minute. One minute, we can be highly committed to the organization. The next minute, on hearing about a decision we disagree with, we can lose commitment. That means that it is one of the most sensitive aspects of the model for managers to work with.

There is a classic story about commitment. This is a story of a pig and a hen who were very good friends. Since they were such good friends and got along well, the hen suggested to the pig that they go into business together. The pig also thought it was a good idea and asked the hen what kind of business she was thinking about. The hen said she thought they could open a restaurant chain that would serve ham and eggs. "Great idea, and it sounds like a good strategy," said the pig. "But there is one problem. *What is mere contribution for you is total commitment for me.*"

Commitment grows out of clarity and agreement with purpose, clarity and agreement with roles, and feedback systems that let us know if we are on target. But purpose, roles, feedback, and commitment cannot stand alone. They need a foundation—the four pillars.

30

*Four Pillars of the OPO*

The four pillars are truth telling, choice, regard, and renewal.

*Truth Telling.* Truth telling is not a question of moralizing or doing right. It is a question of stating what is—that is, generating valid data. Truth telling provides the organization with valid data about the world. There is no guessing about it; no information is withheld. It is a simple sharing of what is.

*Think for a moment about your organization. When you think of the concept of truth telling, where would you rank your organization on a ten-point scale?*

| 1 | 2 | 3 | 4 | 5 | 6 | 7 | 8 | 9 | 10 |
|---|---|---|---|---|---|---|---|---|---|
| Low | | | | | | | | | High |

*What would be the reason for your choice?*

Louis Thomas states the following about lying:

As I understand it, a human being cannot tell a lie, even a small one, without setting off a kind of smoke alarm somewhere deep in a dark lobule of the brain, resulting in the sudden discharge of nerve impulses or the sudden outpouring of neural hormones of some sort or both. The outcome recorded by the lie detector gadgetry is a highly reproducible cascade of changes in the electrical conductivity of the skin, the heart rate, the manner of breathing, similar to the responses to various kinds of stress. Lying, then, is stressful, even when we do it for protection or relief or escape or profit, or just for the pure pleasure of lying and getting away with it. It is a strain, distressing enough to

31

cause the emission of signals to and from the central nervous system warning that something has gone wrong. It is in a pure, physiological sense an unnatural act [1984, p. 128].

Truth telling is a natural act with many dimensions. The point is that no organization can exist without good data flowing within it and between the organization and the society around. Truth telling is the lifeblood of the organization.

Over the last few years, I have had an opportunity to visit with many gurus in the field of organizational behavior. Whenever the opportunity has arisen, I have asked the following question. "If you were to pick one element of organizational behavior that you consider most important, what would it be?" The response has consistently been the same: truthful communication.

Perhaps this is obvious. However, over and over, experts find truthful communication to be critical to organizational functioning. Schutz provides an excellent discussion of truth telling in organizations in his book *The Truth Option* (1984). It is the great releaser of energy. Like the child in the story "The Emperor Has No Clothes" who pointed out that the emperor had nothing on, truth telling breaks spells.

*Choice.* Choice has to do with options. It has to do with being conscious of the available options. Where do choices emerge? They emerge from a context where truth telling is going on. There is no greater gift than to be with others who are truth tellers. Why? They give us information we are able to use to identify options. Choices become valid in the context of good data. Yet even without good data, choices are made. Choices

can be active or passive. The passive voice sees the world acting on it, and it reacts to the world. The passive voice is des-
tined to be a victim of circumstances. The active voice assumes
the posture of decision making. Regardless of the circumstances,
the active voice is asking the question, "What choice do I want
to make in light of these conditions?"

*Think for a moment about your organization. When you think
of the concept of choice, where would you rank your organization
on a ten-point scale?*

| 1 | 2 | 3 | 4 | 5 | 6 | 7 | 8 | 9 | 10 |
|---|---|---|---|---|---|---|---|---|-----|
| Low | | | | | | | | | High |

*What would be the reason for your choice?*

Frankl (1963) provides a dramatic discussion of choice.
Reflecting on what most of us would consider the ultimate out-
of-control situation—the concentration camps of World War
II—he says that "in the concentration camp, every circumstance
conspires to make the prisoner lose his hold. All the familiar
goals in life are snatched away. What alone remains is 'the last
of human freedoms'—the ability to 'choose one's attitude in a
given set of circumstances.'"

Frankl continues as follows:

The experience of camp life shows that man does
have a choice of action. There were enough examples, often of a heroic nature, which proved that apa-
thy could be overcome, irritability suppressed. Man
can preserve a vestige of spiritual freedom, of in-
dependence of mind, even in such terrible conditions

of psychic and physical stress. We who lived in concentration camps can remember the men who walked
through the huts comforting others, giving away their
last piece of bread. They may have been few in number, but they offer sufficient proof that everything can
be taken from a man but one thing: The last of human freedoms to choose one's attitude in any given
set of circumstances, to choose one's own way. . . . In
the final analysis, it becomes clear that the sort of
person the prisoner became was the result of an inner
decision and not the result of a camp influence alone
[p. 105].

Fritz (1989) emphasizes that choice is the key to living cre-
atively. He argues that "the way you activate the seeds of your
creation is by making choices about the results you want to create" (p. 163). He describes eight ways of making ineffective
choices (pp. 166–171):

1. *Choice by limitation.* Choosing what seems possible or
   reasonable. By doing so, we compromise and cut ourselves off from what we really want. Health care suffers
   a good deal from this.
2. *Choice by indirectness.* This is choosing the process instead of the result we are after. This is the difference
   between choosing to eat health foods or choosing to be
   healthy. This is doing things right instead of doing the
   right things.
3. *Choice by elimination.* We put ourselves in the corner so
   that only one choice makes sense to us.
4. *Choice by default.* We choose not to choose and in the

process a choice is made. It appears to happen without choice. Some in health care see health care reform in this light. If we wait long enough (and maybe we have), the choices will be made for us.

5. *Conditional choice.* If this . . . then . . . What we do is place conditions on choices. The result is watered down choices. We avoid the results we want.

6. *Choice by reaction.* Choice is made under pressure to relieve the stress or the tension of the moment. Within health care, we often resort to this type of choosing. The emergency room mentality runs through our organizations—we wait for the ambulance to come with the unknown.

7. *Choice by consensus.* Here we make decisions as a group. This may necessitate subordinating our own preferences.

8. *Choice by adverse possession.* What I have was chosen by the cosmos. The power of creation determined this.

Fritz emphasizes that the key is to choose the results we are after. No excuses. No partial wants. The goal is to determine the results we are after and make a conscious choice to pursue them.

An OPO recognizes that it is continually making choices. Change means constant choice.

*Regard.* Regard has to do with valuing self and others. It is in valuing self that the truth telling and choices become most life giving. When I am not being honest with myself or valuing myself, I have low regard for myself and experience limitations and barriers.

*Think for a moment about your organization. When you think of the concept of regard, where would you rank your organization on a ten-point scale?*

| 1 | 2 | 3 | 4 | 5 | 6 | 7 | 8 | 9 | 10 |
|---|---|---|---|---|---|---|---|---|---|
| Low | | | | | | | | | High |

*What would be the reason for your choice?*

Think about yourself for a moment. Remember a time when you were pleased with yourself. You felt very good about who you were. Now remember a time when you felt down on yourself. Your self-respect was low. How did your sense of self-esteem impact your view of those around you and the work environment? The other half of the discussion involves regard for others. A vital part of an alive organization is that the members show respect toward one another.

Regard is a critical pillar of the on-purpose organization. When we do not have high self-regard, we have a limited ability to function effectively in an on-purpose manner.

*Renewal.* Organizations all go through cycles. They need renewal. Renewal is what allows them to prosper and grow in response to the changing environment. The central thesis of Senge's (1990) work on the learning organization is that organizations need to learn how to learn. That is what renewal is all about—learning how we continue to learn as a team and an organization. This principle of organizational lifelong learning is critical to health care organizations. Think for a moment about our changing environments. To survive, we need to be constantly learning. And the learning does not involve one in-

36

dividual continuously learning. The whole organization must continue to learn from the environment.

*Think for a moment about your organization. When you think of the concept of renewal, where would you rank your organization on a ten-point scale?*

| 1 | 2 | 3 | 4 | 5 | 6 | 7 | 8 | 9 | 10 |
|---|---|---|---|---|---|---|---|---|---|
| Low | | | | | | | | | High |

*What would be the reason for your choice?*

Another concept that is important here is that of the resilient organization. The *resilient organization* is one that lasts. It is able to take in information from its environment and use that information to adjust strategies.

Truth, choice, regard, and renewal are the foundations on which an OPO is built. But the community in which the health care organization is found is the main reason for the organization's existence.

## Community

Just as the individual is dependent on the tension between the external and the internal environment, so too is the organization. If the external environment does not support life, the individual will not survive. If the internal environment does not process the products from the external environment, the individual will not survive. Both environments are needed for survival.

The same is true with the organization. The external environment needs to support the organization with markets and raw material. Otherwise it cannot survive. The organization needs the sanction of society to exist. That is why I believe that all organizations exist to serve the community. We may disagree with the values of a particular organization, but the fact that it exists says that somehow it is addressing the needs of the community. The organization also needs to have a highly tuned internal environment to take from the environment and effectively return to the environment. The organization needs both environments. In the past, those of us involved in health care organizations have tended to assume the community is there for our benefit. Now we are beginning to see our organizations as existing for the good of the community.

Table 1.1 illustrates the interrelationship of the internal and external environments of an OPO.

The ultimate question for organizations is this: Does the environment accept and support the organization? If the answer

Table 1.1. Internal and External Environments of an OPO.

|  | *Internal* | *External* |
|---|---|---|
| Purpose | The purpose of the organization. Its reason for being. | How the organization's purpose fits with the societal purpose. |
| Roles | The various functions the organization needs to carry out to achieve its purpose. | The role the organization plays in the community. |
| Feedback | The important pieces of information the organization needs to have to determine if it is being successful. | The community assessment of the impact of the organization on its well-being. |
| Commitment | Commitment that the organization has to carrying out its purpose. | Commitment the organization has to the organization and the organization's commitment to the community. |

is yes, the next step is to look at the organization and see how it might do its job better. If the answer is no, the next step is to find something the environment will support or move to another environment. This becomes the ultimate example of customer service. The environment is the ultimate customer of the organization. If the customer is satisfied, the organization has an opportunity to continue serving it. If the customer is not satisfied, the organization will go out of business.

Organizations have constant shifting of purpose. Individuals, work units, and organizations all have life cycles. Every organizational start-up has within it the seeds of its own decay. Stated another way, inertia is built into it. If it is not constantly fed and attended to, it will slow down and begin to decay in earnest. That is why it is critical for an OPO to constantly reaffirm its purpose and mission, engage in role clarification, monitor the way feedback is given, and attend to levels of commitment. This is the way the organization can prevent premature difficulties.

## OPO Questionnaire

The OPO questionnaire in Exhibit 1.1 is designed to assist you in determining the amount of alignment within your organization or work unit. It will help you identify areas where you are on target and areas you need to pay more attention to. The questionnaire asks you to respond to questions on purpose, role, feedback, and commitment.

Some suggestions for use include:

Step 1: Develop the objectives for the use of the questionnaire. What is it you are trying to accomplish? What outcomes are you after?

Step 2: Communicate the objectives to the organization

THE COMMON BOND

Exhibit 1.1. On-Purpose Questionnaire: A Survey.

Using the scale below, circle your response to the right of each item. The top line is "what is." The second line is "what is desired."

1—Not at all
2—To a very limited degree
3—To a limited degree
4—To some degree
5—To a great degree
6—To a very great degree

*Four Components of the OPO*

The first set of questions pertains to the major components of the OPO.

*Purpose*

1. Are values discussed in meetings in this organization?  1 2 3 4 5 6
1 2 3 4 5 6

2. Does this organization attempt to promote a clear set of values?  1 2 3 4 5 6
1 2 3 4 5 6

3. Do your personal values fit those of this organization?  1 2 3 4 5 6
1 2 3 4 5 6

4. Does this organization project a clear vision of its future?  1 2 3 4 5 6
1 2 3 4 5 6

5. Do you agree with that organizational vision?  1 2 3 4 5 6
1 2 3 4 5 6

6. Do you understand the central purpose of this organization?  1 2 3 4 5 6
1 2 3 4 5 6

7. Do you agree with the central purpose of this organization?  1 2 3 4 5 6
1 2 3 4 5 6

8. Do you understand the priorities of this organization?  1 2 3 4 5 6
1 2 3 4 5 6

9. Does this organization have a clearly defined mission?  1 2 3 4 5 6
1 2 3 4 5 6

10. Do you agree with that mission?  1 2 3 4 5 6
1 2 3 4 5 6

11. Do you agree with the priorities of this organization?  1 2 3 4 5 6
1 2 3 4 5 6

40

Exhibit 1.1. On-Purpose Questionnaire: A Survey, Cont'd.

---

*Roles*

12. Do you understand what your role is in the organization?

   1 2 3 4 5 6
   1 2 3 4 5 6

13. Do you agree with that role?

   1 2 3 4 5 6
   1 2 3 4 5 6

14. Is your role central to the organization?

   1 2 3 4 5 6
   1 2 3 4 5 6

15. Is your role clearly linked to others in the organization?

   1 2 3 4 5 6
   1 2 3 4 5 6

16. Is your role of value to the organization?

   1 2 3 4 5 6
   1 2 3 4 5 6

17. Do you understand how job tasks are assigned in this organization?

   1 2 3 4 5 6
   1 2 3 4 5 6

18. Do managers in this organization believe that the interests of this organization and those of individuals are inseparable?

   1 2 3 4 5 6
   1 2 3 4 5 6

19. Are you kept up to date with regard to your job responsibilities?

   1 2 3 4 5 6
   1 2 3 4 5 6

20. Do you and your manager agree on standards for good performance?

   1 2 3 4 5 6
   1 2 3 4 5 6

21. Are your manager's expectations of your job performance reasonable?

   1 2 3 4 5 6
   1 2 3 4 5 6

22. Do you know what is expected of you?

   1 2 3 4 5 6
   1 2 3 4 5 6

23. Are you clear about how your role and responsibilities relate to those of others?

   1 2 3 4 5 6
   1 2 3 4 5 6

24. Are you confused about your job responsibilities?

   1 2 3 4 5 6
   1 2 3 4 5 6

25. Is this organization able to tolerate ambiguity in roles?

   1 2 3 4 5 6
   1 2 3 4 5 6

*Feedback*

26. Do you receive adequate feedback on the outcomes of your job performance?

   1 2 3 4 5 6
   1 2 3 4 5 6

Exhibit 1.1. On-Purpose Questionnaire: A Survey, Cont'd.

---

27. Do you know whether or not your work is satisfactory?  1 2 3 4 5 6
    1 2 3 4 5 6

28. Does your manager provide both constructive criticism and positive feedback in your performance-review session?  1 2 3 4 5 6
    1 2 3 4 5 6

29. Does your manager help you understand how you can contribute to achieving department objectives?  1 2 3 4 5 6
    1 2 3 4 5 6

30. Does your manager give you the information you need to do your job well?  1 2 3 4 5 6
    1 2 3 4 5 6

31. Are you satisfied with the information you receive about what is going on in this organization?  1 2 3 4 5 6
    1 2 3 4 5 6

32. Does this organization solicit feedback from employees on its priorities?  1 2 3 4 5 6
    1 2 3 4 5 6

33. Are problems in this organization solved through open communication?  1 2 3 4 5 6
    1 2 3 4 5 6

34. Are oral communications in this organization clear and understandable?  1 2 3 4 5 6
    1 2 3 4 5 6

35. Are the policies of this organization clearly explained to you?  1 2 3 4 5 6
    1 2 3 4 5 6

36. Are written communications in this organization clear and understandable?  1 2 3 4 5 6
    1 2 3 4 5 6

37. Are employees in this organization kept well informed?  1 2 3 4 5 6
    1 2 3 4 5 6

38. Does this organization solicit feedback from employees on its administrative policies?  1 2 3 4 5 6
    1 2 3 4 5 6

39. Is it possible in this organization for you to communicate directly with people two or more levels above you?  1 2 3 4 5 6
    1 2 3 4 5 6

40. Do you understand how you are supposed to behave in this organization?  1 2 3 4 5 6
    1 2 3 4 5 6

*Commitment*

41. Are you willing to put forward a great deal of effort beyond what is normally expected to make this organization successful?  1 2 3 4 5 6
    1 2 3 4 5 6

Exhibit 1.1. On-Purpose Questionnaire: A Survey, Cont'd.

| | |
|---|---|
| 42. Do you feel strong loyalty to this organization? | 1 2 3 4 5 6<br>1 2 3 4 5 6 |
| 43. Does this organization inspire the best in you in the way of job performance? | 1 2 3 4 5 6<br>1 2 3 4 5 6 |
| 44. Are you proud to tell others you are part of this organization? | 1 2 3 4 5 6<br>1 2 3 4 5 6 |
| 45. Do people in this organization take pride in the excellence of their performance? | 1 2 3 4 5 6<br>1 2 3 4 5 6 |
| 46. Is there an atmosphere of fun in this organization? | 1 2 3 4 5 6<br>1 2 3 4 5 6 |
| 47. Is this organization interested in what you think? | 1 2 3 4 5 6<br>1 2 3 4 5 6 |
| 48. Is this a good place to work? | 1 2 3 4 5 6<br>1 2 3 4 5 6 |
| 49. Is this organization loyal to its employees? | 1 2 3 4 5 6<br>1 2 3 4 5 6 |
| 50. Does this organization invest in people? | 1 2 3 4 5 6<br>1 2 3 4 5 6 |
| 51. Does this organization place value on enjoying work? | 1 2 3 4 5 6<br>1 2 3 4 5 6 |
| 52. Do you believe that this is an ethical organization? | 1 2 3 4 5 6<br>1 2 3 4 5 6 |

### Four Pillars of the OPO

The next set of questions pertains to the four pillars that contribute the foundation of the OPO.

### Truth Telling

| | |
|---|---|
| 53. Do members of this organization practice truth telling to one another? | 1 2 3 4 5 6<br>1 2 3 4 5 6 |
| 54. Do you trust the communications and information you receive in this organization? | 1 2 3 4 5 6<br>1 2 3 4 5 6 |
| 55. Does this organization value the contribution of its employees? | 1 2 3 4 5 6<br>1 2 3 4 5 6 |

Exhibit 1.1. On-Purpose Questionnaire: A Survey, Cont'd.

56. Do you feel free to communicate authentically with your manager?

1 2 3 4 5 6
1 2 3 4 5 6

57. Does your manager attempt to work through differences in viewpoints with you?

1 2 3 4 5 6
1 2 3 4 5 6

58. Does this organization encourage you to look on the manager as someone to talk openly and freely to?

1 2 3 4 5 6
1 2 3 4 5 6

59. Do you feel free to discuss ethical concerns with your manager?

1 2 3 4 5 6
1 2 3 4 5 6

### Choice

60. Does this organization encourage you to take responsibility for your choices?

1 2 3 4 5 6
1 2 3 4 5 6

61. Does this organization encourage individuals to take responsibility for carrying out agreements?

1 2 3 4 5 6
1 2 3 4 5 6

### Regard

62. Do people in this organization have respect for one another?

1 2 3 4 5 6
1 2 3 4 5 6

63. Does this organization encourage people to make suggestions?

1 2 3 4 5 6
1 2 3 4 5 6

64. Does this organization encourage people to listen to each other?

1 2 3 4 5 6
1 2 3 4 5 6

65. Does this organization emphasize confrontation?

1 2 3 4 5 6
1 2 3 4 5 6

66. Are you expected to confront interpersonal problems in your work group?

1 2 3 4 5 6
1 2 3 4 5 6

67. Do your co-workers treat you with respect?

1 2 3 4 5 6
1 2 3 4 5 6

68. Is there a spirit of teamwork in your work group?

1 2 3 4 5 6
1 2 3 4 5 6

69. Is there a climate of trust in this organization?

1 2 3 4 5 6
1 2 3 4 5 6

70. Does this organization celebrate its successes?

1 2 3 4 5 6
1 2 3 4 5 6

Exhibit 1.1. On-Purpose Questionnaire: A Survey, Cont'd.

---

*Renewal*

71. Are people in this organization encouraged to initiate    1 2 3 4 5 6
    projects that they think are important?                    1 2 3 4 5 6

72. Is there emphasis on innovation in this organization?      1 2 3 4 5 6
                                                               1 2 3 4 5 6

73. Is this organization quick to use improved work methods?   1 2 3 4 5 6
                                                               1 2 3 4 5 6

74. Does this organization encourage improvement when          1 2 3 4 5 6
    things are going well?                                     1 2 3 4 5 6

75. Is this organization sensitive to the emotional effects    1 2 3 4 5 6
    of change?                                                 1 2 3 4 5 6

76. Is innovation rewarded in this organization?               1 2 3 4 5 6
                                                               1 2 3 4 5 6

*Community*

77. Is this organization making a worthwhile contribution      1 2 3 4 5 6
    to the community?                                          1 2 3 4 5 6

78. Does this organization stay adequately informed about      1 2 3 4 5 6
    the outside environment?                                   1 2 3 4 5 6

79. Is this organization sensitive to changes in its           1 2 3 4 5 6
    external environment?                                      1 2 3 4 5 6

80. Does this organization emphasize being the "best" in       1 2 3 4 5 6
    its industry?                                              1 2 3 4 5 6

81. Do you feel that this organization is respected in the     1 2 3 4 5 6
    community?                                                 1 2 3 4 5 6

82. Is this organization's industry healthy?                   1 2 3 4 5 6
                                                               1 2 3 4 5 6

83. Is this organization making a meaningful contribution      1 2 3 4 5 6
    to society?                                                1 2 3 4 5 6

---

or work unit in which you are using the questionnaire. Explain how it will be used and how it will be useful. Also be clear that it is anonymous—individual responses will not be reported.

Step 3: Fill out the questionnaire.

Step 4: Based on the questionnaire, identify the gaps between expectations and reality. This questionnaire is designed to make the process of gap identification easy. Simply look at "what is" and "what is desired" and where the significant gaps are.

Step 5: Develop an action plan for the priority gaps. Much material in this book can be used to develop specific steps.

## Conclusion

This chapter has introduced the model that will guide the remainder of this book. As we have seen, it has four basic components: purpose, roles, feedback, and commitment. These four components are built on the four pillars: truth telling, choice, regard, and renewal.

Whether discussing the organization or the work unit, we constantly need to ask the following questions:

1. Do we understand purpose? Do we agree with that purpose?
2. Do we understand role? Do we agree with role?
3. What feedback do we need if we are on target with purpose and role? How do we obtain that feedback?
4. What level of commitment do we have to purpose and role?
5. What is the quality of the data in our organization— that is, what is the degree of truth telling?
6. Are we intentional about the choices we are making?
7. Do we have respect for and regard for one another in the organization?
8. How do we plan for renewal and continuous improvement?

However, do not let the simplicity of the model be decep-
tive. As we move along, we will begin to unfold the layers of
the onion skin to reveal further layers of complexity. The following chapters will address the OPO model at the individual,
departmental, and organizational levels.

# CHAPTER TWO

# The Shifting Boundaries of the Organization

All along, we have been talking about the larger system which embeds the smaller one, much as a bed embeds a body that itself embeds a heart that embeds a blood vessel, etc. But this language fails to capture the very important idea that the larger system may be the future world. In this sense of larger, the larger system is infinite, stretching endlessly into the future generations. It also stretches endlessly into the past, but management sciences are not interested in this sector of the larger system except as a source of data, as they somewhat naively think they can do nothing about it.

—C. West Churchman,
*The Systems Approach*

SYSTEMS THINKING INVOLVES LOOKING at organizations in many different ways. The organization can be seen as having a set of entities (parts of the system), the attributes of those entities, and the relationships between those entities. One approach to systems thinking is seeing systems as layers of interrelated elements. The following chapters are based on the *onion skin model* (Figure 2.1). This model approaches a system in the same way that you would approach peeling an onion. One layer leads to the next, which leads to the next, and so on. Obviously, this approach is somewhat artificial, since the layers overlap. But each layer has unique properties that we need to consider. In the case of an organization, the primary layer of the system is the organization itself. The organization establishes the mission and purpose. In doing so, it defines the boundaries of the other layers. However, even the organization is embedded in another layer—the community.

The second layer is that of the work unit. This is where the organization's functions are carried out. In some settings, the work unit is equivalent to the department. In other settings, the department is an additional distinct level and may be composed of work units. The work unit is charged with providing a service or product for the organization. That ser-

Figure 2.1. Onion Skin Model.

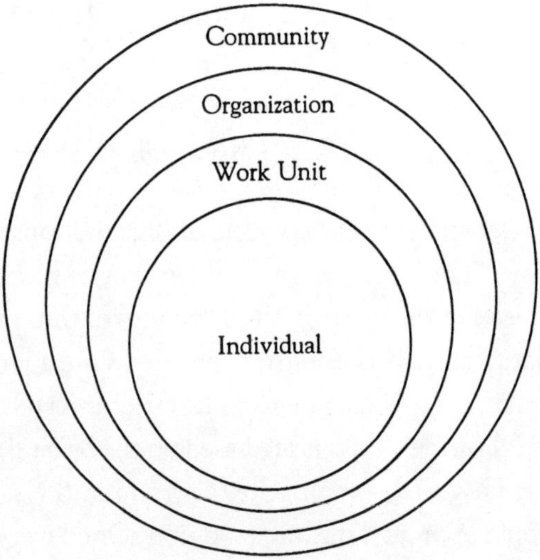

vice or product may be for another work unit within the organization or for an external customer. The work unit brings the expectations of the organization together with the expectations of the individuals who make up the work unit and do the actual work.

The third layer consists of the individuals who do the work. The individual employee is the ultimate building block of the organization, because this is where the work actually gets done. The efforts of these individuals result in a product or service for the work unit that allows the organization to provide products and services to the community.

This chapter applies the OPO model to the organizational layer of the "onion" depicted in Figure 2.1. Much that has been said earlier regarding the OPO model carries over to this chapter, which focuses on specific organizational strategies for building the OPO structure. In thinking about changing the organization, we need to think about a process that takes place over several years. Unless it is revolutionary and crisis driven, change does not happen overnight. A well-established organization often has considerable inertia to change, which comes from doing things the same way over a long period of time. When we talk about adopting the OPO model, we are talking about changing organizational culture. Therefore, it will be useful to spend some time discussing organizational culture.

## Organizational Culture

Organizational culture has been an interest of mine for a long time (Ulschak, 1989). This interest grew out of experiences that had nothing to do with organizations. Fresh out of high school, I decided that it would be worth my time to travel around the world before entering college. So I did. For a couple of years, I traveled from country to country through Europe, the Middle East, and Asia. My travels gave me a great awareness of cultural diversity. The differences were easy to see—standards of politeness varied, religious symbolism took different forms, and so on. Different cultures had different ways of doing things.

That is true of organizational cultures as well. In some organizations, the culture is readily apparent—for example, it can involve a specific dress code. But cultural standards are less apparent in other organizations. And of course you will get into trouble if you do not conform to them, no matter how subtle they may be.

Think for a moment about the following organizational snapshots, which I initially discussed in my chapter in *Productivity and Performance Management in Health Care Institutions* (1989). The first describes organization A:

*Structure.* The organizational structure is flat. This means there are few layers between the first-line supervisor and top management. The organization is set to work from a matrix design, which means when new projects come along, project teams or task forces are set up.

*Decision making.* Decision making is done quickly and efficiently. The CEO makes many decisions on the spot. The general operating norm is that the organization cannot wait for long decision-making processes. Decision making may happen in informal ways—for example, in impromptu gatherings in hallways or elsewhere—or in formal meetings using formal processes.

*View of managers.* Managers are viewed as major assets to the organization, which spends significant dollars in management recruitment, selection, development, training, and compensation. Managers are hired because they were successful cutting-edge managers in their previous positions and are expected to continue to be on the cutting edge. They are to be decision makers. The general operating principle is that it is easier to ask for forgiveness than permission.

*Compensation.* Compensation is built around the merit system. Individuals are compensated based on their ability to meet objectives and standards. Some team incentives are included for work on project teams and task forces.

*Patients.* The organization has a strong service emphasis. Patient information is aggressively sought. The organization is constantly monitoring patient feedback and takes that feedback to the highest levels of the organization. Patients are seen as customers, and every effort is made to ensure as pleasant a stay for them and their families as possible.

Organization B, in contrast, has the following characteristics:

*Structure.* Hierarchical. There are three or four layers between the first-line supervisor and the CEO. The chain of command plays a central role. In discussing new projects, it is important to determine in whose areas those projects belong.

*Decision making.* Decision making occurs at the highest levels. Lengthy processes exist to insure the "right" decision is made. If new items come up, they need to wait until the start of the decision process—for example, until the fiscal year begins. Responsiveness is slow but methodical.

*View of managers.* Managers are rewarded for following the system. Many of them have grown up in the system and have learned to observe its rules. Conservative actions are encouraged. The key operating principle is to keep upper management informed of every move.

*Compensation.* Compensation is based on some merit but mainly longevity. Longtime service and loyalty to the health care organization are of primary importance.

*Patients.* "Patients come to us." The attitude is one of: "We are the ones who know health care; they need to trust in us and the years we have in the community." Some questions are asked regarding patients' experience of the health care organization, but these are limited.

How would it feel for you to be part of organization A? Organization B? Do you have a preference regarding which organization you would like to work with? In reality, neither has the "right" corporate culture; each has a corporate culture that has its own unique flavoring. The effectiveness of each will depend on how the culture matches with the marketplace in which it finds itself.

What is organizational culture? The most useful definition is Schein's (1985, p. 9): Organizational culture is "a pattern of basic assumptions—invented, discovered, or developed by a given group as it learns to cope with its problems of external adaptation and internal integration—that has worked well enough to be considered valid and, therefore, to be taught to new members as the correct way to perceive, think, and feel in relation to those problems." Schein's definition has several important components:

1. *Culture is a pattern of basic assumptions.* First and foremost, culture is a set of underlying patterns. Culture provides the rulebook for how to succeed in the organization. It provides the model for success. It is not simplistic; it is like a finely woven garment with intricate patterns.

An implication is that it is not easy to get to know culture. In fact, experts debate whether culture is really knowable. Superficial aspects of culture are readily seen—for example, a dress code, a particular way of doing work, and so on. However, the deeper aspects of culture are not readily accessible. Even people within the organization may not have a conscious sense of why something is done the way it is. They only know that it is the right way to do it. And some argue that even if culture is knowable, it is not easily changeable.

2. *Culture is learned or discovered as the organization copes with surviving in the environment and integrating itself internally.* A key aspect of this definition is that culture is learned as the organization grows and develops. Implicit is the importance of understanding organizational growth cycles and the critical incidents in the life of an organization. Each critical event is a time of testing the basic assumptions. Will they continue to work? Will the organization survive? As the life cycle of the organization changes, so do the purpose and roles. Organizational learning is an ongoing process that does not end. The organization needs to learn to survive (Senge, 1990).

3. *The learnings have worked sufficiently well to be taught to new members as the way work should be done.* The members of the organization believe strongly enough in the way they get work done that the new members will be taught "the way." A key part of orienting new members to the organization is socializing them according to traditional values: "This is how we do things here. This is the way we have been successful in the past." In an organization that is aware of its culture, the recruitment and selection process will be focused not only on the technical skills the potential member might have but also on the question of how this person fits with the organization's culture.

The orientation programs will be designed to teach the organization's cultural expectations. A classic example is the orientation program at Disney World. Orientation is seen as a time of teaching "the culture." A key purpose of that program is to get new recruits to know what the culture expects and to accept those expectations.

The OPO model depends on teaching new members what it means to be part of an OPO. Purpose is a major focus of orientation. Organizational stories need to be told to the new inductees to convey a sense of the organization's purpose.

Culture is a history of what has worked for the organization. It is the road map for successful behaviors. And then change hits. An example involves health care organizations that were settled into basic assumptions about life when DRGs were introduced. The way of doing business changed. Old assumptions were no longer useful. Change impacted the culture. An OPO is designed to facilitate the management of change. This flexibility is part of the culture of the OPO organization. This type of organization is designed to be a learning organization.

A significant aspect of the definition of culture is that the learned patterns become assumptions. The patterns become so ingrained that the typical member of the organization is not fully aware that the patterns are driving forces. This creates a certain "amnesia" to the culture itself. We do it this way because we have always done it this way. The superficial cultural material, such as dress codes, may be readily apparent, but the deeper cultural assumptions are not. This also means that members of the culture may not be the best people to ask about their culture. They will be oblivious to the deepest aspects of the culture.

This recalls the story of the preparation of the Thanksgiving ham. As father is preparing the ham for the family's Thanksgiving dinner, he cuts both ends off the ham. When someone asks him why, he says that the ham "breathes" better this way and, consequently, it cooks better. And his father always did it this way. So the person goes to his father and asks him, "Why do you cut the ends off the ham?" The response is, "So the ham can breathe better. And my father always did it that way." So the person goes to the grandfather and asks him about the ham. His response: "I cut both ends off because the pan was too small." Once ingrained, the reasons for particular actions may no longer be clear. You do it because that is the way it is done. People of the culture may not know why they do it; they just do it.

Implicit in this definition is that culture is not easy to get at. Measuring an organization's culture will not happen by passing around a questionnaire or doing surface observations. The best that is achieved from these methods is surface data. The roots of the culture run deep. The basic patterns are deep and connected. It may take years of living in the culture and observing it before the deeper assumptions come through. Parts of a culture are visible, but the key assumptions are hidden.

How is culture built? What is its origin? Schein (1985, pp. 224–237) describes the following primary and secondary ways in which leaders build culture. These primary and secondary reasons become clues to building the OPO culture:

1. What leaders pay attention to, measure, and control is a key way that the culture becomes embedded. *What is controlled for happens.* If the leaders' attention is seen as a spotlight, whatever ends up in the spotlight gets rein-

forced. If leaders expect on-purpose behaviors and put the spotlight on them, they will get on-purpose behaviors.

2. *Leaders' reactions to critical incidents and crises are crucial.* Intense feelings are the seedbed for organizational culture. During crises, basic assumptions are revealed and the leader shows what is really important. An organization may have lots of verbiage about what is important—the actions in the time of crisis show what is really important. This is when leaders need to "walk the talk." The value core shows through in times of crisis.

3. *Role modeling and teaching are deliberate.* What is it that the leader actually role models? If the leader values ethical behavior and actively role models this, then it becomes embedded in the culture. We are all well aware of the importance of top-down modeling. To have top management role model a desired management behavior is the ultimate in management development. There is a clear message about commitment to the behaviors and the organization.

4. *Criteria for allocation of rewards and status are known and established.* The culture then knows the rules for working together. Behaviors that are "on purpose" get rewarded. Those that are not, do not.

5. *Criteria for recruitment, selection, promotion, retirement, and excommunication are defined and acted upon.* Again, the concept of internal congruence is important. An organization that has a stated value that certain actions will result in excommunication but then does not act on them when the actions occur, creates an inconsis-

tency in the system. The "on-purpose" organization has defined the playing field. Potential members do not have to guess. They know.

There are secondary methods as well. Again, Schein (1985, pp. 237–242) identifies these as follows:

1. *Organizational design.* The design of the organization can reinforce the culture that is desired. Take the reporting relation of human resources. To whom the function reports indicates its role in the organization. The structure is a value statement of the organization. It reflects what is seen as important for the organization. For example, a teaching hospital will have a value statement about academic affairs by having a senior management position with that title in it.

2. *Organizational systems and procedures.* Procedures and policies are mundane and yet vital for the organization. For example, termination policy may say a good deal about the culture of the organization with respect to human relations.

3. *Design of physical space, facades, and building.* The design of the building will say things about the culture. For example, I once toured a hospital where the administrative offices were lavishly furnished and spacious. The Nursing Administration offices were barren. The message was clear.

4. *Stories, legends, myths.* Stories about critical incidents provide hints regarding culture. One example is the infamous voice mail incident. Within a health care organization, voice mail was introduced. When a physician

leader called radiology and got voice mail, he became upset and immediately went to the director of radiology. He walked into the office, walked up to the desk, dialed the phone, handed it to the director and said—"What do you hear?" The story had become widespread in the organization.

5. *Formal statements of organizational philosophy, creeds, and charters.* The formal statements are hints as to what is believed to be true about the desired culture. Look at what is on the walls. Most health care organizations have organizational statements on the walls. Maybe there are only pictures—yet behind the picture is a story. What did it take to get that picture on the wall? Dollars? Community service?

The elements listed become useful clues for what needs to happen to facilitate organizational change and cultural change. If we want to introduce a culture built around the OPO model, the ten points become clues for what might be done.

In an OPO, there is a deliberate attempt to build a culture that is clear about purpose, role, feedback, and levels of commitment. The organization is deliberate about communicating culture to those within and outside the organization.

This brings us to the question of change. Can organizations change culture? The answer is a resounding yes . . . and no. The quick response is one of yes. Look at what happened to health care organizations as a result of the shift in reimbursement systems. The cultures of health care organizations changed. However, this did not happen quickly or easily. With respect to change, we need to speak in terms of years.

What does change involve? Here are five requirements:

1. Understanding the current culture and implications of change for that culture
2. Knowing what vision you are moving the culture toward
3. An action plan for the steps to be taken
4. Benchmarks to see that we are moving in the right directions
5. Top-down role modeling of the skills and the direction

The process is not easy. But it is workable. The key is knowing what it is you want (purpose and roles), knowing how you will monitor it (feedback), and knowing how you will reward it (commitment).

## The Organization and the OPO Model

What is the starting point of any organization? We have been saying "purpose" thus far in this book. Drucker (1974, p. 79) provides us with a bit of a twist: "With respect to the definition of business, purpose, and business mission, there is only one such focus, one starting point. It is the customer. The customer defines the business."

Figure 2.2 shows what the OPO model looks like when it is expanded to capture the organization. What does this model do? Most important, it provides a framework for thinking about the broader context of the organization. Remember our discussion regarding customers? The penultimate customer is the organization itself. (As Drucker indicates, the ultimate customer is the person dependent on the organization's product or service.) Each individual is there to serve the organization. That

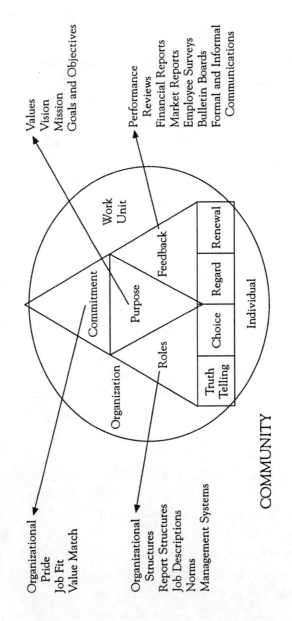

Figure 2.2. Organizational View.

Values
Vision
Mission
Goals and Objectives

Performance
Reviews
Financial Reports
Market Reports
Employee Surveys
Bulletin Boards
Formal and Informal
    Communications

Work
Unit

Commitment

Purpose

Feedback

Organization

Roles

Truth
Telling

Choice

Regard

Renewal

Individual

COMMUNITY

Organizational
Pride
Job Fit
Value Match

Organizational
Structures
Report Structures
Job Descriptions
Norms
Management Systems

service may be to provide the best care possible to a patient or it may be cleaning a patient room. We are there to serve the organization. When we are working in a portion of a department or a department within the organization, we need to be sensitive to the impact of our work on the overall organization. Health care organizations are highly complex, and changes in one part of an organization almost always mean changes in other parts. Changing the procedures in a lab work-up impacts others within the organization. The value of the organizational model is that it enables us to think about how a change is impacting the overall purpose, roles, commitment, or feedback systems in the organization.

What does this mean when we look at our components? The next four sections will address each individually.

*Purpose*

Purpose is the starting point of an OPO. What does it take to get to "purpose"? Greenleaf (1973, p. 9) says that "a mark of a leader . . . is that [he or she] is better than most at pointing the direction. [He or she] always has a goal. It may be a goal arrived at by group consensus; or the leader, acting on inspiration, may simply have said, let's go this way. But the leader always knows what it is and can articulate it for any who are unsure. By clearly stating and restating the goal, the leader gives certainty and purpose to others who may have difficulty in achieving it for themselves."

So where does organizational purpose begin? The natural starting place is with the founding fathers or mothers of an organization. As Schein (1985, p. 319) says, "Organizational culture does not start from scratch or come into being accidentally.

63

Organizations are created by people, and the creators of organizations also create culture through the articulation of their own assumptions. Although the final form of an organization's culture reflects the complex interaction between the thrust provided by the founder, the reactions of the group members and their shared historical experiences, there is little doubt that the initial shaping force is the personality and belief system of the founder." As we noted earlier, a basic reason an organization comes into existence is to serve society. But what other factors cause someone to say, "Here is a need we can address"? Take a few moments with the following questions.

*Think about your current organization. How did it begin? What were the motives and intent of the founding mothers or fathers?*

*What are some of the stories associated with the start-up of your organization? Are there some legends there?*

*Look around your organization for the symbols regarding the start-up of the organization. Whose pictures are on the walls and why? Where did the building get its name? If there was a large donor, why did he or she choose to give?*

I have had the privilege of being part of a start-up organization. Based on that experience, I was able to study three other organizations as they started up. The start-up organization I was part of began because the founding leader had a purpose. That purpose was to establish a world-class cancer research center in Florida. Why? Two important reasons. First, he had friends who had bouts with cancer—including one who died at an early age. He himself had had cancer. Second, he recognized that Florida has one of the highest rates of cancer in the country.

That was the motivation. He took the battle to the state legislature and "won" the funding for the establishment of the Moffitt Cancer Center and Research Institute. The actual funding came from a tax on cigarettes.

How an organization takes its first steps is critical to its growth and development. It is useful to know what those steps were like for your organization. Think about the following questions: How was the organization birthed? What is its lifeline? What happened as decision makers appeared on the scene with variations on purpose? These new decision makers may be the "customers." Perhaps the customers want something different from what the founder wanted. To stay in business, a change in the service or product may need to be made. Perhaps a new management team comes into existence. Now it begins to put its collective fingerprint on the organization.

In many settings, a board of directors comes into existence. In most health care organizations, the board is the legal guardian of the purpose and mission of the organization. It has the fiduciary responsibility. The board naturally becomes involved in changes to that basic mission. And the administration carries out the wishes of the board.

Real-life scenarios can involve a multitude of combinations of the above. Sometimes, the board is a board in name only. The members are there to enjoy the amenities of being board members. What is important is that planners consider the role of the board as part of the question of organizational purpose.

*Think about your organization. If you have a board, answer these questions: What is the role of the board in your organization? What is its interface with administration?*

*If you were to ask board members about the mission of the organization, what would they say? (Next step—ask them!)*

*If you were to ask board members what they think the purpose of your organization is, what would they say?*

Assume you have decided that you want to build an OPO. Where do you begin? There are two options. The first is that you are starting from scratch—a new organization start-up. The second involves "renewal," if you are working with an existing purpose statement and want to reaffirm or change it. In either case, the process is similar.

*Step 1: Establishing the groundwork.* Identify why you want to establish the organization and the outcomes that you have in mind. What service or product will you be delivering? Who are the customers for this service or product? Do you know their requirements? Do you have the decision-making group's "sanction" to do this? And do you have the energy? The answer to the last question has to be yes. The primary leadership role is to facilitate the vision and purpose of the organization. The name for it is *purposing*. Vaill (1989, p. 52) defines purposing as "a continuous stream of actions by an organization's formal leadership that has the effect of inducing clarity, consensus, and commitment regarding the organization's basic purposes." Purposing is ongoing and dynamic; it changes over time and over the organization's life cycle.

Purposing is the responsibility of senior leadership (administrative and board), which keeps adjusting the purpose of the organization to the changing times and circumstances. It presupposes that what makes sense for the organization today may shift and change tomorrow. The role of senior management and others is to adjust accordingly. The result of step 1 is a deci-sion (commitment) to move forward.

*Step 2: Deciding the "who."* This is the decision about who finally determines purpose. There are two major options at this point. One is that the leader begins to redefine purpose. This person assumes responsibility for developing or revising the pur-pose statement. If the leader is a visionary who has a clear and strong vision of where the organization needs to go, this can be very workable. It might also be that the leader is able to pick up on the "wisdom" of the organization. In other words, the vision has already been articulated by others within the organization, and the leader simply nurtures that vision and allows it to grow.

For example, in one setting which I have been part of, the facility brought in a strong physician administrator who was also a strong academic. She knew the hospital side of the busi-ness as well as the academic structures. She had strong views on group practice and provided the vision—here is what we need to do to get where we need to get. Her vision was strong and clear.

The second option is deciding a cast of people to be involved. This could include the board, members of the management team, customers, suppliers, and others. This is the most excit-ing alternative because a multitude of viewpoints are involved. Another setting I worked with had a group of strong middle managers. Most of them were very involved in their professional societies and were strong individuals. The result—the vision process involved them heavily.

Ultimately, the customers of the service or product you are providing resolve the question of purpose. They have the ultimate vote. If you are not in touch with them, you will be out of business.

*Step 3: Determining the scope of the work.* This step involves laying out the plan of attack. Here is how the process will go in a step-by-step manner. The scope of the work involves essentially three movements. The first is visioning. The second is "what is." The third is bridging the gap between vision and reality. If you cut away the multitude of steps involved in most processes, you will find that these three steps make up the core.

Visioning allows us to project what can be. If I begin with a focus on "what is," I may confine myself to just that. Visioning says, "Here is what we can be." The definition of "what is" is a critical part of developing the purpose statement. Your definition needs to be as precise as possible. "What is" takes the hard facts of your organization into account. It gets input from customers, suppliers, and others. It is a reality test. The next step is to bridge the gap. Now is the time to begin thinking about the movement from "what is" to the vision. If the gap in purpose is minimal, you may have little or no work ahead of you. But if the gap is large, you may be faced with a major challenge.

*Step 4: Publishing.* Publishing needs to happen at two points. The first is when you have a draft of your purpose statement. This provides a tool for others to give you feedback. The second is the final copy. It is important to date this copy. Be sure to put it up on the wall—or on the back of your business cards, name tags, and so on. Make sure the word gets out.

*Step 5: Doing the care and feeding.* Last, you need to have a plan for how you will keep the purpose statement alive. This is the care and feeding of it. How can you keep the spotlight on it? As you walk around, ask questions about purpose. When key organizational questions are being decided, use purpose as the plumb line. As personnel policies are developed, revisit purpose statements. The goal is to keep the spotlight on purpose in all the activities of the organization. The constant question is—how does this contribute to purpose?

Again, let us return to the quotation from Farr at the beginning of Chapter One. For me, the impressive aspect of this statement is that purpose is the all-encompassing aspect of organizational life. Without a sense of purpose, there is no way to measure organizational success.

The statement defines organizational integrity. Organizational integrity occurs when the organization acts on purpose. The organization is not judged according to purpose, but according to whether it acts on its purpose.

In addition, Farr says the following:

> To have integrity, an organization must be staffed by people who are totally in support of its purpose, and who act in total commitment to it. To the extent that they do not, their actions become inappropriate, they are not on-purpose, and integrity decreases.
>
> For individuals to be in total commitment and support of an organization's purpose, those purposes must be appropriate to the individual's purposes, as must the actions required to attain them. In other words, the purposes and actions of the organization must enable the individual to act fully in support of this personal integrity [Farr, 1984].

This statement brings together the concept of the individual building blocks and the organizational building block. Organizational purpose must support individual purpose, just as individual purpose must support organizational purpose.

Given the statements of purpose and the statements about subpurposes, we now hire for those purposes. We say to individuals, "This is the purpose of this organization," and they can enroll or not enroll in the organization. The statement of purpose also determines what our style of leadership will be and what we will train our managers to do. In addition, we use the on-purpose behaviors as the benchmarks for determining rewards and punishments.

The only way the organization can work is if individuals work in a truthful manner, taking responsibility for themselves and acting in support of others who have the interest of the organization at heart.

*Roles*

Here we look at two aspects of role. The first is *internal*—the roles within the organization; the second is *external*, involving the role of the organization in the community.

The following components of an organization define internal roles:

- Organizational structures
- Report structures
- Management structures
- Norms
- Decision-making structures
- Job descriptions

The development of organizational structures is one of senior management's major responsibilities. Various tools aid in defining these structures.

Organizational charts are an example of such a tool. One of the stories regarding the origins of organizational charts goes like this. In the early 1900s, a major train wreck occurred in the Northeast. In trying to find out who was responsible for the wreck, the investigators asked each person who they reported to and for what. The result was an organizational chart. The original intent of the organizational chart was to determine blame. Unfortunately, that is still true in some organizations today.

Organizational charts are useful in giving an overview of how the organization is structured and how formal relationships are defined. However, this implies that the charts are complete and up-to-date and that the organization actually works like the charts indicate. In most organizations, the charts represent very little. They are stagnant and represent a past organizational structure. This is unfortunate. Organizational charts that reflect the relationship of departments to work flow are an underutilized tool that can potentially be valuable for the organization.

A problem with most organizational charts is that they only represent a top-down approach. They identify a person's status. They do not show the work-process relationships. However, organizational charts that represent relationships and work flow can be invaluable. As a friend of mine says, "The only valuable organizational chart is a work-flow chart."

Another way that roles get defined in organizations is through report structures. These will typically be laid out on the organizational chart. This chart can be expanded to include other key relationships: Who does this person tend to consult with? Who does the person relate to most frequently?

Management charts have the same editorials. They are useful in seeing a snapshot of what is going on. To be more useful, they need to be expanded. For example, a management chart that defines the level of decision making at each level of management is very useful. Management charts that indicate client and supplier relationships are also useful. One suggestion: draw lots of circles on the management structure chart to indicate relationships.

Finally, job descriptions define the formal roles and responsibilities of a position. Typically, there will be linkages within a particular job description. Job descriptions are useful if they provide good information. For example, job descriptions based on work flow make sense. But job descriptions based solely on report relations are questionable.

What is being said here? First, the formal tools for defining roles within the organization are important and necessary. The problem is that we have largely passed over them and have made them repositories of useless information. In so doing, we minimize their real value to the organization. The problem: they are typically out of touch. The solution: they need to be made dynamic and reflective of work flow. How is that done? By providing more information about what really happens with work flow and relationships. Here are the suppliers. Here are the customers. Here are our requirements. Here are our customers' requirements. Now the organizational structures, management structures, decision structures, and job description come alive.

The structures discussed so far address only the formal structures. What about the feelings of people within those formal structures? What about informal role expectations? Within any organization, there are formal activities and interactions. These are typically represented by organizational charts and job descriptions. Along with those formal activities and interactions come sentiments. People have feelings about what they do and the discussions they have. A natural outgrowth of those formal interactions and activities are informal interactions and activities. As people work together, they begin to form relationships. Maybe they discuss children. Maybe it is hobbies. The informal discussions take place. Next, they might join a bowling team or play softball together. The informal activities begin to develop. Any organization, then, needs to be seen as a combination of formal and informal activities and interactions and sentiments.

So, we have defined the internal roles. What about the external? What role is the organization expected to play in the community? What are the community's expectations of the organization? The organization's expectations of the community?

This becomes a question of customers and suppliers again. The leaders of the organization need to do the following:

1. Identify who the key customers and suppliers are within the community.
2. Meet with those customers and find out their requirements. Do we know what is really important to the customer? If so, how do we know this? What is our evidence?
3. Based on the above, develop a role statement that defines the roles and relationships the organization has within the community. What are the key relationships?

One of the more exciting examples of the way health care is taking on a new role in the community is the Linn County story. Linn County, Iowa, has begun an extensive process of soliciting community involvement and participation in building a healthier county. Their health care organizations have defined their roles in novel ways. These organizations facilitated public and private groups in identifying the vision of a healthier Linn County, then had the same groups articulate the goals for a healthier county (Healing Linn County, 1992).

This process of defining the organization's role needs to be deliberate. Most organizations just fall into relationships within the community. A member of the board may be connected with a particular organization, and the organization mysteriously becomes connected with that organization as well. The role should be a conscious strategy, not a haphazard one.

To reiterate, organizational roles—both internal and external—need to be defined.

## Feedback

Bennis and Nanus (1985, p. 92) make an important point about feedback in their discussion of leaders and managers:

We have here one of the clearest distinctions between the leader and the manager. By focusing attention on a vision, the leader operates on the emotional and spiritual resources of the organization, on its values, commitment, and aspirations. The manager, by contrast, operates on the physical resources of the organization, on its capital, human skills, raw materials, and technology. Any competent manager can make it possible for people in the organization to earn a living. An excellent manager can see to it that the work is done productively and efficiently on schedule and with a high level of quality. It remains for the effective leader, however, to help people in the organization know pride and satisfaction in their work. Good leaders often inspire the followers to high levels of achievement by showing them how their work contributes to worthwhile ends.

The purpose of feedback systems is to show how the work of the organization is progressing. How does the organization know it is doing well? How does the organization know it is not doing well? Feedback systems provide the organization with data. Some of these feedback systems include:

- Formal and informal communications
- Performance reviews
- Financial indicators
- Market survey data
- Consumer surveys
- Infection rates
- Risk management information

The list could go on. This is especially true as we think of the abundance of information available to health care organizations. The important question is the usefulness of the feedback. Are we collecting information that is helpful to us as we make decisions about service and products, both now and for the future?

Our starting point is purpose and roles. Having defined purpose and roles, we have established the universe for the data we need. We need data that will tell us how we are proceeding with purpose and roles. As we defined purpose, we identified vision. How do we determine the indicators that we need to monitor our journey? In the section on roles, we discussed what internal and external roles we wanted. Now we need to identify monitors that will allow us to track them.

In the traditional business strategy approach, there are four major focal points for collecting feedback:

1. *Business analysis.* How are we doing as a business? How healthy is our bottom line? Are we functioning "on purpose?" How are our products and services?
2. *Competitive analysis.* What options do our customers have? Why are they choosing those options? What are our competitors doing better than we are doing?
3. *Customer analysis.* What customers are we serving? What are their requirements? How do we know if we are meeting those requirements? What is important for them in selecting us?
4. *Benchmarking analysis.* What services and products we provide are important to the customer? Who among our competitors is best in these areas? What do they do and how do they do it? What must we do to match or surpass them?

Feedback is information back to us about how we are doing.

*Take a moment to think through the following. Review the purpose statement you have developed. What are the key elements you defined as part of purpose? Now, what information do you need if the organization is to stay on purpose?*

- *Business analysis*
- *Competitive analysis*

76

- *Customer analysis*
- *Benchmarking analysis*

*What is the source of that information? People? Agencies? How often do you need to gather that information? Who needs to collect that information?*

*Now take a moment to think about roles. What were the key external and internal role clarifications that were done? What information do you need to monitor to see if you are staying on track or not? What is the source of that information? People? Agencies? How frequently do you need to collect it? Who will be responsible for collecting it?*

The questions are simple. When they are answered carefully, they provide the needed direction.

Feedback allows the organization to know if it is on track or not. It is the compass that points the direction that we are going in.

### Commitment

Much has been written about commitment in the organization. I believe it is a by-product of other factors that have already been discussed. It also has one other prerequisite—integrity. Drucker (1974, p. 462) points out, "The final proof of the sincerity and seriousness of management is uncompromising emphasis on integrity of character. This above all has to be symbolized in management's people decisions, for it is character through which leadership is exercised; it is character that sets the example and is imitated."

We saw earlier that the right level of commitment is a major asset to any organization. The questions we are concerned with are the following: How do we get and keep employees who are committed to their jobs, the work unit, and the organization? How do we prevent poor job fits? How do we stop inappropriate turnover?

The issue comes to this. We want individuals who can find meaning in their work, connect with that meaning, and have a sense of contributing to the organization. The result is a feeling of pride in the organization. A tall order!

Commitment fuels the organization. It will include such things as personal satisfaction, wage and salary plans, pride, job enrichments, and the value match between the individual and the organization. The focus of this section is on organizational pride. If people find their jobs meaningful, if work units provide social interactions and a small-group identity, the key remaining factor is organizational pride. That grows from people's sense that the organization they are working with has integrity.

*Think for a moment about the following question: Remember an organization that you have been part of (or know) that was involved in something considered "unethical." What was your feeling and response to the organization?*

If you have had that experience, you must have noticed that your feeling of commitment and investment changed rapidly. While discussions of ethics are not unusual in health care institutions, typically these discussions have to do with medical ethics. Ethical issues associated with technology, quality of life, decisions involving do-not-resuscitate policies and procedures, AIDS testing, and so on most often receive scrutiny. However, another significant aspect of ethics deals with the administrative management of the health care organization.

The assumption I am making here is that ethical behavior in organizations, and specifically on the part of administrators and managers, has a great impact on organizational pride. Organizational pride in turn is intimately linked to commitment. Individuals may feel uncomfortable with certain decisions made by a management team. However, if they trust the basic ethical core of the decisions, they will be uncomfortable but will not let those decisions erode their own commitment to the organization. On the other hand, if the employees have a sense that the administrative or management decisions are unethical, at that point the core of trust in the organization is eroded. The organization will experience significant losses in the areas of productivity and performance. Why? The commitment to the organization will be significantly impacted.

*Take a moment and just think to yourself: When you think about ethics, what comes to your mind? What is your working definition? Make some notes to yourself about your definition of ethics.*

Ethics, as defined in this chapter, involve "the identification and practice of what constitutes good and bad conduct in the workplace." Obviously, built into the definition of good and bad conduct are some further assumptions. Typically, society defines the terms *good conduct* and *bad conduct*.

For example, we have determined, not only ethically but also legally, that discriminatory practices are not good for us as a society. They contradict a value we hold. Consequently, we have a variety of equal employment opportunity rules and regulations that organizations need to observe.

In health care organizations, we have also defined practices based on personal preferences, for the most part, to be bad or questionable. A decision based on personal preference would be, "If I like you, you get a promotion; if I don't like you, you don't get a promotion." We have defined choices based on accepted published criteria and standards as good. Instead of just personal preference, it is a matter of "Did the employees meet certain goals? Did they meet certain standards?" And so on.

We choose to work for organizations that have ethical value cores that match our own values. If we do not, our quality of work life diminishes very rapidly. We end up dissatisfied and move elsewhere. There is a process of self-selection involved: "I am going to select an organization that fits my values and my ethics." This means that organizational values need to be part of discussions in recruitment and selection. That is the "prevention" approach to unnecessary dissatisfaction and turnover.

Several beliefs regarding ethics and ethical behavior are behind this section. First of all, good ethics make good business sense. Davis, Frederick, and Blomstrom (1980, pp. 51–52) refer to the *iron law of social responsibility*. This law says simply, "Organizations that tend to abuse their power will go out of business." An organization that society begins to regard as unethical will quickly begin to find its bottom line impacted. An organization that functions in a way that is contrary to the interests of the immediate community in which it finds itself will encounter extreme opposition. Good ethics make good business sense, and good ethical organizations make good neighbors.

A second belief is that all management decisions have an ethical component. All decisions have a value core. Within that value base is a definition of what is good and what is bad. That means that regardless of the decision, there will be an ethical component to it.

Think about decisions that your senior management team has made in the past few weeks. And then think about the ethical base that you have used to make those decisions. Even decisions that might seem relatively trite have an ethical core. However, frequently the ethical core exists just on the edge of our awareness. We are making decisions automatically, based on that half-understood set of assumptions.

A third belief is that effective management is a result of perceived ethical management. Think about that for a moment. An organization can forgive a management group for bad decisions. However, if a decision is perceived to be poor in an ethical sense, the parameters of forgiveness become much narrower. The key operational concepts are perception and perceived ethical management.

A fourth belief is that ethical decisions are often not cut-and-dried. In some settings, they may be black or white, but in most settings, they are going to be shades of gray. That means that they will be both frustrating and intriguing. They will be frustrating for those who want a very simple answer. They will be intriguing for those who ask, "How do we make the best decision given the particular situation?"

How do we make the practice of ethical decision making a common expectation among us? The starting place is the boardroom. We need to provide a welcome mat for discussions regarding the question of ethics.

Here are a few practice questions for you to work with.

*Think about yourself as manager. If you were to make a statement to your employees about ethics, what would you say to them? When you think of the statement you just made in response to the first question, what would be an example of an ethical issue you recently had that is consistent or inconsistent with that statement?*

*Take a moment to think about your boss. What would your boss say to you about ethics? What does your boss's behavior say to you about ethics?*

The above questions are guidelines that can be useful in helping you think through your role in ethical decision making within the organization.

Blanchard and Peale (1988) describe five basic ethical principles for the organization. These are the "five P's" of organizational ethical conduct:

1. *Purpose.* Ethical standards need to be communicated in a statement of purpose. Just as there is a mission statement about the organization that talks about markets, the direction of the organization, and so on, there are also ethical standards that need to be communicated. The values the organization believes in, expected modes of conduct for the organization's members, and so forth need to be communicated in a statement of purpose as well. The core of the OPO model comes through in this way. Purpose needs to be there before the rest makes sense. Purpose needs to be a mirror of organizational values.

2. *Pride.* Organizational pride is the result of how people feel about themselves and the organization. Pride comes

with a sense of implementing good, ethical decisions. This was discussed earlier when it was mentioned that employees will forgive a bad decsiion but will not forgive an unethical decision. An unethical decision will erode morale.

3. *Patience.* The organization is unwilling to make short-term gains that are inconsistent with the core value at the cost of long-term interests. Short-term gains that violate a value core may be the ultimate downfall of the organization.

4. *Persistence.* The organization does what it says it is going to do. On an individual level, trust is built when individuals say what they are going to do and then carry it out. Organizational trust is the same. In organizations, trust is built when the organization does what it says it is going to do. It carries through on its word.

5. *Perspective.* Managers take time to reflect on where they are. This may appear in annual retreats, quarterly meetings, and so on where the work of the organization is reflected on. In addition, prospects of the year to come are reflected on as well. Management takes time to look at that.

When the preceding principles are followed, the result is an organization that people are proud to be members of. When employees are out in the community and someone asks them about their organization, they talk proudly about where they work. When others hear of their organization, they congratulate them on working there. If people are proud of the organization they work for, many policies and procedures, administrative decisions, and bureaucratic inconveniences will be forgiven. If not, those items will become problematic.

The workbook in the appendix contains a step-by-step walkthrough in reviewing commitment.

*Community*

The community is the environment in which the organization finds itself. This consists of the health care trends, regulatory bodies, boards, licensing groups, vendors, professional associations, physical community, and so on. The health care environment is a complex one that dramatically impacts the business of health care. That is why environment is such an important consideration.

The community is the "host" of the organization. It is in the environment that the organization survives or does not survive. Just as an individual or work unit within an organization may not survive if it deviates significantly from the organizational culture, the organization itself will not last long if it conflicts with the environment. Previously the concept of the iron law of responsibility was mentioned. Any organization that abuses its power will eventually lose it.

A number of specific areas need to be addressed when thinking of the organizational fit with the environment. The first is the value core. The second is the market core. The third is the resource core.

The *value core* is the starting point for the organizational fit. The value core looks at the values society has and then matches those with the organization. While this is not always clear, if those value cores do not match up, the organization will have difficulty surviving. This is particularly true in health care organizations, where the nature of the organization has to do with quality of life. When a decision is made not to provide an expensive organ transplant because of a lack of funds or because of the determination that the dollars would best be used in a different way, a major value statement is being made. The important point: the organization was produced by the environment in which it finds itself. If the organization strays significantly from that environment, it will be brought into line.

The second core is the *market core*. In a market-driven society such as ours, the market is what determines if the health care organization is offering the market what it wants. The customer is society. In the health care world, this becomes very complex. The product is health care. The customer wants the very best at the lowest possible price in a timely manner. Society has to face issues of technology costs, quality-of-life issues, rising health care costs, and so on. And the core is the marketplace. This is a critical point.

The third core is the *resource core*. The resource core consists of the technological resources needed for high-tech procedures as well as the human resources needed to run a health care organization. Anyone who has lived through a nursing shortage knows what the implications are for the organization.

The point is both obvious and dramatic. The organization operates with the sanction of the environment. When the environment revokes that sanction, the organization no longer exists.

## Conclusion

The organization ultimately comes together when it is "on purpose" or purposeful. The organization has first defined its purpose. It has then structured itself to fit that purpose. It has communicated that purpose throughout the membership, both within and outside of the community. Recruitment, selection, orientation, training, and reward systems are based on that purpose. At any time, all members of the organization know what their purpose is and how it fits into the overall purpose of the organization.

The OPO is in a constant process of role clarification and refinement. As the environment changes, so do the role definitions. The OPO has committed itself to being as clear as possible about role and role changes.

In addition, the organization has designed feedback systems that reflect key criteria for success. These criteria measure how on purpose the organization is. And the organization strives for appropriate levels of commitment and investment, both internally and externally.

Resource B provides a step-by-step walk-through of the process of building an OPO. Like a blueprint, it will provide directions, but the final building is still to be built.

CHAPTER THREE

# Integration and Differentiation in Work Units

We managers must recognize that in this almost sudden, compulsive search for connection and a sense of community, business has an unprecedented opportunity to create a special place, which in the old days we thought of as just a place to work. . . . We managers have the opportunity to lead and direct people in that ever more powerful bond of common enterprise, and at the same time to create a place of friendship, deep personal connections, and neighborhood. . . . So how about this for a new management bumper sticker: *If You're Not Creating Community, You're Not Managing.*

—James A. Autry,
*Love and Profit*

IN THINKING ABOUT ORGANIZATIONS, an image comes to mind. As a child growing up in the Dakotas, each spring I would witness the rising of the Missouri River. There would be a time of flooding as the little mountain streams that fed the Missouri in Montana brought the runoff from the winter snows and the spring rains. The Missouri would overflow its banks whenever it could. It had great force and strength. Later in the year, the

Missouri would be a narrow thread of water flowing through the banks that were cut during flooding. It was nowhere near as mighty and powerful as the springtime Missouri. The banks that had been cut to accommodate the torrents of spring now held a little meandering river. In both cases, the Missouri depended on hundreds of small tributaries to contribute to its greatness. Without those feeder streams, it was nothing. And, in fact, as water upstream was drawn off for other purposes—irrigation, water management, and so on—the final strength of the Missouri was compromised.

What does this have to do with this book? The individual and work units become the tributaries which feed the rest of the organization and give the final organization its strength and might. At times, those tributaries cause the banks of the organization to almost overflow. At other times, they fall neatly within the banks. But, the organization's strength comes from the individuals feeding those work units that feed the overall organization. If those tributaries disappear, the total organization will go dry. But if the tributaries remain full of ideas and energy, the organization flows strong. The OPO approach means that tributaries are focused and flowing. They all contribute to the organization's strength.

The organization sets the stage for the OPO. It defines purpose and roles, establishes feedback systems, and creates the climate for commitment. Therefore, the first layer of the onion skin model is the organization. However, the work of the organization is so complex that it has to be broken into smaller units. One key to the organization, then, is how the workforce is organized to get the work done. In the language of organizational theory, we are talking about *integration* and *differentia-*

*tion.* Because different groups have to do different things to get the work of the organization done, the process needs to be integrated. Structure is one way this integration is managed. Organizational structure defines relationships and integrates the work process.

At the same time, differentiation is also necessary. The complexity of the work demands differentiation. Differentiation means the work is divided up. Small groups have responsibility for certain aspects of getting the work done. In health care, we have "specialized" in specialization. There may be as many as 450 job descriptions within a single health care organization. This field has become so complex that the American Hospital Association publishes a handbook on departments of health care organizations (Goldberg and Buttaro, 1990).

To return to our river metaphor, I like to think of integration and differentiation as a tide ebbing and flowing. Health care organizations are in a constant flux back and forth between the two. At the point where we find high levels of integration, we can expect the movement toward differentiation, and vice versa. Changing times mean that the flow is even greater. Today, the concept of seamless health care organizations focuses on the customer—while we may have tremendous differentiation in the organization, the customer needs to have a sense of seamlessness.

In Chapter Two, we discussed the organization itself. The work unit represents the next major layer in the onion skin model. The work unit is the immediate group that the individual is a member of. Examples may be nursing services, a group of unit clerks working in the same area, environmental service people working in the area, secretaries, nursing assistants, and so on. Typically, the work unit is geographically intact—that is, all members of the work unit are in the same location. The work unit has a defined responsibility for a function or work process. The work unit depends on the organization to provide the overall direction and mission and on the individuals within it to work together to get the work done. It is the critical infrastructure in the organization. In health care, almost all work gets done through teams.

This chapter focuses on the OPO model as it applies to work units. It covers both formal and informal aspects of work units.

## Formal Versus Informal Structures

To get the work of the organization done, work units are established in a formal sense. However, in the process of doing their jobs, members of the work unit develop sentiments or feelings about what is happening. Those feelings invite informal activities and informal interactions.

### Formal Structures

When organizations put individuals together in formal work units, typically it is because these work units make sense for the organization. Rationales for work units include the following:

1. The work unit is a logical subset of the organization. It may be logical for the health care organization to have all the finance people together in one unit. Or it could be logical to create a product-line approach where intact teams can be formed. Another example might be a cardiac team. Or it would make sense for nurses to be part of the nursing division. The logic is that likes (however defined) belong with likes. This is *specialization*. Take the specialists in an area and group them

together. The specialists build on one another's ideas and increase their level of competence.

2. The work unit provides the organization with some element of control. By putting individuals in work units, the organization can create something known as *management structures* to watch over the units and see that everyone is producing. The organization has created a way to integrate the various functions. In the hierarchical organization, the ultimate integrator is the CEO—or at least that is the implication. By sitting in the driver's seat, the CEO oversees coordination of vice presidents, who oversee the coordinating of work unit directors, who oversee the direction of their work units, and so on. Today the demand is to be fluid.

3. The work unit represents some unique function of the organization. When the unit has been properly defined, the work unit encompasses a function or set of functions for the organization. It becomes an entity with its own vision, purpose, and mission to perform. It has internal and external customers and suppliers. It needs to know who those customers and suppliers are, what is required of them, and how they are doing.

We have been talking about the organization from a formal standpoint. Typically, there are three major types of formal work units. The first involves a *functional* approach. According to this design, the organization is divided into unique functions, which then contribute to the organization. In the health care organization, the functional approach may be to put all the accounting people in one work unit, the nursing people in another work unit, and so forth. The key is that individuals who have similar functions are grouped together. Likes belong with likes. This is the typical hospital structure.

The good news about this approach is that it allows the specialists the opportunity to be among specialists. If you have all the education people together in the same unit, there is an economy of scale. People reinforce each other. The bad news is that this structure can get clumsy in rapidly changing times, since it can be slow and inefficient. This structure also promotes the development of "turfs." Departmental goals and objectives may drive the health care organization instead of the other way around. For example, in one setting, the information systems strategic plan drove the organization. It was highly technical and costly.

The second major way of forming work units is through a *client-centered* or *product-oriented* approach. In this approach, the organization is structured around specific client groups. Each work unit includes all the functions necessary for it to come up with the final product or service. For example, in this product-line approach, the goal might be to turn cancer care into a product line. That work unit will include the patient care staff, fiscal people, marketing people, and so on. A team is formed around the desired results and supports the product. Many of the patient-centered innovative approaches are compatible with a client-centered approach. The unit is focused with one end in mind—the patient. One example of this is a cancer center's organization around programs. Programs are based on organ site; they might include a breast program, a lung program, or a head-and-neck program. In the programs, there is a nurse manager, physician leader, and administrator. Whether patients are being treated on an inpatient or outpatient basis, the team follows them throughout their stay. Another example of patient focus is a patient-focused orthopedic unit that

I am familiar with. All key patient care functions happen within the unit. The unit has an X-ray unit, lab, rehab, admitting, and business office. And it is immediately outside the operating room. An orthopedic patient needs to go to only one place—the orthopedic unit.

The good news about this approach is that the team can adapt to changing conditions rapidly. The product team knows if volume drops off, so it can take corrective action quickly. Another key advantage in health care is that the costs for creating that product line are more readily identifiable. We are more apt to know what the costs and revenues are. The bad news is that duplication may exist within the system. Instead of a small number of individuals meeting public relations needs, every team has its own public relations person. At the same time, specialists on the team may feel cut off from the others in their field.

The last type of work unit is created through a *matrix* approach. This approach attempts to combine the best features of the other two approaches. A matrix organization crosses the functional lines and forms product teams that are a cross section of the organization. The assignment to a particular team is for the life of the project. That may be one month or until retirement. In health care, matrix work groups become project management groups. We call it *product-line management.*

The good news about this approach is that the benefits of the functional organization can be combined with the benefits of the product organization. The bad news is that individuals may retain their loyalties to the functional unit and be reluctant to become part of the team.

With the advent of Total Quality Management, work units

are being organized around processes rather than functions. This is similar to product-line management, since the key integrating force is the required work process. If that is patient care, all the pieces of the patient care process are articulated and laid out. The work unit, then, becomes a combination of people who touch that work process.

Health care work units may be organized in numerous ways, and none of them are "pure." Given that, how do we decide to structure? The major driving forces are the organization's mission and purpose and its environment. Structure is a tool to help the organization organize its resources so that the organization can get its work done most effectively. The key question remains the following: Will this type of organizational structure help or hinder our ability to fulfill our purpose?

*Informal Structures*

Behind every structure there is an informal structure. For example, the medical records work unit is organized to promote the flow of patient information to the appropriate health care providers. Formal activities take place to properly record the information coming in and see that the information is secure. To accomplish the tasks, members of the work unit have formal interactions. Initially, these formal interactions may be with orientation and job training. In the process of doing work, feelings develop about the work itself, co-workers, the work environment, and so on. This is a natural occurrence within any human organization. At the same time, the informal work unit begins to emerge. The informal activities may be such things as taking coffee breaks together or going out for lunch, or even taking part in the work unit softball team. Informal activities lead to informal interactions—talking about family, hobbies, vacations, and so forth. All work units have informal as well as formal interactions. Try this experiment. At random, walk into any work unit in your health care organization. Ask the first person you see what the function and purpose of that work unit is and how it is organized. Now, ask this question: "If you need to get something done around here, what do you actually do?" Given truthful communications, you will now begin to get at the informal structure. The goal of the OPO is to have significant overlap between the formal and informal interactions.

The goal is to have the informal organization support and complement the formal organization. When it does so, the work unit is on purpose and remains targeted. When it does not, the informal activities can actually begin to overwhelm the formal ones. A counterculture can develop that pulls energies away from the formal work unit. This can be extremely disruptive to the organization.

Elsewhere I have discussed organizational and work-unit culture (Ulschak, 1989). With respect to the concept of subcultures, options immediately present themselves. The first is that the subculture of a particular work unit is on purpose with the organization. It is in line with the organization. It is supportive of its mission to the organization. The second type of subculture is on a parallel track to the organization. Information resources is an example. Certainly, information resources supports the organization, yet it runs parallel to the organization. Within the information resources group, norms may differ from the organization, but this does not significantly impact what goes on. Then there is the counterculture subgroup. This can be positive or negative. In either case, the counterculture group goes its own way and the organization be damned. The culture of the group may be more potent then the culture of the organization. When it goes counter to the organization, a major misuse of resources can result.

Health care organizations depend on the work of teams. Our biggest challenge is that many of the work units border on the counterculture because of their strong boundaries. Just walk into a nursing unit. You will find one type of work-unit culture. Now walk into the lab. Here you find a different variation. Now go to the business office. Again there is a different version. What we need is that common bond that crosses boundaries.

The lesson? We have formal and informal structures. Our goal is to have the informal support the formal.

## The Work Unit and the OPO Model

Earlier, I stated that health care organizations cannot get their work done without teams. As Reddy and Jamison (1988, p. 35) say, "Without teamwork, we cannot fully experience productive community." Now the question becomes: How can the OPO model be useful for the work unit? The purpose of this section is to answer that question. The OPO model is an excellent tool for understanding a work unit and for making decisions about what can make the work unit more effective and efficient. A key assumption: almost any significant work in health care is done through teams.

The goal of the OPO model at the work-unit level is to create clarity of purpose, clarity of roles, appropriate feedback systems, and appropriate levels of commitment. When those elements are in place, the work unit is ready to carry out its work. And those elements need to apply to individual members as well. Each member needs to be seen as a vital component of the work unit. That means that each member needs to have a clear understanding of what needs to happen, how it needs to happen, and when it needs to happen. The question for the manager is how to bring about alignment within the work unit.

The added challenge of the work unit is this: the manager now needs to bring together others to get the work done. Instead of one person's purpose, roles, feedback, and commitment, the manager needs to bring together multiple people and get them targeted on common purpose, roles, feedback, and commitment.

*Purpose*

The first step in applying the OPO model to the work unit is to raise questions related to purpose: What is the purpose of this work unit? What is its mission? What are its core values? How do the above fit with the organization's purpose? Mission? Core values?

The goal of the OPO model is to develop for the work unit a purpose statement that is in alignment with the organization and that members of the work unit clearly understand and agree to. This is where the power of the organization is unleashed. It is only when these questions are answered that the energies of the work unit can be harnessed. This is the role of leadership at the work-unit level. Conger and Kanungo (1988, p. 136) state: "The essential work of the organizational [or team] leader is defining, constructing, and gaining commitment to a set of shared values, beliefs, and norms about change, goals, and people working together. That is, defining, building, and involving people in the organization's culture. This is the primary task work of organizational leaders, and it is the reason that the three themes of change, goals, and people working together must be built into the leader's vision."

Leadership at the work-unit level is responsible for carrying out the sanction the organization has given the work unit. The organization has provided resources to the work unit to get something done. The unit may have been given an explicit statement or charge. In reality, most organizations function on the basis of "inheritance." We inherit a particular work unit and assume that it has been given a certain responsibility to carry out.

One of the more challenging experiences of my life has been being a member of the senior management team in the start-up of a new facility. From this experience, I have learned that it is critical to articulate the obvious. For instance, instead of assuming that we know what a lab is about, we need to give the lab a charge and then let the lab work with that charge to refine and reform it. Do not assume that the people will know or agree with the charge. This is the role of work-unit leadership.

The starting place for reviewing the work unit is purpose. There is only one way to begin and that is by asking questions about what has been, what currently is, and what can be.

*Think for a moment about the work unit that you are currently in. Answer the following questions. What was the founding reason for this work unit? Was there a particular person responsible for its founding? Who was it designed to serve? What were the dreams for it?*

*What is the purpose of this work unit? What is the core reason for its existence?*

*Think about mission. The mission statement is a statement of the business you are in and the customers you serve. Now take a few moments and define mission for your work unit. What are your products and services? Who are your customers? What are their requirements?*

*As you think about purpose and the mission statement, what are the core values around which this work unit is built? How do they come out in terms of the mission statement and the purpose statement?*

*Now think about the key functions of the work unit. What are these key functions?*

Take some time to review what you have written down. See what you have written as "draft" material. Let yourself "play" with the concepts. Now ask the question, "Who are the other people in this organization that I need to begin to talk to about purpose, mission, and values?" There are some obvious answers— your boss, perhaps your boss's boss, other members of the work unit, users of your services, and so on. It is important for you to lay your thoughts on the table for others to review. In that review, negotiation begins.

One valuable exercise for work units is based on Block's "vision of greatness" (1987). This exercise asks, "If our work unit were doing things in a 'great' manner, what would it look like? What would we be doing? How would we be doing it? How would we be treating one another? How would we be treating others?" The exercise is outlined below.

*This is an exercise in developing a vision of greatness for this work unit. Do not let the word greatness get in your way. It is deliber-*

ately in the title to encourage you to let yourself dream. As Green-leaf (1973, p. 9) states: "For something great to happen, there must be a great dream. Behind every great achievement is a dreamer of great dreams. Much more than a dreamer is required to bring it to reality: but the dream must be there first." This exercise will have you focus your preferred future for the work unit. It is a "frontier" that you would like to see us move toward. It is a future that the work unit may not live up to but it becomes something to move toward.

Here are some guidelines for the exercise:

1. Do not be practical. The purpose is to dream.
2. The vision should be compelling for you.
3. The vision comes from the heart.
4. If the vision sounds unrealistic and you might be embar-rassed to read it in public, you are on the right track.

Most of all, enjoy the exercise and let yourself think about what might be.

### Focus on Clients

The first part of the vision of greatness focuses on the client groups with which you work. Here are some questions to consider as you develop your ideal of how you might relate to these groups:

1. If they were our only client group, how would we treat them?
2. When our clients express frustration and disappointment with us, how can we use that frustration and disappointment as a learning so we can improve?
3. How do we deliver bad news to our clients?
4. How do we handle situations when our clients let us down?

*Think about these questions (and others you might have) and write your ideas for a statement of greatness directed at how we would like to deal with our clients.*

## Focus on How We Treat Each Other

*The first part of the vision of greatness looked at how you deal with your client groups. This second part looks at how you deal with each other in the work unit. Here are some questions to help you focus:*

1. *How do you want support expressed? Do you want to be left alone? Recognized?*
2. *How do you want conflict and disagreement handled?*
3. *What balance do you want between team and individual effort?*

*Take some time and write down your ideas for the vision of greatness.*

## Focus on Products and Services

*The third part of the vision of greatness deals with products and services.*

1. *What would our products and services look like?*
2. *What would be the process of evaluating the products and services?*
3. *How do we balance the desire for products and services with the limited resources we have to deliver?*
4. *What accountability do we have for poor quality? Excellent quality?*
5. *How do we celebrate our successes and learn from the failures with our products and services?*

*Use these questions as a starting point for statements of greatness. Write down those statements.*

The heart of every work unit is its statement of purpose. Pascarella and Frohman (1989) provide a number of questions that need to be answered in developing a purpose statement. Here are some of those questions.

The first question that needs to be answered is, "Are you prepared to write a purpose statement?" Purpose statements take time to write. They require energy. Do you have the time and energy? Purpose statements involve others. This means time to get their input. In general, a good deal of work will be involved. Do you think the benefits outweigh the costs? Answer these questions for yourself: Are you prepared to take on this exercise? If the answer is yes, what are the benefits that you expect to get from it?

The first question is to do or not do it. The next questions are concerned with the actual writing of the purpose statement. Here are those guides:

1. *Make sure that the work-unit director is committed to the process of defining purpose.* Remember that in the process of defining purpose, some things are defined "in" and some things are defined "out." Not everyone will agree with these choices. Recently, I have been working with an organization in which the major problem identified by the employees was a lack of leadership. And, the board of the organization was recruiting heavily for a nationally known leader. A question recently was raised about what will happen when the organization hires someone who has a firm direction. There will be a major parting of the ways for some members of the organization. They will realize that the organization is not going in the direction they would like to see it go in.

2. *Make a preliminary draft of the material.* One of the major

blocks in writing a purpose statement is perfectionism. The work-unit director will want to write the perfect purpose statement at the first draft. However, that does not work for most of us. We need to begin and just "do it." As some friends of mine say—pretend you have something important to say and then say it.

3. *Determine the data needed to fill in the draft and begin to collect them.* Focus on the success factors. You need to identify what data are needed as you go through the process. This part of writing a purpose statement is frequently overlooked. The response might be, "What do you mean, collecting data—that sounds more like a research project."

The reality is that you will need to collect data. The data might be what your boss thinks, what your subordinates think, what your peers think, and so forth. Or they may mean benchmarks—that is, going out to other organizations that have similar work units and talking with them about purpose.

4. *Take time to envision the future.* Later in this chapter, we will talk about a process for envisioning the future. Whatever process is used, it is critical to think about the desired state for the work unit. What are we really after? What do we really want to create? That needs to be part of the purpose statement process.

5. *Redraft with a focus on what the success factors will be for today and for tomorrow.* If you are successful, what does that mean? What does it mean for your services and products? What does it mean for the customers you service? What does it mean for suppliers?

6. *Test the statement on some other audiences.* As mentioned earlier, this step is critical. Test the statement on others. Let

them have an opportunity to respond to you. One audience is your work unit. Have the work unit critique the statement. Another audience might be the management group at your facility. Present it to the management team. And, most important, present it to your key customers.

An important point to remember: the work unit is within the context of the rest of the organization. That means that the organization has already charged the work unit with a particular purpose. And the purpose statement of the work unit has to be supportive of the organizational purpose statement.

The process of writing a purpose statement is an excellent way to develop ownership of the purpose statement by the key stakeholders. If the process ends up with a purpose statement different from the one originally given by the organization, it is important to discuss and negotiate the differences. If there is a discrepancy between what is and what is desired, it is better to identify that gap and get it out in the open than to leave it hidden. The process is ultimately a win-win situation for the work unit because of the clarification and reconciliation of differences.

Once the purpose statement is written, circulate it to other work units for their comments. Since they are the ones who "use" your work unit, they become an invaluable resource for comments to you. This also invites them to be greater stakeholders in your specific work unit. Finally, by publishing the statement in this way, you also have a new level of accountability.

Purpose is the natural place to start in building the on-purpose work unit. Once it is defined, it provides the structure on which the other components of the OPO model rest.

The goal—building an on-purpose work unit that is congruent with the organization.

*Roles*

When we discussed roles at the organizational level, we identified how important role clarity was for the organization. This is just as true at the work-unit level. Maehr and Braskamp (1986, p. 40) make the following statement: "Before we can ask why a person engages in one activity but not another, we have to make sure that both activities were, in fact, regarded as viable options. People will act in terms of what they perceive to be available to them in any given situation; that is, they will act in terms of what they perceive as possible. . . . When we wonder why a person does or does not do something, we must consider first whether that something is a viable option in his or her world." This is what role clarity is all about—making sure that what is being asked is a viable and agreed-on option.

Role definition at the work-unit level consists of two parts. One part is role clarity with other work units. Do other work units understand what the role of your work unit is? Do they know what to expect of your work unit and how to access its services and products?

The other part is role clarity within the work unit itself. Do members within the work unit have role clarity? The first is an external focus, and the second is an internal focus.

First, the external focus. One of the major challenges of the health care organization is bridging separate and highly independent work units. Frequent reference has been made to this throughout this book. While the work units often envision themselves as highly independent, they actually are highly dependent. Every work unit has feeder work units that supply them with services and products that allow them to produce services and products. Think about a nursing unit. The unit is very dependent on other work units to provide patients, to clean rooms, to maintain the physical features of the unit, provide lab services, provide computer linkages, and so on. Every work unit in a health care facility has dependencies. Every work unit is a "customer" of other work units. And, as a customer, it is dependent on that work unit to supply it with goods and services.

Every work unit is also a supplier of others. Others depend on it for some resource. If that resource is not there in a timely or quality way, the workings of the dependent work unit can be hampered. When we truly understand this, we recognize how limited it is to reward individuals for actions. The health care organization is filled with people and work units "feeding" and "being fed" by others. Rewarding individual performance is misguided. Individuals are able to perform because others supply them what they need in order to produce.

*Think for a moment about your work unit—how is it dependent on other work units? Make a list of work units you depend on for goods and services. These are your suppliers.*

*Now think for a moment about who is dependent on you for goods and services. These are your customers.*

The obvious next questions are the following: Are we meeting the expectations of the customers and suppliers? What do they require of us? How do we know that? That is called meeting the customer's requirements. Finding out customer requirements is as simple as setting up meetings with the customers and talking with them about requirements. With your customers, you want to know what is important for them in receiving services and products from you.

The three questions that need to be answered are:

1. What are my customer's requirements?
2. Are we meeting those requirements?
3. How do we know we are meeting those requirements?

With suppliers, the questions become reversed. With suppliers, the questions are:

1. Do the suppliers know our requirements?
2. How do we know they know our requirements?
3. Do we provide them with data on how they are meeting the requirements?

Identifying dependencies between work units is a most interesting exercise to do within health care organizations. The dependencies between work units are clearly seen. And when the dependencies are identified and discussed openly, greater efficiencies become possible. One exercise I have used is to structure a meeting of work-unit heads around dependencies. To begin with, one work unit outlines its purpose and functions. Then other work units discuss how they are dependent on the first work unit. The customer-supplied linkages are clearly made.

The second look is the internal look within the work unit. When the inputs enter the system (your work unit), something happens that creates outputs. What happens, and how does it happen? In systems thinking, this looks at what value gets added to the inputs before they become products of the work unit. Is there clarity within the work unit regarding who is doing what to achieve those results?

The concept of customers and suppliers works equally well when we think internal to the work unit. Each member of the work unit needs to understand who the customers and suppliers

107

are and what their requirements are. What is important to them in receiving the products and services? Have these requirements been communicated? Are they measured?

It is exciting when members of a work unit talk about who they see as their customers and who they see as their suppliers. These can be lively and animated discussions. They also allow members of the work unit to identify their key processes.

A number of tools are useful for work-unit role clarity. Two of these include the following:

1. *High-level flowcharting of the work unit.* The first step in role clarity is to understand the key work processes. Take some time with the members of the work unit to flowchart the processes for which the work unit is responsible. Frequently, the process of flowcharting results in significant discussion about who is responsible for what, when. And, more important, it provides everyone with a picture of what really happens, as opposed to what is supposed to happen.

The steps are simple. Begin by identifying the starting and ending points of the work process you want to study. Next, capture each major activity or decision that happens between the start point and the end point. Typically, there are eight to twelve key points. An important guideline is to focus on how the process is done now. When you have completed the flowchart of the process as it exists, you are in a position to ask how the process might be improved.

One recent example of flowcharting leading to greater role clarity comes from a reference lab. The lab was receiving specimens from outside groups—hospitals and physician offices. The lab process was fine. However, the billing occurred after the specimen had already been processed. That left the biller with the task of finding out who was going to pay. By changing the process and getting the biller into it up front, many problems were solved. The flowcharting process helped all the parties involved to understand each other's roles.

2. *Role matrix.* The role matrix is a chart listing the key activities of the work unit down the left side (Scholtes, 1989). Members of the work unit are listed across the top (rows). The task is to fill in who is responsible for what. Exhibit 3.1 illustrates this. This approach combines the flowchart with the people who are involved in it. The result: greater role clarification.

Exhibit 3.1. Sample Role Matrix.

| *Activities* | *Person 1* | *Person 2* | *Person 3* | *Person 4* |
|---|---|---|---|---|
| Activity 1 | | | | |
| Activity 2 | | | | |
| Activity 3 | | | | |
| Activity 4 | | | | |
| Activity 5 | | | | |

So far, we have talked about common understandings of roles. Do we understand our role? Do we understand how others see our role? Another aspect is that of how members feel about their role. Do they feel that their role is important to the organization? Do they feel that their role makes a difference?

A useful tool to answer the question of role efficacy is the one developed by Pareek (1980, p. 143). The questionnaire in Exhibit 3.2 is based on his work.

Exhibit 3.2. Role Efficacy Questionnaire.

---

*Exhibit 3.2 is designed to help you assess the clarity of your role efficacy. Take a few moments to respond to the questions:*

Using the scale below, circle your response to the right of each item. The first scale is "what is." The second scale is "what is desired."

1—Not at all
2—To a very limited degree
3—To a limited degree
4—To some degree
5—To a great degree
6—To a very great degree

1. My role is central to this organization.
   1 2 3 4 5 6
   1 2 3 4 5 6

2. My role in this organization allows me to use my strengths.
   1 2 3 4 5 6
   1 2 3 4 5 6

3. I take the initiative in responding to others in this organization.
   1 2 3 4 5 6
   1 2 3 4 5 6

4. I have opportunities for new and innovative activities.
   1 2 3 4 5 6
   1 2 3 4 5 6

5. My role is clearly linked with that of others in the organization.
   1 2 3 4 5 6
   1 2 3 4 5 6

6. My role allows me to give help as well as receive help.
   1 2 3 4 5 6
   1 2 3 4 5 6

7. My role is of value to the larger group.
   1 2 3 4 5 6
   1 2 3 4 5 6

8. My role allows me to exercise influence with others.
   1 2 3 4 5 6
   1 2 3 4 5 6

9. My role allows me to grow and develop personally.
   1 2 3 4 5 6
   1 2 3 4 5 6

10. My role allows me to confront problems and problem solve effectively.
    1 2 3 4 5 6
    1 2 3 4 5 6

---

Role clarity within the work unit and between work units is critical to a well-run organization. Role clarity provides:

1. Common understandings about who does what and when
2. Common understandings of expectations and requirements
3. Common understandings of the scope of responsibilities

One final thought. Think for a minute about birds flying in a flock. Have you ever wondered why they do not run into each other? Or why they are able to fly even in turbulence? There is an answer to this mystery.

Birds are able to fly together because three simple rules are ingrained. First, they fly at a minimum distance from each other. Second, they all fly at about the same speed. Third, they are constantly flying toward the center. These are simply rules that cause a group of individual birds to make it south each year.

How might these rules apply to work groups? First, the group needs to stay in close communication (flying at a minimum distance). Second, the group members help one another out (flying at more or less the same speed). Third, the group keeps its purpose in mind and continually moves toward it (moving toward the center). Simple rules for going the distance.

*Feedback*

Feedback in the work unit is the fuel of productivity. One of the quotes that I like to use in talking about feedback comes from Johnson. He tells the story of learning jazz:

> In thinking about the creative, my memory often turns to a jazz class that I took when I was about 12

years old. The concept of improvisation was new to
me. I learned about it through the experience of making mistakes. Looking back, I can see that the word
'mistake' evolved through three successive meanings
for me. First was the delightful, devious discovery that
in jazz a mistake could be turned into a new riff and
no one would be the wiser. Then came the unsettling
recognition that the riffs I trickily chose to cover my
errors were often the most exciting parts of what I
played. The instructor encouraged me to purposefully
make mistakes. The mistakes became discovery spaces
where I could let my creativity play in the music.
Final realization, both enlightening and bewildering,
was the clear fact that whenever the music really
worked, it was in an important sense a mistake. I saw
that whether what I was playing was overly improvisa-
tional or written, it was my willingness to let the un-
expected into each note that made it music [1986, p. 45].

When is an action a mistake? When is it on target? How
does a work unit know when it is on target? How does the work
unit know that it is getting down what it needs to do? How
does it know that it is serving the internal and external clients
and suppliers of the work unit? Health care organizations are
rich collectors of data. There are monthly financial statements,
quality assurance reports, FTE reports, budgeted and unbud-
geted hours, and so on. Feedback systems are prevalent in health
care. Clearly, feedback is vital for a work unit. It is the only
way it can know if it is on or off target. The questions here
become:

What types of feedback are given? Is that required feedback?

When is the feedback given?

How frequent is the feedback?

How useful is the feedback?

First, think about the type of feedback.

*Take a moment to answer the following questions about your work unit. What type of feedback do you get as a work unit? What form does it come on? Is it written? Verbal? Both? Make an inventory of types.*

*Now the question of "when." When do you get feedback? Do you get it immediately? After a while? What is the frequency of feedback? Often? Rarely?*

*How useful is the information you receive? A feature of the information age is that an abundance of data exists. Computers can spit out more data than we can digest. The key is useful information. Think about the feedback you get and rate it according to its usefulness for you.*

Now think about the type of feedback you would prefer and the ways you might obtain it.

Feedback has many sources. First, there are the financial feedback systems. Since most work units have an expense/revenue budget for the fiscal year, that represents a major source of feedback. Typically, each month work-unit managers receive feedback and can determine if they are on budget. At the end of the fiscal year, feedback regarding the final results of the budget is also provided.

Another source of feedback is the person-hour budget. This is the number of human resources hours that are used within the work unit. Again, depending on the system, there is a feedback schedule each month and/or at the end of the year. Attached to this budget may be a work-unit budget. This is a budget that reflects the work units of a work unit. When combined with the person-hour budget, it can be used to determine the relative productivity of that particular work unit.

Still another source of feedback for work-unit managers is work-unit goals and objectives. Depending on the organization, every work unit will have the objectives set for the year, months, and year ahead. Those objectives may be reviewed on a monthly basis, quarterly basis, or annual basis.

Perhaps one of the most important and least used sources of feedback is from the "customers" of the work unit. The work unit, on a regular basis, needs to ask customers if it is meeting their requirements and how the work unit might be more useful for them. This should be a "real-time" assessment of customer satisfaction.

Depending on the health care organization, a number of other indicators may provide the work-unit director with an understanding of targets that are being met or not being met. Examples are quality assurance reports, incident reports, infection reports, turnover reports, and so on. Each provides the work-unit manager with a quantitative way to measure the impact of the work unit on the functioning of the organization.

Implied in this discussion is that the work-unit director needs to identify any necessary types of information. That means that the earlier steps of identifying purpose and roles are vital. It is useful to identify the key work-unit processes, to flowchart those processes, and then to identify the critical success factors to measure.

How do the members of the work unit know they are successful? Within the work unit, feedback systems need to be in place for the individuals. A typical feedback system is the performance review. Whether done annually, semiannually, quarterly, or daily, this is still one of the most widely used mechanisms for providing the work-unit employee with feedback. It is also one of the most political—for example, "If I give too many 5 percent raises, I will have to answer to . . . " In addition, it can be one of the most abused feedback systems. That is why there are libraries on the art and science of giving performance reviews.

Let us say we really are interested in feedback for the work unit. How do we get it? The formula is simple. We get a table in the cafeteria and invite our customers and suppliers over for a one-on-one discussion. "Can we talk?" Much of what has been discussed regarding feedback is a "has been"—that is, it is history. A financial report is history. It reveals what has been. A turnover report from human resources brings to light a historical fact. If there is a desire to be more current, the informal channels can be accessed. This is a proactive way to search out the data. Most organizations have individuals who are especially good with the informal communication channels. Get in with them. Have them put you on their information-to-be-shared-with list. And develop your own informal communications network. Then you will be in a better position to find out what is happening within the work unit.

Without feedback, the work unit simply does not know when it has strayed off target. It does not know when it no longer is servicing its customers. It is like playing volleyball with blind-folds on—you are never sure where you are hitting the ball or when the ball is coming back.

## Commitment

The question is not whether we are committed; it is what are we committed to. Maehr and Braskamp (1986, p. 6) say this about motivation: "It can be effectively argued that for most purposes motivational problems are problems of resource distribution. The issue is not really whether a person is motivated, but rather how, to what ends, and in what ways the person is motivated. The assumption is that all people are motivated to do something; the question is what they are motivated to do."

How do we get people to invest in the work unit? We know that the issue is not one of unmotivated people. The question is how to get them motivated in appropriate ways. That becomes a question of leadership.

One of the classic stories of motivation is found in Mark Twain (1876/1981). The story is this: Tom Sawyer has been sentenced to paint thirty yards of board fence nine feet high. His friends come along and make fun of him working.

"Hey, old chap, you gotta work, huh?"

"Why, it's you Ben, I weren't noticing."

"Say, I'm going swimmin', I am. Don't you wish you could? But, of course, you'd ruther work, wouldn't you. Course you would."

Tom contemplated the boy a bit and said, "What do you call work?"

"Why, ain't that work?"

Tom resumed his whitewashing and answered carelessly, "Well, maybe it is and maybe it isn't. All I know is it suits Tom Sawyer."

"Oh come now, you don't mean to let on that you like it?"

The brush continued to move. "I don't see why I oughtn't to like it. Does a boy get a chance to whitewash a fence every day?"

That put the thing in a new light. Ben stopped nibbling his apple. Tom swept his brush daintily back and forth, stepped back to note the effect, added a touch here and there, criticized the effect again. Ben watched every move, getting more and more interested, more and more absorbed. Presently, he said, "Say, Tom, let me whitewash a little" [p. 14].

So, how do we get the work done? By making it attractive! We do not get a chance everyday to do this kind of work. Again, there are two important aspects. The first is commitment to the overall organization, and the second is commitment to the work unit itself.

Much of what we have talked about so far in this chapter impacts the individual employee's commitment to the work unit and to the organization. Assume that we have done the following. First, in sessions within the work unit, members discussed and drafted the work unit's purpose statement. They discussed at length questions of clients and suppliers and determined the customer's requirements and their requirements of the suppliers. They explored questions of values and so forth. They defined the key work processes.

Next, they spent times with roles. What roles do they have? What is expected of them? What do they expect of others? Again, there were discussions, debate, and decisions.

Finally, the feedback system was discussed. The basic questions asked were the following: What do we need feedback on? How frequently do we need it? What will we do with it? Who do we need it from? Feedback systems are in place, and the work unit has regular information on performance. This includes the problems it is encountering and the contribution it is making to the organization.

So, what do the employees have? They have information. They know what the work unit is about. If they disagree with it, they can leave. If they agree, they can stay and prosper. Also, they know what is expected of them. That means they do not have to spend time guessing about expectations, tasks, responsibilities, and so on. They know. They know because, on a regular basis, they get information from the organization on how they are doing.

What has been built is a work unit that provides choice through good information and involvement. In their book *Getting Commitment at Work* (1990), Thomas and Thomas propose a three-step approach to gaining commitment at work. Each step involves the manager and the employee. In the "dance" of these steps, commitment is built, maintained, and enhanced. As Thomas and Thomas point out, commitment begins in the recruitment process and carries over to day one.

*Step 1: Creating commitment between managers and the new employee.* For new employees, getting along with the manager is even more important than liking the job. Think back to your first day on the job. It was probably one filled with reservations about how you were doing. You asked yourself questions like, "Will I fit in here?" "Will I make it here?" For managers to create commitment in new employees, they need to:

1. Discuss work relations in the employment interviews. They should talk about roles, purpose, feedback, and expectations for commitment.
2. Interview instead of interrogate.
3. Carefully explain the reporting structure.
4. Recruit and hire their own employees rather than letting someone else do it. Human resources may question this at times. But the reality is that new employees will live in the family of the manager.

What do the prospective employees need to be doing during this early interview time? Here are some of the points they need to be concerned about.

1. Discuss work relations with the potential boss. Talk about purpose, roles, feedback, and commitment.
2. Appreciate a thorough evaluation of their skills. The more questions that can get answered now, the better.
3. Recruit their own manager. Remember, recruitment works two ways.

*Step 2: Creating commitment to the employee agreements.* Common expectations need to be established. These involve pay, benefits, working conditions, job title, and job content. For managers to create a mutually satisfactory employee agreement, they need to:

1. Use a checklist of information about employment terms

and conditions, including job content, organization, performance expectations, salary, and benefits.
2. Give candidates a written job offer to review before
they make a final commitment, with job title, salary,
reporting status, beginning date, and other details in it.
3. Establish realistic expectations of what the initial job
will be. Give candidates a picture of the first few weeks
on the job.
4. Confirm understandings and agreement about employee
terms by active listening. Give employees a moment to
say, "Here is what I am hearing" as they hear you talk.

Now it is time to turn to the prospective employees. With
their boss, applicants need to:

1. Use a checklist to gather information they want to
gather about the job, including salary, benefits, job content, organization, and so on.
2. Ask for a written job offer before they resign their current job.
3. Establish realistic expectations about what the initial
job will be like.
4. Confirm understandings and agreements by active
listening.

*Step 3: Creating commitment for new employees in the work
group.* What do new employees need to do to prepare for a new
job? Here are some tips. One of the kindest things managers
can do is pave the way for new employees.

Managers can create employee support for new workers in
a number of ways. These include the following:

1. Inform all employees about the job vacancy and qualification requirements.
2. Involve employees in recruiting new employees before and after hiring.
3. Involve employees in selecting new employees.
4. Give new employees background before you turn them loose in the group.

For the new employees, there is also a list of things to do. These include:

1. Be positive about the new job.
2. Let your manager know you need help before you ask your co-workers.
3. Show an interest in your co-workers.
4. Let your co-workers know that you respect their abilities and need their support.

The above are the ingredients of the "perfect match." They provide a starting place for commitment to take root and grow. There is nothing magical about this perfect match. It involves several ingredients. First, there is truth telling. Both parties need to be clear about what they want and need. They need to tell the truth. Second, there is choice all through the process. It is choice based on truth telling—that is, on good data. Third, there is mutual respect. The parties are respectful of each other. Both know that a poor employee beginning will lead to problems. Commitment begins the moment the "employment game" begins.

Some other suggestions for building commitment are:

• Make commitment an agenda item for work-unit meetings. Many managers have never asked employees about commitment. Ask people what their commitment level is.

- Provide permission to vary commitment levels from time to time. As was mentioned earlier, there are shifts and changes with commitment. A personal or family crisis will change the level of commitment. Disagreement with what is happening can change levels of agreement. Provide the permission that it is okay to vary commitment. But be sure you clarify what the boundaries of "okay" are.
- Remember that commitment is a by-product of other things. When issues of commitment come up, raise questions about clarity of purpose, roles, and feedback.

## Case Study: Building Alignment

The purpose of this case study is to provide an example of building organizational alignment within a health care organization. The process used is not radical or new. Rather, it is a "meat-and-potatoes" approach. The outcome of the process brings departmental objectives in line with the organizational objectives. In other words, there is organizational alignment.

The facility on which this case study is based is a 200-bed acute care hospital. The only work prior to the retreat discussed in the case study was done by senior management. The senior management team, along with the board of directors and physicians, developed a draft of five organizational objectives. While the organization was accustomed to retreats, it was not accustomed to a retreat where the goal was to build departmental alignment with the organizational objectives.

An assumption of the workshop was that senior management are responsible for defining the mission and goals for the organization. This is a hierarchical, top-to-bottom approach. However, first-line supervisors and middle management are responsible for producing the actions that get the results that meet the objectives. This is a bottom-up approach. In other words, senior management decides the "what," and the core of the organization decides the "how."

The agenda for the first day of the retreat was as follows:

- Introduction/Overview of Workshop
- Review of the Strategic Plan—that is, the draft objectives decided on by senior management
- Department Visioning and Departmental "What Is" Statements

On the second day, the agenda consisted of these items:

- Defining the Gaps Between "What Is" and the Visions
- Building Commitment

An important goal was for individuals to have the opportunity to exchange information and opinions throughout the workshop. The result was consensus building. The retreat opened with an exercise that invited individuals in the room to pair up with other individuals they normally were not with. During this paired-up time, they were to discuss the following: What they wanted for themselves from the retreat, what they wanted from others, what they did not want to see happen, and what they were willing to do to see that they got what they wanted from the retreat.

These responses then were discussed and recorded on flip

charts in front of the room. The stage had been set for the next phase—the draft objectives.

## Strategic Plan

At this point, senior management presented the draft objectives they had developed for the next twenty-four months. As expected, senior management had spent significant time thinking about these objectives. However, since this was the first time that many of the participants had heard the objectives, they had numerous questions. An important goal was to get those questions raised and answered.

To manage the question-and-answer time, participants were first asked to break into smaller groups to discuss their questions regarding the objectives. This provided them with the opportunity to identify issues to be discussed as well as areas of agreement. The goal: engage the objectives with dialogue.

Senior management's role was to define objectives. It then became the department's responsibility to identify what was needed to carry out a particular objective. The departments needed to identify what was being asked of them and their resources.

At the conclusion of the senior management presentation on strategic plan, departmental directors had an opportunity to identify which objectives impacted their departments most. Out of the five major objectives, two were clearly resource intensive and impacted almost all departments. These were the "vital few" that would use most of the resources.

## Visioning

Now came time for visioning. Visions are descriptions of a desired future state. Department directors were asked the following questions:

1. What is the mission of your department?
2. What key functions do you carry out?
3. Who are your primary customers and suppliers?
4. What organizational structure is needed to get you to that vision? FTEs and relationships?
5. What budget will be needed?

Each department responded to these questions. It was recognized that the vision would not be completely defined during these two days. However, it was important for departments to begin to identify their vision and how that vision came into alignment with the organization.

The decision to do visioning before a discussion of the "what is" was deliberate, because discussions of "what is" frequently can immediately put boundaries around people's thinking. We put ourselves in boxes. Therefore, we chose to talk first about vision and then, in the next section of the workshop, to discuss "what is."

After the visioning sessions, departments were given an opportunity to discuss in the total group what they saw as their vision for their departments. This was followed by a time of interaction with others. The result was clarification. There was clarification both of points of agreement and of points of disagreement on departmental visions. It was not unusual for department directors to express surprise that a particular department was or was not doing a specific function.

The "what is" part of the day began with a discussion of why it is important to identify specifics about current functioning now that we had discussed our visioning. Again, department directors were asked to respond to a series of questions:

1. What is your current mission—that is, the organization's charge that you are to carry out?

2. What are your primary functions?
3. Who are their current suppliers?
4. Who are your primary customers—both internal and external?
5. What is your current organizational chart?
6. What is your current budget?

The goal of this time was to have each department grounded as firmly as possible in the current conditions. The questions provided a starting point for them to identify the current realities they were facing.

This proved to be an extremely important time for the department managers. While there was some discussion as department managers talked about vision, vision is more futuristic. In the discussions about "what is," there was much discussion about how people were impacted by others, differences in how individuals and department managers saw the missions of different departments, and so on. In other words, the discussion became extremely lively during this phase of the workshop. The tendency for individuals was to say, "In order for me to meet the strategic plan vision, I will need $x$ additional FTEs or more resources." It became a discussion of the question, "How could current resources be shifted to meet the strategic objectives?"

*Gap*

We were now into the morning of the second day, which provided an opportunity to look at the gap between vision and actuality. Participants were given a short introduction on the importance of identifying gap.

The participants then were broken into smaller groups, which began to do gap analysis. They went back to visions and "what is" from the first day and began to identify key gaps. They summarized gaps, wrote them on newsprint, and presented them to the total group.

Again, within the group, a significant amount of discussion took place regarding how gaps might be addressed. Participants recognized that this workshop was simply the start. Much of the work of the workshop was to identify key areas where gap analysis had to go to greater depth. This was the beginning of their work.

*Closing*

The workshop closed with a discussion of how to build support for the vision. Participants engaged in an activity in which they were asked to identify the following: (1) individuals who would be ardently against what they were about, (2) individuals who would be on their side, and (3) individuals who would be "fence sitters." The department managers were asked to develop plans for how they would take the vision, the "what is," and the gap analysis and begin to build support for what they needed to do. Everyone left with a plan in hand.

*Summary*

The objectives of the workshop were to

- Review and discuss the current strategic plan
- Develop departmental strategies that were in alignment with that strategic plan
- Provide a forum for departmental directors to communi-

127

cate to each other their vision, current conditions, and what they needed in order to meet the organization's strategies

The report of senior management and the department managers was that, indeed, those objectives were met. They were also very clear that the work had just begun. In many ways, the retreat had developed a table of contents for a book yet to be written. The chapters that describe in detail the summations represented by the table of contents were developed as the department managers and senior management went back to work within the organization.

To make sure that loops were closed, senior management set additional meeting dates to get progress reports from departments.

Participants agreed that the key outcome of the retreat was that department objectives and resources were brought into alignment with the overall organizational strategic objectives and plans.

And the participants were highly enthusiastic about discussions that had begun among the group. Many of them described a relationship change from being adversaries to being allies.

## Conclusion

The work unit has an in-between role. The organization has created the work unit to provide a service or product to either an external or an internal customer. That means the organization has set the agenda for the work unit. At the same time, the work unit is composed of individuals who need to understand the function of the work unit so they can be productive. The organization says what needs to happen. The work unit responds with how it can meet the organization's expectations.

The individual is our next layer in the onion skin model. The individual represents the ultimate building block of the organization.

CHAPTER FOUR

# The Individual, the Core of the System

*If you follow your bliss, you put yourself on a kind of track that has been there all the while, waiting for you, and the life that you ought to be living is the one that you are living. Wherever you are, if you are following your bliss, you are enjoying that refreshment, that life within you all the time.*

— Joseph Campbell,
*The Power of Myth*

WE HAVE TALKED about the overall organization. We have talked about work units. What is the ultimate building block of an organization? The individual is the heart of the organization. This is especially true in health care organizations. These organizations are labor intensive and depend on people to deliver services and products. Precisely because health care organizations are labor intensive, the individual becomes the fundamental building block.

The purpose of this chapter is to apply the OPO model to the individual. Just as this model is usefully applied to the other layers of the onion skin, it is usefully applied to the individual. The key factor that needs to be understood with regard to the individual is perceptions: How does the individual view the world? Therefore, the chapter begins with a discussion of perceptions. The topic of perceptions is not new for us in health care administration, but it is crucial enough to revisit. Following the introductory remarks on perceptions, the chapter turns to the OPO model as it applies to individuals. The goal is to provide you with a way to enhance the individual's sense of purpose, roles, feedback, and commitment to the work unit and organization.

Behind the thinking in this chapter is Kurt Lewin's model of human behavior. Lewin is one of the greats in the study of organizational and human behavior. Part of his beauty is being able to state in a very simple way a very complex dynamic. Lewin's model of human behavior is:

$$Behavior = f(p \times e)$$

(B)ehavior is a function of the (p)erson and his or her (e)nvironment. If we want to understand why a person does what he or she does, we need to look at the interaction of the person and the environment. Take the classic case of a successful employee who is transferred to another department. And, let us even build the story more and say that the reason for the transfer was a promotion for outstanding work. A few months later, we find that the individual is no longer successful and the department and the individual are unhappy. Or the reverse. We take an individual who is having performance problems and put him or her in a department where suddenly we find that the person is successful. Behavior is a function of the person and the environment. Deming takes this even further when he states that 90 percent of "people problems" are not people problems at all. They are process problems, that is, problems related to the environment in which the individual is performing.

132

When Lewin's model is applied to this chapter, the key point is that we need to consider both the individual and the environment when we are trying to understand behavior.

## Perceptions

The starting point for understanding behavior is understanding the world the behavior is coming from. This is the world of perceptions. We act based on our perceptions of reality. Reality does not matter; what matters is how we perceive it. Perceptions are what trigger our attitudes and behaviors toward another person or situation. Think for a moment about the following scenario. You are about to go into a patient's room. Your experience has been that the patient is hostile and does not like people coming into the room. How do your perceptions about the patient impact your entrance into the room?

Now, suppose that you are about to enter a patient's room where you have the perception that the patient likes to have you there. How does that impact you as you move into the room? In both settings, the actions are the same—going into a room. However, your perceptions differ, and I suspect these different perceptions will influence your behavior.

Grinder and Bandler (1975, p. 3) talk about the "maps" we make of our world. They state:

Human beings live in a real world. We do not, how-ever, operate directly or immediately upon the world, but rather we operate within that world using a map or a series of maps of that world to guide our be-havior within it. These maps or representational sys-tems necessarily differ from territory that they model

133

by three universal processes of human modeling: generalization, deletion, and distortion. When people come to us in therapy expressing pain and dissatisfaction, the limitations which they experience are typically in their representation of the world and not in the world itself.

This is what the world of perceptions is about.

Native Americans have the following saying: "Do not judge another person until you have walked in their moccasins." If we are truly interested in understanding the behavior of others, we need to understand their frame of reference. What is their map? How do they make sense of the world around them?

Some might ask questions like the following: Why care about the perceptions of others? Why bother to understand where they are coming from? The primary reason is that perceptions form the basis for behavior. And they form the basis for performance. How the individual is perceiving the world is the ultimate bottom line to performance. If we want to have maximum use of this resource—this ultimate building block—we need to understand perceptions.

We especially need to be attuned to our own perceptions. What is the most important tool that you bring to your role as manager, administrator, or whatever? Is it your understanding of health care systems? Patient care systems? Admitting processes? Financial reimbursement? No, none of these. The most important tool you bring to the management setting is yourself (Ulschak, 1988b). That is your key tool. Weisbord (1987, p. 141) states this clearly: "If we wish to find out what works, we must start with our own values and personal situations. Management is best conceived as a constructive, self-fulfilling prophesy acting in ways to make happen what we most believe in. It is, at bottom, an exercise of moral imagination."

Managers and administrators must have an understanding of their perceptions and how they act on them. This is critically important, and it is especially true when working in a value-laden field such as health care. Self-understanding is the bottom line of understanding organizational behavior. Frequently, failure to understand one's own behavior is the source of many organizational and work-unit problems.

Generally, the goal is to understand how the other person is behaving. Can we understand these other people (employees) so we can motivate them more? However, the interesting paradox is that to understand that other person's world, we need to understand our own world of perceptions.

Think for a moment about individuals who do not have self-understanding. They are likely to project their needs on other people in ways that will eventually interfere with effective working relationships. For example, if managers need to be needed by co-workers, there is a high probability that that need will eventually reduce their effectiveness. They will be more interested in being needed than in being effective managers. They may end up being the type of boss who continually creates crises so that the need to be needed does not go "unfed." A lack of self-understanding is a filter system that blocks out certain signals. The tighter our filter, the less we are able to see the impact of our behavior on others or be aware of how our perceptions are driving our behavior. Instead of being enlightened, we continue to be "endarkened."

The greatest tool that individuals bring to the health care

setting is their self-understanding and awareness. It is that self-understanding that allows for an effective working relationship. It is that self-understanding that allows individuals to make most effective use of their technical skills. And it is that self-understanding that allows for effective understanding of the world of others.

*Precept language* is one model that is useful in understanding perceptions, how they are formed, and how they function. The concept of precept language was developed by John and Joyce Weir. The material presented here is taken from material they have presented in a workshop setting (Ulschak, 1988a). Figure 4.1 depicts the model.

*Precept language begins with filter 1—our sensory channels.* Think for a moment about how we physically take in information from the environment. The journey to forming a perception and a response to an event or a person begins with sensa-

Figure 4.1. Precept Language.

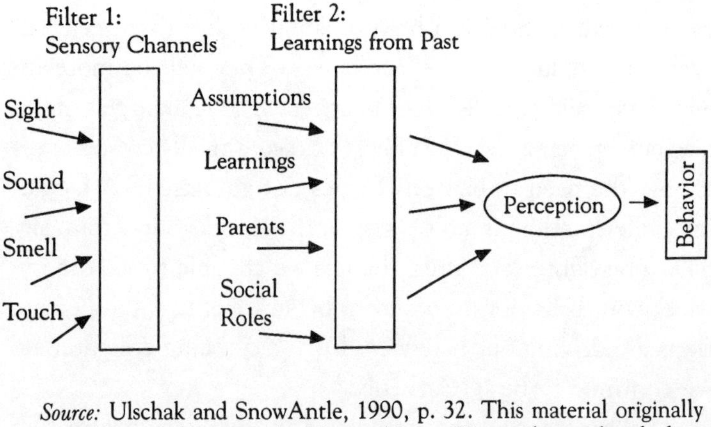

*Source:* Ulschak and SnowAntle, 1990, p. 32. This material originally came from a workshop given by John and Joyce Weir and is used with their permission.

136

tions that are channeled to our brain via our sensory inputs. The sensory inputs include sight, sound, smell, touch, and so on. But we have physical limitations on what our sensors can take in. If our physical hearing is not accurate, we may miss important data and respond inappropriately to the person we are working with. My kids say, "Dad, are you deaf? I am talking to you!" If our seeing is limited, we may not physically see a particular item. If you are dependent on glasses and take them off to read this book, you may find that you are limited in what makes sense to you. Filter 1 represents the physical limitations we have to receiving the sensations from our environment. It is important to know that the employee who never listens may actually not be hearing (as opposed to ignoring) you.

*Think for a moment about filter 1. What are some examples you have of misunderstandings that grew out of a shortcoming of one of the sensory channels?*

*Filter 2 is composed of our past learnings that impact the passage of sensations.* We may have learned not to hear certain things. For instance, if something "not nice" is said about someone, we may not hear it because we have learned not to hear certain things. Or we may have learned not to see certain things. For example, if two people are in conflict, we may have learned not to see the conflict. Our past learnings about the world and what is okay and not okay to take in filter what we let ourselves see, hear, feel, and so on. Each of us has survived to this point by living by rules established (at least at one point in our lives) by parents or parent substitutes. From those early learnings, we have taken key assumptions about the world and about ourselves. These now are filters that impact what we allow ourselves to take in and what our perceptions will be.

These filters can be thought of as scripts. Scripts are unconscious decisions that we have made regarding ourselves and the world early in life. Consequently, they were made with limited information in a context where the need to survive was paramount. Script theory says that these early learnings about how to survive in the world become preconscious and impact behaviors in later years. For example, if individuals have decided that they cannot do anything right, they may constantly err at the last moment and not make it. Or they may make it but never let themselves sense that they have made it. Others may decide at this early age not to be close to others and find that no matter how hard they try, they simply do not get close to anyone.

These learned messages carry over to behaviors. They become filters that allow in only certain messages. Typically, those messages are congruent with the early decision. The early messages result in a belief system that in turn results in behavior.

The important point is that each of us has formed certain assumptions about ourselves and the world around us. These assumptions influence what information we will allow to pass through our senses to form our perceptions. The learnings that we have picked up from our environment form this second filter. Having been raised in a fairly traditional German-Hungarian household on the plains of the Dakotas, I learned that anger was best kept in. In later life, that meant that I was quick to spot anger in others but not open to sharing my own with others. For a period of time, that resulted in a "nice guy" syndrome. My blind side had to do with my own expression of anger. It took me a while to become comfortable expressing my anger. This was a past learning that needed to be overcome.

*Take a moment and think about filter 2. What are some examples you have of misunderstandings that grew out of filter 2?*

*After passing through the two filters, a perception is formed by the individual.* At this point, perceptions are formed. From those perceptions, actions will follow. The action may be a thought, a feeling, a physical movement, and so on. For example, a manager has just heard an employee request time off. If the manager believes that people really are out to circumvent the system, the logical next step may be to call the employee's motives into question. The manager's belief system leads to certain ways of perceiving reality as well as to certain actions. The behavior and thoughts we see in ourselves and in the people we are working with are the result of actions based on perceptions.

These two filters allow only certain material to register in our consciousness. The physical filters will actually prevent us from seeing or hearing. The learning filters will determine what we ought to think or feel about a certain situation. In both cases, we end up running on limited information from our environment. If we realize that we and the people that we are working with are both coming from our own set of perceptions, we are in a better position for dialogue and understanding. We can move from attributing certain actions and behaviors to personality issues to thinking of them as learning issues. Learning issues we can address. Personality issues are non-problem-solving dead ends.

Perceptions lead to behavior. Behavior results in a response to it. The response to the behavior is noted in our perceptions. And the cycle begins again.

So we arrive at understanding. What about change? Are

we locked into the filters from our past? No, we are not. The foundation of change is awareness of the filters. If we want to change, the first thing we need to do is to become aware of those filters that impact our perceptions and influence our behaviors. Once we get them into our awareness, we can begin to work with them. That means change. The steps:

Step 1: Become aware of the filters.

Step 2: Decide whether to change them.

Step 3: Change. Simply do it.

We have talked a good deal about perceptions and the link to behaviors—how it is that our behavior is a function of perceptions. Many books have been written on this topic, and it is the foundation for this chapter. In the remainder of this chapter, the OPO model is applied to individual behavior.

## The Individual and the OPO Model

This chapter focuses on applying the OPO model to the individual. As with other chapters, the goal is to make the discussion as interactive as possible and provide you with tools.

Think about the resources that you manage as a health care professional. They include time, space and space utilization, budget dollars, machines and material, and people. Further, the people resources are composed of skills, abilities, knowledge, and so forth. How these resources are applied to the task at hand determines the effectiveness and efficiency of the organization.

Since health care is so labor dependent, the labor component is the most critical. That is why the individual is referenced as the basic building block of the work unit and organization. If the individual accepts or "enrolls in" the mission of the work unit and the organization, the result is a committed individual. This committed individual then becomes the source of the performance and productivity of the work unit and the organization.

How does the OPO model come into play with productivity and performance? In the integrated organization, individuals have a clear sense of alignment between the organization's purpose and their own sense of purpose. There is a common bond between the two. In addition, individuals know what is expected of them and what they expect in return from the organization. Since roles are clear, a degree of predictability comes into play. Furthermore, individuals receive feedback that allows them to know how they are doing. Feedback is the scorecard. These things provide the basis for commitment. That means the individual is invited to invest in the organization. The goal of effective leadership is to make this happen.

In the remaining pages of this chapter, each step of the model will be discussed; hints will be provided for addressing each component as it relates to the individual. We will start with purpose. Again, the core of the OPO begins with the question of purpose.

*Purpose*

The first component of the model is individual purpose and meaning. "At the heart of living with vision is purpose. Purpose is what compels us to take a stand, to act with such conviction that we may surprise ourselves, and ultimately it is what fulfills us. We live from purpose at times, without even knowing it. Without purpose, life is at best incomplete, at worst, futile. Our sense of purpose is what connects us to ourselves and to all life" (Marks, 1989, p. 60).

As employees view the organization, do they sense that their purpose and meaning in life can be nurtured in this organization? In this section, we want to explore some of the important aspects of individual purpose and meaning and how that individual purpose and meaning connect to the work unit and the organization.

*Take a moment to think about the following questions: Think about a time when you were "purposeless." You felt that your life or job or task had little or no meaning. Take a few moments to write down your thoughts, feelings, or actions.*

*Now remember a time when you were filled with purpose. Your life was "purpose-full." Your life or job or tasks had great meaning for you. Note the thoughts, feelings, and behaviors that went along with this.*

Compare the two sets of thoughts. What are the primary differences? Are there any similarities? Typically, the message is clear. When we lack purpose, our lives (and jobs) lack direction. Like an out-of-focus camera, our lives take on a hazy tint and lose clarity.

However, the opposite is also true. When we reflect on the moments of being on purpose, our lives had clarity and direction. In a scene in the first *Karate Kid* movie, the old man shows the kid how to throw a karate punch by focusing the energy of the punch in the heel of the hand. By doing so, the energy flows solid and direct to the target. There is no dissipation of the energy. The same is true of being on purpose as an individual. *On purpose* means our energies are targeted and focused.

One exercise that helps focus the power of being on purpose is the following:

*First, have individuals pair up. The goal of one individual is to walk from point A in the room to point B (somewhere on the other side of the room). The partner extends an arm and in so doing presents a barrier to the individual walking from point A to point B. In the first part of the exercise, the individual walking is supposed to focus on the problem of the arm being in the way. Typically, the individual does not make it to the other side of the room. The person gets stuck at the arm.*

*In the second part of the exercise, the individual walking focuses on a target on the other side of the room. The person focuses on the destination instead of on the barrier to achievement—that is, on the desired result. And the individual achieves it.*

What is the point of this exercise? It is a quick way to demonstrate the power of focusing on the desired result—that is, to reach a spot on the other side of the room—rather than focusing on the problem of the blocks. When the focus is on the barriers, the barriers become the end points. When the focus is on results, the barrier becomes secondary. The barrier is merely a problem to be solved. What this little exercise demonstrates is the power of focusing on purpose.

Being in touch with life's purpose means life becomes full— we become "life-full." When there is a loss of purpose, life becomes empty. The ultimate cosmic joke is that about the time we have defined our purpose, our life situation changes, and we need to rethink purpose.

There are many ways to focus the topic of individual purpose. We can discuss it theologically. What is some deity's purpose for our life? We can discuss it from a secular perspective. What is the purpose of life? Why is this happening to me? We can discuss it practically. What is the purpose of this particular task? Whatever the context, the importance of purpose remains the same. When we are able to assign meaning to our lives and task, we have a tremendous amount of energy. Purpose gives us that meaning. Without a sense of purpose, we drift and lose focus.

Now for the ultimate question: How do we discover purpose? This is the question that people have been asking gurus for centuries. Teachers have been asked this question, and they ask it of themselves. In the opening quotation in this chapter, Campbell provides a clue when he talks about following one's bliss. Using his lead, "following our bliss" is a sign that we are on purpose with ourselves. The starting point seems to be discovering our bliss. That is not always easy!

Paulson, Brown, and Wolfe (1988, p. 59) suggest that a key aspect of discovering purpose is through the recognition of choice:

Living on purpose simply means becoming aware enough of living so that you are at choice about your experience and what you want to do. You notice your content and your experience of your content and you get yourself to choice about it. You may choose to experience it emotionally, but at least you have chosen.

You may think about content in a particular way, but you have chosen to think about it that way. You can decide to think and experience in a way that lightens the situation for you. You will not be controlled by some mysterious feeling or thought pattern that you no longer remember because you know what is and you are at choice.

The point: The way to live on purpose is to become aware of choices. Earlier, we noted that awareness is the first step to change. The next step is recognition that we are making choices. Do this one step at a time.

One useful area to target is our value core. Why the value core? A sense of purpose comes because we have a sense of being in alignment with our value core. There are many ways to explore our values. Two options are (1) self-discussion, and (2) indirect observation. In the first, we ask ourselves what we value. Typically, the response is one that indicates what we think our values should be or what we think we would like them to be.

Spend a few minutes with the following exercise to get at what you think your value core is.

*Imagine that you are about to talk to a child about what is important to you in your life. This child might be your son or daughter or an imagined child relative or friend. What would you say to that child?*

*Now that you have a list, think about each item you put down on the list and ask yourself, "When was the last time I acted on this value?" Be specific about when it was, what the issue was, and who was there. Would you question any of the items you have listed?*

145

Some years ago, a friend of mine helped me through a difficult decision I was making regarding work and family obligations by asking me, "Imagine you could do one of the following for the next three months."

1. You would get a work assignment that would be very exciting and important to the hospital. You would work on it day and night and receive tremendous acclaim for its success.
2. You take your children on a three-month tour of the Rockies in a camper. For three months, you enjoy them and you have a great time.

Now, whichever your choice, you die. At the funeral, which of these would you prefer:

1. Your boss's coming to your son and talking to him about how great you were as an employee.
2. Your son's going to your boss and talking to him about how great you were as a father.

The value choice was clear—and so was my response.

The second way is through observation. Behaviors are an accurate source of information about values that are actually acted out. Here are two ways to look at values in action. First is the time audit. A time audit reviews how time is spent. A time log is formed to track time use over a specific period of time. Then the time usage is analyzed for the values that are implicit and explicit in the audit. This is a powerful exercise to monitor if values in action match the spoken values. Ultimately, time is *life*. All we have is time. So how we spend our time is how we spend our lives. The following is an exercise that will help you look at this.

*How we manage our time is one of the best clues to our values. The exercise is simple. Do a time audit of your time usage. For one week, monitor how you spend your time. At the end of the day, note how that day was spent. Then, at the end of the week, sit down with your time log and note the categories of how your time was spent. You now have a listing of how you actually spend your time. What does that tell you about what you value? What values are implicit in how you are spending your time? How are the learnings similar to and different from what you say you value?*

A companion exercise is the checkbook. Go back through your spending habits and see what you are spending money on. Let that be the guide to what it is you value. Analyzing how you spend your money is an excellent way to get at action values.

*One way to look at your values is by not looking directly at them but looking at them over your shoulder (so to speak). Take some time with your checkbook. Go through and look at your spending habits. Now think about what is behind the spending habits. What values are you expressing through how you spend or manage your money?*

There are many other exercises that are designed to assist you in thinking through what values are operational in your life today. Once you are aware of what is important to you—and what you have chosen for yourself—purpose begins to emerge.

So far, the discussion of purpose and values has deliberately focused on you. That is by design. As was mentioned earlier, the starting point has to be with you. However, you can take the same exercises and apply them to others. You can look at how others structure their time, spend their resources, and so on and talk with them about the values reflected in this.

Step 1 is knowing what is important and publicly affirming those important things. This step involves listening to self with a keen, sensitive ear. Listening to self is a major source for life learning.

Step 2 is pulling together those things that are important to you and letting them "cook." *Cooking* means that they need a time of reflective thoughtfulness. Frequently this is a time of "endarkenment." You may feel that you are exploring what is important and yet not be sure. It is the early stage of articulating meaning and purpose. A good friend of mine flags this time as one when she "talks herself into clarity." It is a time of talking to self and others. The following exercise helps some with this.

*This is an exercise to assist you in developing your personal vision of greatness. Do not let the word greatness throw you. If you were to create your ideal world where you were functioning with greatness, what would that world look like to you? What is your vision of personal greatness? What would you be doing? What would you be feeling? How would you be relating to others? How would you be relating to yourself? P.S. If you find yourself blocked, searching for the right answer, start by just "making it up."*

Once the vision is in a draft state, the next step is to share it with a few others you know and trust. Each time you share it, think about the parts of it that fit you and the parts that do not. Embellish it as you share it with others. Show your enthusiasm for it.

Another use of the vision of greatness is in relationships. This involves defining a vision of greatness for a special relationship that you are in or one that you would like to be in.

One example of a vision of greatness in marriage is the following passage, which was written by a friend of mine:

> In the past weeks, I have been pondering the meaning of purpose-full relationships. And I have been thinking about this in the context of a vision of greatness for marriage. A vision of greatness for marriage simply asks us to dream about what greatness would mean in this relationship. Here are some of my thoughts.
>
> Marriage is to be a purpose-full relationship. So what does purpose-full mean to me? The ultimate purpose is to be life giving and life-full for you and me—the marriage partners. Life giving and life-full mean that the marriage relationship needs to enhance our ability to give love, receive love, and feel competent in our life's work. Life-full also means creative energies are unleashed.
>
> Behaviors that honor life-fullness are on-purpose behaviors. Behaviors that subtract from life-fullness are off purpose and need to be confronted. On-purpose behaviors include truth telling—that is, saying what is true for each of us, taking responsibility for self and our thinking and feeling, and increasing our self-responsibility. Off-purpose behaviors are non-truth-telling behaviors— that is, withholding from each other important self-truths, manipulation, and behaviors that diminish self and other.
>
> A purpose-full relationship means that the relationship honors self and honors other. Purpose-full means that the full range of feelings exist in the relationship and are honored. Conflicts are seen as the cutting edge of the relationship and productive.
>
> In purpose-full, life-full relationships, we need to have sensitivity to times of respite. Just as there are times of

stretching and risk within the relationship, there need to be agreed-on times of calm and quiet. While there are times of risk and stretching, there also needs to be caretaking. Fear is to be honored and respected but is not a sufficient condition for backing off of risk. Fear is to be honored and discussed.

Secrets have their role in the purpose-full relationship. However, when secrets violate the spirit of the relationship, they need to be openly discussed. Our operating norm needs to be that when we spend time debating whether a secret should be told or not, that the secret needs to be told.

Commitment is the core of a purpose-full marriage. Without commitment, there is no energy to move through the hard times of the relationship. Commitment needs to be to the purpose of the relationship. Commitment is to behaviors that reinforce the purpose of the relationship.

An important part of the purpose-full marriage is parenting. Parenting needs to be seen as a mutual task whose core is relating to the children in ways that are truthful, build mutual self-regard, and encourage self-responsibility. As a result of being part of this family unit, our children should have a sense of being loved, a sense of knowing what it is like to love, and a sense of their own ability to make sense of the world. Simply stated, purpose-full marriage honors the children and invites them to life-full, purpose-full existence.

A purpose-full approach also extends to the roles that we have with others outside of the marriage. Part of being purpose-full is recognizing that we cannot be all things to each other. Part of having life-full relationships with each other is recognizing that there will be significant other people in our lives. Those others will be significant for each of us in our individual development and in our development together.

In general, within the life-full relationship, there needs to be truthfulness, self-regard and regard for others, and responsibility for relationships both inside and outside the marriage.

The lesson thus far is that the identification of purpose is not always what it initially appears to be. It takes some time and energy to explore it. At one time in my life, I had the privilege of working with Native Americans in the Dakotas. During that time, I was introduced to the concepts of vision quest and the writing of Black Elk. Vision quest among the Lakota was a long arduous process that was not entered into lightly. It extended over weeks or months. It involved the decision to take the vision quest, time spent with a "guide," time in the sweat lodge, time in isolation, deprivation of food, and other measures. A vision quest involved personal pain and suffering. Out of the quest emerged the personal vision. I sometimes find myself chuckling as I do half-day or full-day retreats with teams and organizations to look at vision. Vision quests cannot be achieved in a single night or a weekend. I have begun to refer to this type of retreat as "McVisions"—fast-food visions.

The paradox—vision quests are not easy to do, and yet they are simple. They simply involve following your bliss.

The process of thinking about and defining meaning and purpose happens. Then there is a high likelihood that circumstances will shift. Purpose is not the same throughout life. It changes. At one point in life, purpose is to survive school. At

151

another time, it is to find someone to live with. At another time, it has to do with parenting. Later when we discuss feedback, one of the important points we will make is that feedback allows us to keep track of the changes in purpose.

For the health care manager, purpose has two aspects, the personal side and the work side. The personal side is what we have been talking about. It is people's sense of meaning in what they are about.

The work side is more basic. Do individuals understand the purpose of their work? Do they understand the organization's purpose? The department's purpose? The first question is one of understanding. The second question is one of agreement. Do individuals agree with the organization's or work unit's definition of purpose? This is a question of alignment with the purpose. In the work context, both questions are important.

The concept of vocation is important. Some in the workplace feel called to do the job they are doing. The job is more than just something they do to earn money for other things. The job is their calling. All their time and energy go into workplace activities. Their life can be consumed by the workplace.

For a friend of mine who is a nurse, nursing is a calling. Her core identity is as a nurse. She spends countless hours each week in nursing work and related activities. When asked who she is, her response is, "I am first and always a nurse." Another friend of mine is a nurse who sees nursing as "a job." She defines herself first and foremost as a mother. That is what is important for her. Her work supports her real love, which is parenting.

One last comment. Remember that the organization's primary role is to define its purpose. This allows work units and individuals to decide if there is enough overlap between them and the organization to work for the organization. The organization's purpose and the individual's purpose needs to be aligned. If they are not, serious consequences such as intentional and unintentional sabotage may result. When the individual deliberately does things that prevent the organization from achieving its purpose, we call that *sabotage*. When the individual unintentionally does things that get in the way of the organization, we refer to this as *accidental sabotage*.

## Roles

Personal boundaries are critical for us. "Being well grounded is the result of having a clear sense of your own boundary, a clear sense of what is going on inside, and a feeling of calm readiness for what is to come. . . . Significantly, good grounding involves physical as well as mental stability, for managers as well as athletes. Well grounded, the manager can listen without feeling threatened, without imagining that someone is trying to manipulate or doing something to him or her, and without interpreting or predicting hidden meanings in advance" (Herman & Korenich, 1977, p. 67). Roles provide us with boundaries.

Remember that roles are a set of expectations, responsibilities, and tasks. These are the expectations the individual has for the organization and the expectations the organization has for the individual. In today's world, rapidly changing roles coincide with the rapidly changing organizations. There was a time when we all knew what it meant to be a man. There was a time when we all knew what it meant to be a woman. There was a time when we knew what it meant to be a manager or director. Today, we know we have much to learn. All of this represents shifting and changing of roles.

All of us perform a multitude of roles. We wear many hats. The following exercise, based on Lauderdale's "role mapping" concept (1982, p. 128), will help focus on roles.

*Take a few moments and identify some of the roles you have in life (parent, teacher, husband, lover, friend, manager, and so on). List them on a sheet of paper. Next, for each role, identify with a 1 (little clarity) to 5 (very clear) how clear you are about the role expectations.*

Now, think about the exercise that you just did. What roles had role clarity? What roles were lacking in role clarity? How important is it that there be clarity in that role? As you reflect on the exercise, what are key learnings or relearnings for you?

For the individual, the concept of role clarity is critical. Why does this topic take on importance? Let me ask the question of you.

*Think back to a time when you were having role conflicts. These may have been conflicts between your role as worker with your role as parent. Or they may have been conflicts involving your work roles. What were the thoughts and feelings that you had at the time? Take a moment and jot them down.*

*Now take a minute and think about a time when you had definite role clarity. You felt strong because you knew the expectations for you and what you needed to do. What were the thoughts and feelings that went along with that?*

Now take some time to reflect on the two settings. The time of role confusion probably involved frustration, confusion, false starts, anxiety, and so on. The time of role clarity had a sense of being productive and making a contribution. That was your personal experience. Now imagine what it is like when, within an organization, significant numbers of persons feel they do not know what their roles are. In that type of organization, the wonder is that any work at all gets done.

One of the most useful tools I have found for looking at the question of individuals and their roles within organizations is *pinch theory* (Scherer, 1975). The model is illustrated in Figure 4.2.

The pinch model begins with some relationship coming into existence. In our case, it is the relationship between the organization and the employee. Each party puts its best foot forward. In the classic job interview, prospective employees put their best foot forward. But when asked about weakness, they will proudly and humbly state that they are not perfect. The organization is doing the same thing. "Here is our best side— and of course, there are some downsides to working here." They eventually arrive at a mutual agreement regarding roles and relationships. In the case of the initial employment interviews, if both parties are comfortable, the decision is made to proceed.

Then the work begins. The most productive time is the time when there is a sense of mutual agreement regarding roles and responsibilities. However, as time passes, there are "pinches." Pinches are those small yet discernible sensations like, "I thought he was going to do that, but now he wants me to do it." "What did he mean by that comment to me?" "When they hired me, I thought that one of the benefits was . . . " "Who is going to do that part?" And so on. The pinch is a deviation from what was expected to happen. It is the realization that there is a gap between what was expected and what is actully happening. The

Figure 4.2. Pinch Model.

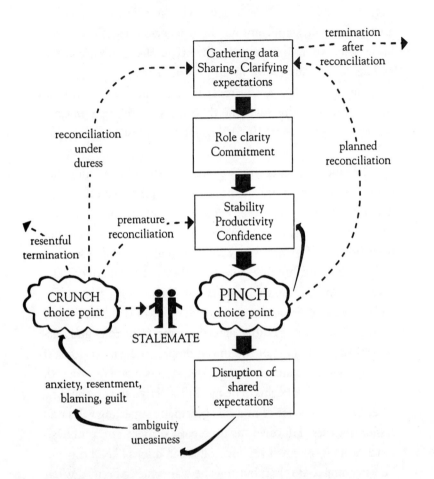

*Source:* "A Model for Couples: How Two Can Grow Together," by J. J. Sherwood and J. J. Scherer, 1975, February, *Journal for Small Group Behavior,* p. 112-1. Reprinted with permission. Earlier version of model appeared originally in J. Gidewell & J. Sherwood (1973) "Planned Renegotiation" in *Group Facilitators Handbook.* San Diego, CA: University Associates.

choice each time a pinch appears is to ignore it in the hope that it will go away or to confront it.

The best advice is to confront pinches when you find yourself thinking about them for more than a few minutes. If you find yourself thinking over and over, "Boy, did he let me down," that is a sign that the pinch should be confronted. The purpose of the confrontation is not to blame the other person. The purpose is to go back to the initial agreement and renegotiate it with the person. The dialogue may be as simple as, "When you said that, I was surprised. I was expecting . . . " The goal is to focus the discussion on the gap between what was expected and what actually happened.

The problem with ignoring pinches is that they may have a tendency to collect and build. In the literature of transactional analysis, this is referred to as *stamp collecting.* Those of you familiar with collecting redemption stamps at the store will readily understand stamp collecting. You buy an item and get the value-added stamps. You then paste the stamps in a stamp collection book. At some point, you are able to cash the stamps in (redeem them) for some free item. You get a free gift.

Stamp collecting in the emotional sense is very similar. As you go through your day or week, you collect emotional stamps. For example, assume you collect anger stamps. Someone says something to you, and you smile. But you open your mental stamp book and paste in an "anger" stamp. The next person comments on your clothing, and you place another "anger" stamp in the book. This continues until you reach the point where your book is full, and the next person who says something to you gets "dumped on." That person gets the whole load of your wrath. When you cash in the stamps, you even have a momentary sense of righteousness and indignation. This is the essence of stamp collecting.

If you do not confront pinches, one possible result is that you will build up a collection of pinches (stamps) until they become a crunch. Unconfronted pinches add up to a significant number of stamps in the stamp book. When the book finally is filled, the crunch happens and you have a serious relational problem. The options are:

1. *To leave the relationship.* This can be a costly choice, since it means leaving it all behind. For the employee, it means leaving the organization. This means leaving behind a collection of benefits and friends. Also, if the leaving happens under negative circumstances, there is a good chance that the person leaves "dumb." Leaving "dumb" means that the person does not leave with a good sense of what happened. The employee has not learned anything that can be applied to future work settings.

2. *To smooth over the relationship and try to start over.* One problem to be avoided is smoothing over the gap in expectations too quickly. The result could be that the problem repeats itself in the near future. This is akin to the couple who decide to smooth over their differences without addressing them—they are bound to repeat the same mistakes.

3. *To do nothing.* Simply let the gap in expectations or the stamps collect. Get a bigger stamp book. This is a situation where the individual can become paralyzed with inaction. Burnout can be the result.

4. *To renegotiate the relationship.* While this is time consuming, it is the preferred option. It means going back to the gaps

in hopes and assumptions and renegotiating the original expectations. This can be a scary time, because it once again puts the relationship on the line. Raising the questions may result in unwanted answers. As a result, people may leave the organization. However, if they do leave after the period of clarification, they have the option of leaving "smart"—they leave having learned how better to survive in future organizations.

A key assumption of the pinch model is that pinches are a given. There is no way to avoid them. They will occur. In any relationship, there will be gaps in expectations. This is especially true in the world of health care. With so many changes happening, it is a given that there will be changes in expectations. The only choice we have is to manage the pinches.

The following case study illustrates the use of the pinch model for enhancing role clarity.

Mary was in a difficult situation. She had reached the peak of her ability to climb the corporate ladder in her current position. In the organization's eyes, she was still a valuable resource, and several of the key executives did not want her to leave. They proposed that a new position be created. And the offer was made to Mary.

Mary was called into the CEO's office, and the new position was explained. It was a definite promotion, and it created a new division within the company. The CEO had several reports that he was willing to have now report to Mary instead. However, he did indicate that those reports still needed access to him and that he needed access to them.

Mary raised a question at this point. Would this not

mean almost a dual report? The CEO responded that there was only one report but that he needed access. He added that this was true for any member of the organization.

Mary accepted. For a time things went well. Expectations were clear, and when they were not clear, it was excused as being a new position.

After a few months, Mary was beginning to feel definite pinches. The pinches were "small" but important to her. There were several occasions where "her reports" went directly to the CEO. The CEO would hold meetings with the direct reports and provide direction to them without informing Mary. Enough of this. Mary set up a meeting with the CEO.

During the CEO meeting, Mary discussed the pinch as she felt it and how it was a problem for her. The others involved were being caught between two sets of priorities. Mary would have her listing and the CEO would have his. When conflict occurred, Mary would have to work it out with the CEO. The job was good but needed to be kept in the loop. The CEO agreed to include her in the loop more often.

The problem continued. Mary had another pinch meeting with the CEO. Again the feelings were well received and Mary was "heard." But the meetings ended with only temporary remedies.

Mary began to find herself being angry and frustrated as time wore on. Meetings would be held—decisions would be made—and she would find out about them later. When she found out, she would confront the CEO in a positive way. He was most apologetic, and a temporary fix would happen. But now Mary stopped going with pinches. She started talking to a couple of co-workers about the terrible way decisions were made. The complaining had begun. And Mary began to go beyond complaining; she also clandestinely circulated her résumé.

Crunch time came for Mary when she was sitting in a management meeting and one of her reports gave an updated report to the management team that contained important new information only the CEO and the staff member had been aware of. Mary was livid. She was about to stand and announce her rage and resignation, when she remembered the pinch model. She was poised to make a "dumb resignation." So she stewed instead.

But that night she put her anger to work. She outlined the events of the past eighteen months in a document with a clear identification of her wants and needs. The next day, she set up an appointment with the CEO. In that meeting, she clearly articulated how the position was not working and what now needed to happen. The result was a phased-out resignation that allowed Mary to leave in a manner that she "learned from" and that the organization "learned from."

This walk-through is a good example of the pinch in action. The pinch provides an opportunity to keep roles clean. It is one model for role negotiation that works well in any relationship.

One last tool for role negotiation with the individual includes the following four questions. They are an efficient way of getting at role clarity.

1. On a one-to-ten scale (ten is high), how clear are you on your role in this organization? What would it take to make it a ten?

161

2. On a one-to-ten scale, how satisfied are you with your role in this organization? What would it take to make it a ten?
3. What are the three things you would like to see changed about your role?
4. Who do you need to talk with to get those things changed?

The two problems most frequently found in working with and within organizations are a lack of role clarity and a lack of clarity of purpose. These two cores frequently block productivity. "Francis's Principle" states that Peter's Principle is wrong. The problem is not that individuals are promoted to levels of incompetence. It is that in the promotion process, the natural shifting of purpose and roles is not appropriately acknowledged. What used to be in alignment now is out of sync. The individual's "performance" begins to drop off, and the organization labels this incompetence. The reality is that the purpose and roles may now be at odds.

Role clarification happens through feedback.

*Feedback*

Feedback is the information that comes back to you to let you know the results of your actions. Literally, the results of what you have done or are doing now confront you. Senge (1990, p. 128) discusses the importance of appropriate feedback. "I would suggest that the fundamental information problem faced by managers is not too little information but too much information. What we most need are ways to know what is important and what is not important, what variables to focus on and which to pay less attention to—and we need ways to do this which can help groups or teams develop shared understanding."

Remember the discussion concerning perception? Behavior is based on perceptions. Perceptions are formed as data come in through the senses. The results of that behavior come back to us and are filtered through our perceptions. This results in another response, and so on. The feedback can be positive, negative, or neutral.

One of the more entertaining and enlightening comments on feedback comes from the film the *One Minute Manager*. In this management training film, feedback is illustrated in the following way. Imagine that you are in a bowling alley where a curtain blocks your view of the pins. Each time you throw the ball, you need to imagine the impact on the pins on the other side. The curtain does not let you see. Without seeing the results of your bowling effort, you will lose interest in the game. The same is true at work.

*Think for a moment about how you get feedback at work. What types of feedback do you receive? Who gives feedback to you? How do you know when you are doing well or not doing well? Take a few moments to construct a small table. In the first column, list the various ways that you get feedback. Be very specific. Perhaps it is performance reviews. Perhaps it is informal talks in the hall. Or you may have a specific productivity indicator. In the second column, identify the frequency of the feedback. Does it happen often? Finally, in the third column, identify the source. Who is it that you get feedback from? Boss? Colleagues? Others?*

There are two major feedback questions. The first is the basic question of whether you get feedback. This can include where you get the feedback as well as the general nature of it—positive, negative, and so on. Second, how useful and valuable is the feedback? Is the feedback the kind of feedback that you can use? Or is it so general that it becomes meaningless?

The first question deals with how people get feedback. Feedback comes through a number of types of communications. There is verbal feedback. This is where individuals verbally state what they are thinking. Then there is the nonverbal feedback— body language. This is often misleading because you can never be sure exactly what those nonverbal gestures mean. You can make some educated guesses, especially if you have read those books on nonverbal communication. But they are still guesses until confirmed by additional information. Then there are written and pictorial communications. These represent discussions of policies and procedures, monthly reports, surveys, and so forth. The various types of communications just mentioned provide feedback. The question is, are you receiving the feedback?

We are constantly getting feedback from the environment around us. Every behavior has a response, even if that response is no response! We receive a continuous stream of feedback. One of the problems we face is data overload. So much data come to us that we need to filter it for what is useful data. We need to be able to forget information, or in computer language, to delete it.

The second question regarding feedback has to do with its value for us. How dependable is it? How relevant is it for us? If we are about to journey out in midwinter in the north country, a weather report might be vital. If we are staying in a heated building all day, the question of weather will become interesting at best. It is important to remember that for feedback to be useful, it needs to be specific to a purpose.

Feedback arrives in a constant stream. Our filters work to screen out some feedback. One skill that is vital to receiving feedback is listening. Understanding feedback from another person requires good listening skills. One standard exercise for listening skills is the following:

*Sit down with a person whose world you would like to better understand. Be face to face with that person. Before you begin the exercise, make a choice to pay close attention. Imagine that you are interested in everything you are about to hear.*

*As the person talks, reflect or rephrase what you are hearing, seeing, and feeling. "What I am hearing you say is . . . " "Sounds like you are saying . . . "*

*Then ask the person for confirmation of what you have heard. Have you heard correctly? Or what parts have you heard correctly and what parts have you missed? When you have demonstrated that you have heard everything correctly, you have earned your right to respond.*

This simple exercise is important in tuning into other people's world and fully hearing their feedback to you. It is essential to go into the exercise with the attitude that you are very interested in understanding what their world is like. That interest is key.

Frequently people find that when they are actively listening to another person, they learn about themselves as well. For example, when they relate to others what they have heard, they are also letting themselves know something about the filters they have in place. In that process, they are telling others as much about themselves as the others are telling them.

A number of exercises are useful for getting feedback. One I frequently use is the JoHari Window (see Figure 4.3).

165

Figure 4.3. JoHari Window.

|  | Others know<br>about me | Others do not<br>know about me |
|---|---|---|
| I know<br>about me | Public Knowledge | Private Life |
| I do not<br>know<br>about me | Blind Spot | Unknown |

Source: J. Luft, Group Processes: An Introduction to Group Dynamics, 1984, p. 60. Reprinted with the permission of Mayfield Publishing Company.

The four windows of the JoHari Window are:

1. *Public knowledge.* This is the window that is known to self and others.
2. *Private life.* This window is known to self but not to others. This is the area of personal secrets.
3. *Blind spot.* This window represents what others know about you that you do not know about yourself. That is why it is referred to as *blind spot.* This is where our filters are most active in shielding us.
4. *Unknown.* These are the areas that are not known to self or others. These are the "yet to be."

The basic assumption of the JoHari Window is that the goal is to expand the areas that are not known to self. This increases our awareness of self and reduces blind spots.

Take some time with the JoHari Window. Think about the area known as public knowledge and private life. What are the items that you would put into the public knowledge box? It might be your position in the organization. Or it might be your marital status. Next, what are points you would make in the private life box? What are secrets that you do not think others know? Now we come to the interesting box. The blind spot. What do others know about you that you are not aware of? One way to find out is to ask others the question, "What do you think my blind spots are?"

The goal of this exercise is learning more about self. One value that is important for all managers is lifelong learning. The more managers understand themselves, the more effective they can be with others. And lifelong learning eats away at the last box—the unknown. The last box will always be there. The goal is to continually reflect on experiences to learn from them.

So far, the discussion has been about feedback to self. What about feedback to others? Assume that you want to communicate accurately to another person. Here are some suggestions from Phillips and Elledge (1989, pp. 37–39):

1. Focus on the job, not the person.
2. Be objective.
3. Be specific.
4. Be open and honest.
5. Use tact and consideration.

Scholtes (1989, pp. 6–24) adds to the list:

1. Acknowledge the need for feedback.
2. Give both positive and negative feedback.

3. Understand the context.
4. Know when to give feedback.
5. Know how to give feedback.
6. Be descriptive.
7. Do not use labels.
8. Do not exaggerate.
9. Do not be judgmental.
10. Speak for yourself.
11. Talk first about yourself, not the other person.
12. Phrase the issue as a statement, not a question.
13. Restrict your feedback to things you know.
14. Help people hear and accept.
15. Know how to receive feedback.
16. Listen carefully.
17. Ask questions for clarity.
18. Acknowledge the feedback.
19. Acknowledge valid points.
20. Take time to sort out what you have heard.

This is a bit of a laundry list. What is important? First and foremost, the other person needs to want feedback. This is the first and most important condition. Those who do not want feedback will not hear it. The starting point for successful feedback is a desire to have it.

Second, feedback is most useful when we have defined purpose and roles. Instead of a shot in the dark, feedback should be targeted. When you are asked to give feedback, ask for a clarification of purpose and roles. When you want feedback, begin by identifying your purpose and roles. Feedback disconnected from purpose is of little value.

Third, keep the feedback focused and objective. Use as many specifics as possible. Keep those specifics directed at how the person is doing "on purpose."

Fourth, the environment is crucial to all feedback. Keep the environment conducive to truth telling. That means that there needs to be regard for self and others present.

Feedback is the glue that holds the OPO model together. At the individual level, it is especially important because the individual is the building block of the organization. If the organization is not feeding back appropriate information or feeding valid information to correct misinformation, the result will be catastrophic. Feedback, at its most basic level, answers the individual question, Am I on target?

Earlier, I mentioned that we are bombarded by feedback. Feedback has the greatest impact when we decide the type of feedback we want and then go after it. We move from being a passive recipient of feedback to being an active player.

Clarity of purpose, clarity of roles, and feedback systems result in a by-product. That by-product is the individual's investment in the organization. The individual has the raw ingredients for commitment.

## Commitment

Commitment—we all want it in the employee. "Commitment begins the moment a manager and a prospective employee shake hands. It either grows or diminishes through your daily actions and interactions" (Thomas & Thomas, 1990, p. 1).

Take a few minutes and respond to the following questions:

*Think for a moment about an experience you have had in a work*

169

*setting or in a relationship setting where you were very committed. What was happening that invited your commitment and investment? Take a few moments to identify a scene and then make notes about it.*

*Now do the reverse. Think of a work setting or a relationship setting where you were not committed. What was happening that invited you not to commit? Take a moment to identify the scene and then make notes about it.*

*If you were to summarize your learnings from the answers to these questions, what would you say?*

In doing this exercise with numbers of persons, some common themes stand out:

1. Commitment occurred when individuals had a sense of purpose.
2. Commitment occurred when individuals felt they were contributing. They knew what they had contributed.
3. As the previous point implied, individuals knew what they had contributed because they received feedback. Out of that came commitment. Commitment is a by-product of purpose, role clarity, and feedback.

*Take a moment and think about your current work setting. On a ten-point scale, with one being low commitment and ten being very high commitment, where are you? What are the factors that caused you to be at that level? Jot down a few comments.*

Commitment can be approached in many ways. One term sometimes used along with the word *commitment* is *investment*. How do we get employees to invest in the organization? Typically, individuals invest when they see the linkage between what the organization is asking of them and their own need fulfill-ment. They invest when there is a sense that the work unit or organization is fulfilling their important needs. Another way of saying this is that the organization helps individuals find meaning in life. This is the critical link between the individ-ual and the organization. Figure 4.4 illustrates this.

Figure 4.4. Need Overlap.

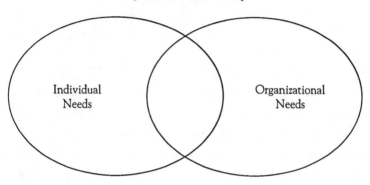

The goal of the health care OPO is to have appropriate over-lap between the two circles. This ensures that mutual invest-ment between the individual and the organization exists.

One way to discuss the commitment of the individual and the organization is the classic behavioral model of stimulus and response. The model is composed of two parts and is shown in Figure 4.5.

Figure 4.5. Stimulus-Response Model.

The organization offers a stimulus, and the individual provides a response. For example, the organization provides an across-the-board salary increase (stimulus) and the individual feels rewarded (response). However, this model is misleading because it does not take some developments into account. Figure 4.6 illustrates what is really happening.

Figure 4.6. Revised Stimulus-Response Model.

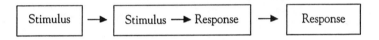

The organization provides a stimulus that enters the individual's internal world. The individual evaluates the stimulus in light of core needs. Based on this evaluation, an internal response is made to the external stimulus. Then there is the external response. In the previous example, the salary increase is designed to make the individual feel rewarded. However, if the person already perceives a salary injustice, the "reward" may increase dissatisfaction. The critical aspect of the revised model is that in order to understand commitment, you need to get inside individuals and understand their internal stimulus and response pattern. That internal stimulus and response pattern has to do with need fulfillment.

The classic literature on rewards distinguishes between intrinsic and extrinsic rewards. Intrinsic rewards are within the individual. One of my colleagues and I joke about why we do what we do. I do it for "fame." She does it for "fortune." I want to do good work because I pride myself on what I create. That is the intrinsic reward system. Extrinsic rewards are external to the individual. Salaries and benefits are examples. My colleague jokes that she does good work because the organization pays her to do it and because of the benefit package she receives. She is motivated by external rewards.

While it is useful at times to break out intrinsic and extrinsic rewards, all rewards are ultimately intrinsic. I work for money (extrinsic) because it allows me to do something for me (intrinsic). That is what the previous discussion on stimulus-response mechanisms points to. The organization gives me a paycheck (stimulus). I receive it and have an internal stimulus. "A paycheck, now I can . . . " Then I make a response. Ultimately, what matters is the internal reaction to the reward presented.

Commitment and investment happen because individuals have a sense of alignment with what is going on. They will get their needs met along with those of the work team and the organization. When that sense is present, they are internally driven.

What core needs should be considered? The following list is not exclusive but offers helpful guidelines. The core needs that impact the stimulus-response process are the following:

- Accomplishment/competence needs
- Structure/control needs
- Social/relational needs
- Creativity/play needs
- Health needs

Each will be discussed.

*Accomplishment/competence needs* cause an individual to invest in an organization. A sense of competence is a major stimulus for performance and productivity. Recently, I had a discussion with a hospital engineer. I asked him what was rewarding in his job. His response was to walk down the hallways of the hospital with me and point out the completed projects. As we walked, he pointed out the projects he had personally been responsible for. Competence that results in a sense of accomplishment is one of the cornerstones of investment.

But competence is more than accomplishment. It is the sense that we are able to respond to the challenges and opportunities that come our way. A synonym is *mastery*. Mastery has to do with an implicit belief that we can cope with what life has to offer us. We are able to ride the rapids as they come along. It is not just mastery of a work setting—it is mastery of life.

*Structure/control needs* are next. All individuals have a need for structure. Structure leads to predictability; it provides the channels for energy and prevents anarchy. Structure helps us make sense of chaos. We need it to make sense of the events about us. Structure can also provide us with a sense of control. Control is the feeling that we can influence our environment. Things do not just happen to us; we can shape events.

Probably the most feared event is that of losing control. Behind the usual lists of fear-provoking events—such as public speaking—is the fear that we will lose control of ourselves or the setting. Our needs for structure and control are important to us as individuals. Moreover, it is important in the health care setting that we provide appropriate structure and control— not too much and not too little.

*Social/relational needs* are especially crucial. We all need to be loved and to love. While it is not usual to use the word *love* in a book such as this, *love* is the most appropriate word to use. The workplace is an important area of our life where social and relational needs get met. Think about the amount of the "awake" day that is spent at work. For many employees, work is not only a place to make money; it is also a place to make friends and have a social life. Some individuals may refuse to take a promotion if it means leaving their work unit. What to the organization is a restructure is for the individual a major shifting of social ties. Work is a place of social interaction and relationships.

Another aspect of this need is recognition. We all need recognition for what we have done. Remember the stimulus-response process? The response of recognition reinforces behaviors. When an individual does something and gets a desired response, the tendency is to repeat it. Most of us know the importance of recognition systems in our health care organizations. We need to enhance them even more.

*Creativity/play needs* are core needs as well. These are illustrated by the engineer mentioned earlier who walks down the hallway proud of the work he has done. Or they can be seen on the part of an individual who has just solved a significant problem. We all have the need to feel creative. A common source of creativity is playfulness. I like to use the word *plurking* to identify appropriate mixtures of working and playing. Plurking is combining the attitude of playfulness with work accomplishment. The result is an individual who stays energized at work. A playful attitude at work energizes work. Recently I was discussing plurking with someone from Apple Computer. She playfully asked, "Do you know the difference between a Boy Scout troop and a group of Apple Computer employees?" I said no and she explained, "The Boy Scouts have adult leadership!" That is an example of playfulness brought into the work setting. A playful attitude at work unleashes creative energies to make improvements in the work processes and work relationships.

*Health needs* are also critical. Reflect on times you felt "unhealthy," and you will realize why this is such an important need. Health has physical, psychological, and spiritual dimensions. Part of my bias is that as health care organizations, we have a responsibility to model healthy work environments.

All individuals bring these and other needs into the workplace. In the past, the misconception was that individual needs should be kept outside of the workplace. The illusion was that employees could put needs into compartments. When individuals walked in the door of the health care organization, they left all personal needs outside. Problems at home were no longer important; for the next eight hours, their focus was work. We now know that that is impossible to do. We are whole human beings, and we inevitably bring our total self to work.

In addition, it is the need fulfillment side or the feeling side of individuals that has the energy. If we want invested, turned-on individuals, we need to invite them to expect need fulfillment at work. The degree to which these needs are met points in the direction of commitment. Use of words such as *commitment, investment, passion, vision,* and so on demands the use of our feeling side as well as our intellectual side. If our employees stop feeling when they walk in the door, they will also stop feeling excitement and enjoyment about work.

Commitment is a feeling. If an organization is really after committed individuals, it will need to be open to the expression of feelings by fully functioning human beings. Organizations that are looking for high levels of performance and productivity in their employees will need to build a corporate culture that supports the expression of feelings and the fulfillment of individual needs as well as organizational needs.

A final characteristic of commitment: it is subject to change. At first glance, this sounds confusing. How can commitment change? Think about it for a moment. Changing an employee's skills and abilities can take weeks, months, or years. Yet commitment can change quickly. For example, a highly committed individual feels unjustly criticized by a supervisor. That event can destroy the individual's commitment in an instant. Instead of a committed individual, the person has become unmotivated or resentful. The reverse can also occcur. An individual who lacks a sense of commitment can readily become committed given the proper conditions—that is, if it becomes apparent that that person's needs will be met. Both the advantage and the disadvantage of commitment is this quality of change.

Commitment, like happiness, is illusory. When you have it, you know it is there. But it can be gone in a moment. What is the foundation for inviting it back? Clarity of purpose, clarity of roles, and adequate feedback on performance.

## Conclusion

The OPO model is a valuable tool for empowering the individual in the organization. The questions the model asks the individual to confront are both simple and profound:

1. Do you understand the purpose of what you are about?
2. Are you in agreement with that purpose?
3. Do you understand the roles you are to perform?
4. Are you in agreement with those roles?

5. Do you know how you will know if you are on purpose and fulfilling the roles?
6. Do you agree with those measures?
7. Do you feel committed to carrying out the organization's purpose?
8. Do you get good information in this organization?
9. Do you feel this organization gives you opportunity for choice?
10. Does this organization value you and what you bring to it?
11. Does this organization provide you with opportunities to grow?

The core of any organization is the individual. The individual is the foundation on which all else is built. Successful organizations know that; unsuccessful organizations do not.

The next four chapters are concerned with the supporting actors for the on-purpose organization. These four actors include leadership, managing conflict, managing change, and problem solving.

CHAPTER FIVE

# *The Path*
# *of the Leader*

All management is people management, and all
leadership is people leadership. The reason for this is
there is nothing that a manager or leader can do that
does not depend for its effectiveness on the meaning
that other people attach to it.

> —Peter Vaill,
> *Managing as a Performing Art*

A GOOD PLACE to begin this chapter is with the following exercise:

*When you think of leaders and leadership, what comes to mind?
What behaviors do you think of? Take a few moments and write
down your thoughts.*

Typically, a leader is seen as someone who is out front leading . . . providing direction . . . issuing orders . . . bringing order
to chaos or performing some other dramatic function. When
asked about leaders, we think of national leaders such as presidents or other politicians. Or we think of leaders in the community—prominent individuals who have influence, wealth, and
prestige. They may be politically or financially successful. Or
they may be individuals we look to because they are wise and
appear to give good advice. (I am reminded of the story of a

prominent professor who asked a student if she knew who Soc-
rates was. She responded "Yes, he was a wise man who gave
people excellent advice. So they poisoned him." Being a leader
is not without its downside!)

Leadership is a topic that is considerably larger than this
chapter, this book, or a set of books. The purpose of this chapter is to discuss leadership in the context of the OPO. Leadership is the core of the OPO model. Leadership makes the decision to be an OPO. Without that decision, there can be no
OPO. In order for the model to function, there must be leadership. Leadership is involved with clarifying, communicating,
and winning acceptance of purpose and roles. Leadership provides feedback to people regarding their work and its impact.
Leadership nurtures appropriate commitment. Leadership permeates the OPO model.

This chapter will provide a definition of leadership, discuss
key aspects of being a leader, describe followership, and then
turn to application of the OPO model.

## Myths and Truths About Leadership

Bennis and Nanus (1985, p. 22) identify several myths about
leadership.

*Myth 1: Leadership is a rare skill.* It rarely happens. Look back
to your reflections on leadership. Did you look to national
figures? Did you look to community leaders? Did you look to
someone who has done an extraordinary deed?

The reality is that leadership is a very common skill. It happens continually at home and work. A parent providing leadership to a family is a daily occurrence. A worker helping her
co-worker clarify direction is providing leadership.

*Myth 2: Leaders are born, not made.* This is the genetic theory of leadership. Some have it, and some do not. If you were lucky enough to be born with it, it is yours. If not, forget it.

Later, this is discussed in greater depth in connection with the topic of leadership traits. A key belief that will be discussed is that leaders are made by the circumstances that allow them to use gifts of their genetic heritage.

*Myth 3: Leaders are charismatic.* This is the concept of leader as "cheerleader." The leader talks, and the audience is swayed by the words and the emotion. Leader is the person who is taking the lead in the charge up the hill.

An example I am familiar with is a surgeon who is charismatic. What I know is that people love to listen to him. Each time he talks, they find their juices flowing. They have a sense of their importance and how their work makes a difference. However, after they leave the room, the juices quickly dry up. It was a good adrenaline rush, but it did not sustain itself.

*Myth 4: Leadership exists only at the top of the organization.* Of course, all of us who have served in the upper hierarchies of an organization know that this is true. You rise to the top of the organization because of your leadership skills.

Wrong! Again, much of our management literature finds that the most important leadership happens at the moment of contact between the product or the service and the provider. It is that frontline person doing the work who is providing the leadership that gets the work of the organization done. As the epigraph to this chapter suggests, the mystery of leadership is that it is relational. It exists between people. That means it is portable: One moment, I am ascribing leadership to a person and the next, I have withdrawn the leadership I have been giving.

*Myth 5: The leader is the one who controls, directs, prods, and manipulates.* It is the leader who has to keep watch over things. If he or she lets up for a moment, the organization could be in serious trouble.

Again, this is misleading. Leadership is the responsibility of everyone in the organization.

If these are the myths about leadership, what are the truths? Key points include the following:

1. *We all have leadership qualities.* Those leadership qualities are with us whether we are at work, at home, on vacation, and so on. For example, you are at work. You look at how the work being done could be done better. You collect some data and present them to your boss. The data make sense, and the boss buys the improvement. You have just taken leadership. Or you are at home. The family cannot decide what to do that evening. The kids want to do one thing. You want to do something else, and your spouse wants a third thing. In the midst of it, you propose a resolution that results in a win-win situation for everyone. You have just exercised leadership.

Recently, I was walking through a hospital cafeteria when I noticed several of the food and nutrition workers going from table to table to see how people were doing. They were genuine about wanting to know how to do their jobs better. At that moment, they were acting out a leadership role.

The important point is that we all have leadership qualities.

2. *Leadership is a function of the person and the environment.* Leadership emerges when an environment supports the leadership qualities of an individual. An implication is that leadership is no longer the prerogative of a single individual. It readily moves from person to person, depending on the current

182

situation. A classic example is a senior manager I used to work for. He was highly successful as a senior manager and was recognized for the leadership he brought to the organization. He was the "old-style" health care manager who knew everyone by name and when their birthdays were. However, the environment of the organization shifted. As a result, my friend became increasingly ineffective as a leader. The skills that once matched the environment so closely now were obstacles. The end result was a termination from the organization. The environment shifted without an equal shift on the part of the individual.

We all know of examples like this involving individuals with outstanding leadership abilities. When the organization changed their role, they became ineffective. The basic message is that leadership is a function of the individual and the environment, not the individual alone. Deming (1986) questions the performance review systems of our organizations on this precise point. What we attribute to individuals really belongs to work processes involving many suppliers and customers. Think about the number of people you depend on to provide you with goods and services to get your work done. This is humbling. We all have significant dependencies on others. This is part of our environment.

3. *Leadership is temporal.* This follows from the earlier discussion. Leadership changes from situation to situation. In one situation, an individual may be perceived as an outstanding leader. Dropped into another setting, the same individual will be seen as ineffective. We are all aware of examples of that from business, from industry, from health care organizations. It is not uncommon to find a shining star who does not make it in the next position.

I have had personal experience with this. Over the years, I have been very successful in the organizations I have worked in as an organizational development person. And I kept saying to myself, "If only I could get into line management, think of the impact I could have . . . " Finally, I got the opportunity to move into a senior management position in an organization, only to find that the skills I had been so successful with were not as effective in this highly political organization. The result was several years of frustration and stress.

4. *Charisma is a special form of leadership.* We tend to equate charisma with leadership. If we walk away from a meeting with our heart pounding and with a feeling of inspiration, we believe that we have been in the presence of a leader. And we may have been. Or we may have been in the presence of a good "motivational speaker" who in another era would have sold us snake oil.

I think of a situation that I was in for a number of years when the organization was searching for the "right CEO." We had a very charismatic leader. The "town meetings" held within the organization were inspiring. We would charge out the door after the meetings ready for the next challenge. But it was a bit like empty calories. There was nothing more. After a short bit, we were hungry again.

Then, along came our leader. He truly was a leader. His approach was low-key. There was no major hype. However, when we left the meetings, we left with the sense of excitement because we had a feeling of vision. We left with substance. He could help us see how the next steps could come about and where we fit in. Our energies were focused.

5. *Leadership means being a servant.* What does this mean?

It means that a leader is able to lead because somehow the leader has captured for the group, for individuals, or for society, a key need or quality of that individual, group, or society.

Have you ever been in front of a group and had them not respect your leadership role? You call for order but nothing happens. You try to get them back on track but to no avail. I used to have a nightmare in which the students walked into the classroom, and, while I tried to teach, they watched television in the back of the room. The experience is one of being out of control.

If you examine leadership, you recognize that at its core it is relationship. Individuals assign leadership to the leader. Without that assignment, you may be able to "boss people around," but you are not a leader. In the richness of the Native American tradition, this concept is seen in its fullest. Leaders emerged according to the issue that the tribe was facing. Whoever had the background or experience in the area was granted the leadership. The greatest warrior led the war party. The greatest hunter led the hunting party. Leadership fell on the shoulders of whoever had the skills that the tribe needed at that moment.

The point is that leadership is not something that is uniquely inherited. It comes through individuals providing the community with a way to move from the current situation to a desired future. It is a blending of qualities and experiences that an individual brings to a setting and the requirements of that setting.

The one function that is true of all leadership in whatever form it takes is that the leader provides the "community" with a sense of how it can move from a current condition to a future condition. That is the basic function of leadership.

185

## *Leadership — Some Definitions*

What is a leader and what is a manager? Bennis and Nanus (1985, p. 21) say that "managers are people who do things right, and leaders are people who do the right thing." They elaborate as follows:

> We have here one of the clearest distinctions be-
> tween the leader and the manager. By focusing atten-
> tion on a vision, the leader operates on the emotional
> and spiritual resources of the organization, on its
> values, commitment, and aspirations. The manager,
> by contrast, operates on the physical resources of the
> organization, on its capital, human skills, raw
> materials, and technology. Any competent manager
> can make it possible for people in the organization to
> earn a living. An excellent manager can see to it that
> the work is done productively and efficiently on
> schedule and with a high level of quality. It remains
> for the effective leader, however, to help people in
> the organization know pride and satisfaction in their
> work [p. 22].

Managers take care of the day-to-day decisions that are necessary and appropriate for the running of a good organization.
Leaders, on the other hand, are not reined in by the day-to-
day decisions or the accomplishment of specific objectives.
Leaders focus attention on vision — what vision means for that
individual, group, or organization — and provide direction on
how to move from current reality to a future reality (vision).

This can be summarized by saying that leaders have the ability to focus attention on a target, communicate that attention, and get others to enroll. Leaders help by putting the spotlight on the target.

Burns (1978, p. 425) defines leadership as "the reciprocal process of mobilizing, by people with certain motives and values, various economic, political, and other resources, in a context of competition and conflict, in order to realize goals independently or mutually held by both the leaders and the followers." Key to this definition is that leaders, again, have the ability to use the available resources in such a way that they and their followers can accomplish what they are about.

Burns goes on to identify two types of leadership, the transactional and the transforming. He states that most leaders and followers have a transactional relationship. *Transactional leadership* involves an exchange of one thing for another—jobs for votes, or subsidies, or campaign contributions. In some ways, we can refer to this as the managerial or administrative role. You put in so many hours, and you get so much reward. It is a transaction.

*Transforming leadership,* on the other hand, is both more complex and more potent. The transforming leader looks beyond current needs to the future. Such a leader seeks ways that employees can be motivated and helps them find paths to satisfy higher needs that engage the full person. This is providing the conditions necessary for empowerment. Empowerment occurs when employees are able to see how they can achieve their personal agendas at the same time the organization is achieving its agendas. Transforming leaders also provide "paradigm shifts," which will be discussed in further detail later.

The transactional leader is a manager. The transforming

leader is a true leader. The manager carries out organizational goals. The leader provides a sense of vision as to what might be. Both are needed.

## Schools of Thought on Leadership

There have been several schools of thought regarding leadership. These schools still influence us today. One of the first schools had to do with *leadership traits*. The leadership trait school said, "Let's proceed to identify leadership traits, and then we will test individuals for those traits. From the test results, we will determine who is and who is not a leader." In other words, "Here are a set of qualities." If you have these qualities, you are a leader. If you do not, you are not a leader." This approach assumes that you are born with leadership skills.

A second approach to leadership focuses on the *environment*. The environment produces leaders; it provides the soil out of which leadership grows. For example, I was raised in the Dakotas. My leadership roots come from being raised on the Heart River in western North Dakota. That is different from being raised in an urban area of the Northeast with access to a different set of resources, such as different political leaders, educational experiences, and so on.

The environment school is a twist on *West Side Story*. Remember that Broadway musical? In it, juvenile delinquents complain to the truant officer that they are a product of their environment. They cannot help themselves because the environment caused them to be juvenile delinquents.

Leaders cannot help it—the environment made them do it!

What makes the most sense? A combination. The position taken in this book is that leadership is a function of person and environment. In reviewing the subject of leadership, we need to take into account the qualities of the individual and the environmental needs.

This section has provided general thoughts on leadership. The next section focuses on the key contributions leaders make to the OPO.

*What Do Leaders Provide?*

Leaders provide any organization or work unit with four main things.

1. *Leaders create a vision of what can be.* This vision can be created in two major ways. First, the leaders themselves have a clear vision or direction. They know what needs to happen. In one setting, the organization brought in a new CEO who brought with her years of experience in creating exactly the kind of organization that was wanted. The leader articulated the vision and how the vision could be achieved. She knew what the organization needed, and she produced it.

Second, the leaders may not have a vision, but they know how to involve others in defining it. Management planning retreats are one method for bringing together participants to create vision. The leader pulls together the people who have pieces of the puzzle and works with them to arrive at a vision. The vision is determined through a participatory style. The result is that group's shared vision. Burns (1978, p. 19) suggests that "the crucial variable . . . is purpose. Some define leadership as leaders making followers do what followers would not otherwise do, or as leaders making followers do what the leaders want them to do; I define leadership as leaders inducing followers to act for certain goals that represent the values and moti-

189

vations and wants and the needs, the aspirations and expectations—of both leaders and followers. And the genius of leadership lies in the manner in which leaders see and act on their own and on their followers' values and motivations."

2. *Leaders articulate the vision.* To a certain degree, this is implied in the first quality. However, whether the vision has been arrived at individually or through a participatory process, it has to be articulated. To whom is it articulated? To the followers, since they are the ones who will carry out the vision. They are the workers. Without the articulation, the vision is not particularly useful. It may shed some light, but it will not provide much guidance.

3. *Leaders enroll others in the vision.* First the vision is created. Then it is articulated. Next, the followers must enroll in it. Because they have accurately portrayed and named a vision, leaders invite investment on the part of followers. Burns (1978, p. 426) puts it this way: "Leaders can also shape and alter and elevate the motives and values and goals of followers through the vital teaching role of leadership. This is transforming leader. The premise of this leadership is that whatever the separate interests persons may hold, they are presently or potentially united in pursuit of higher goals, the realization of which is tested by the achievement of significant change which represents the collective or pooled interest of leaders and followers."

Followers are invited to achieve objectives and goals that they did not think they could achieve. That invitation comes through the articulation of vision. A vision has the potential of enrolling "the heart." That is the vital component of vision. When times get tough, the vision is carried forward by individuals who believe in it. The vision itself invites enrollment.

4. *Leaders act on the vision.* Implicit in all that has been said thus far is that the leadership role moves from simply identifying a vision, articulating the vision, and enrolling in the vision to acting on that vision. Acting on it may be as mundane as putting together action plans—that is, identifying the day-to-day resources that we will need to move from where we currently are to the desired future. Or acting on a vision may involve dramatic symbolic gestures. In one case I know of, the CEO dramatically emphasized the shift away from time clocks by throwing a time clock off the top of a building. Action on vision was dramatic at that moment.

Within management theory, a basic assumption is that you get what you control for. In other words, what you choose to monitor within the organization is what you will get. Once the leader has created, communicated, enrolled, and acted on a vision, there needs to be a process of keeping the spotlight on the desired outcomes—that is, a means of exercising control.

The leader, then, creates a vision, communicates it, enrolls others in it, and acts on it. In those four steps, the leader provides the core of the OPO. Through the maze of events, the leader provides a road map for keeping individuals, work units, and the organization on purpose. The common bond is created.

A different way of viewing leadership comes from Moore and Gillette (1990). Since I began this book using the metaphor of a quest, their approach is of interest. Moore and Gillette suggest that leadership can take four forms:

1. The kingly/queenly
2. The warrior

191

3. The lover
4. The magician

A leader who is *kingly/queenly* provides direction and purpose. This is a higher purpose than the traditional day-to-day purposes. The kingly/queenly leader provides vision and structure.

The leader as *warrior* emphasizes commitment to the purpose and direction of the kingly/queenly. The warrior has the knightly functions of allegiance to the direction that has been set. To carry the metaphor forward, warrior energy is always aligned with kingly/queenly purpose. When the kingly/queenly purpose is absent, warrior energy goes astray, and the sword is used to destroy. When the warrior energy is attached to kingly/queenly purpose, direction and commitment come together. In many ways, the warrior is the manager carrying out the organization's goals.

The idea of the leader as lover may sound strange in a management book. But *lover* evokes the passion of the leader. Leaders need to be passionate about their purpose. Purpose without passion is dry and flat; purpose with passion becomes directed and targeted and energized.

The notion of leaders as *magicians* stresses their competence. Being a magician means having special powers to get things done.

*Take a moment and think about these qualities in relation to yourself: How do you display the kingly/queenly functions? How do you display the warrior functions? How do you display the lover functions? How do you display the magician functions?*

Burns (1978, pp. 460–461) raises four questions that we need to consider in exercising leadership. First, what is our personal interest in being a leader? We need to clarify within ourselves our own personal goal. If our goal is only to secure a livelihood for ourselves, we need to reexamine our desire to be a leader. The leader role transcends self. If we link our career with a cause that rises above considerations of personal success and contributes some social good, we have leadership potential.

Second, who are we seeking to lead? Leadership is a collective process. It emerges from the clash and the congruence of motives and goals of leaders and followers. The goal is to define our potential followers in terms of mutuality of motives.

Third, where are we going? The ultimate test of practical leadership is the realization of intended real change that meets the enduring needs of people.

Fourth, how will we overcome obstacles to realizing our goals? This becomes a question of the motivation of leaders and followers. The obstacles need to be identified and problems solved.

Leadership is relational. It always exists within the context of relationships. Relationship is at the core of even formal, hierarchical leadership. This means that the role of follower needs to be discussed as well. What about followers? What do followers contribute to the equation? What does it mean to be a follower? The next section discusses this aspect of leadership.

*Follower Requirements*

A friend of mine frequently makes the statement that everyone wants to be a leader but no one wants to follow. To be a leader is noble and wonderful, involves calling the shots, and so forth. To be a follower means having to listen to someone else's direction, to be mindless, uncreative, and so on.

193

However, go back to one of the basic assumptions that this chapter is built on. The assumption is that leadership is a temporal experience. That means that it shifts and changes. A leader in one context becomes a follower in another context. A leader in one work setting may be a follower in another setting. A leader at home becomes a follower at work. Leadership is dynamic and shifts and flows from situation to situation. It changes from moment to moment depending on the needs of the organization. That means that we are all leaders and followers. The important implication is that we need to be conscious of when we are followers so that we can carry out this role effectively.

What qualities do followers need to be effective? Here are just a few:

1. *They need to have clarity of purpose and role.* What is the vision? Do they understand what the vision is? Do they agree with it? Does it make sense to them in both their heart and mind? Finally, does meeting the vision allow them a sense of personal meaning? It is critical for followers to have a sense that they are making a contribution. What they do matters.

2. *Good followers take time to define their roles and responsibilities as they look at movement toward vision.* Good followers are constantly challenging leaders about the nature of the vision as well as about how to realize it. Followers are continually raising the question, "What is our role? If there is confusion, how do we clarify confusion? If there is disagreement, how do we recognize that disagreement, focus it, and correct for it?"

3. *A good follower takes responsibility for what is happening.* This implies that there is feedback that allows the follower to actively identify how things are being done and if they are being done effectively. The follower needs to be active, not passive.

4. *Followers monitor levels of commitment.* Effective followers monitor how they are investing or not investing in the vision. Blind followership is not effective followership. Good followership means an ongoing process of truthful, accurate interactions about how resources are being used.

The follower is a full partner with the leader. Think for a moment about what we have learned from the quality movement. One key is that the people who are actually doing the work are the most effective at defining what improvements can and should be made. The worker knows best how to improve the quality of the product and service. The follower is the most knowledgeable about getting the organization from point A to point B.

The follower needs to be invested in the organization and in the vision that the leadership brings to the organization.

## OPO Application

How do the preceding points relate to the OPO model? First, let us talk about leaders and managers. For the leader, the key elements of the model are purpose and commitment. The key leadership function is the creation of purpose and vision. As Burns (1978, p. 455) says, "Leadership is morally purposeful. All leadership is goal oriented. The failure to set goals is a sign of faltering leadership. Successful leadership points in a direction. It is also a vehicle of continuing and achieving purpose."

Leaders are also strong on commitment. Through the creation of vision and articulation of vision, they invite others to enroll in the vision. This means that they invite followers to be invested and committed.

Managers, on the other hand, are strong in role definition

and feedback. Role definition occurs with respect to policies, procedures, job descriptions, and so on. Defining the boundaries determines both the limitations and the opportunities. Key management functions are defining those boundaries and providing people with feedback about how they are fulfilling or not fulfilling role expectations and purpose.

Critical to understanding leaders is to understand that they are going to primarily focus on vision and commitment, and managers are going to primarily focus on roles and feedback. In the OPO, leaders do the following through both words and deeds:

- Define, clarify, and gain commitment to purpose
- Define, clarify, and gain commitment to roles
- Define appropriate and on-target feedback systems
- Invite appropriate levels of commitment
- Create the conditions for truthful communication
- Foster empowerment and taking responsibility
- Create a climate of mutual regard

## Charisma: A Special Consideration

Charismatic leadership is a special form of leadership. Typically, it is charismatic leadership that people refer to when they think of strong leadership. It is that person who in the middle of battle suddenly surges forth and brings order to the troops that are disintegrating. Likewise, it is the charismatic leader who in the midst of chaos and confusion in an organization suddenly takes over and leads the organization out of the crisis.

Crisis becomes intimately linked to the charismatic leader. In fact, Conger and Kanungo (1988, p. 55) state that "it is not only acute crisis that brings out the charismatic leader. Charismatic leadership can arise when crisis is chronic, such as when the ultimate values of a culture are being undermined. . . . Individuals who experience crisis and feel a loss of control over their environments generally are more ready than others to accept the authority of the charismatic leader. . . . Charismatic leaders are more likely to appear in failing organizations or in newly emerging ones that are struggling to survive." They continue as follows: "Transformational charisma cannot develop unless (1) crisis is believed to exist and a strong person of extraordinary powers has been identified, and (2) strong bonds of power and affiliation are established between this leader and the led. Given these conditions, highly charged bonds of communication and a strong collective order of power can be aligned and mobilized into extremely high levels of energy."

So, for charismatic leadership to come forward, crisis needs to exist. Someone needs to be perceived as a person who can lead the organization forward, and very strong bonds are required between the leader and the followers.

In their in-depth treatment of charismatic influence, Conger and Kanungo put forward the following six-part model:

First, there is the leader who has the ability to

- Create a vision
- Express that vision
- Articulate direction
- Act out the vision and direction
- Demonstrate high levels of energy and activity
- Show confidence and commitment
- Act with power

197

Second, there is the follower who

- Has an emotional detachment and trust in the leader
- Is willing to obey
- Has shared beliefs
- Has a low level of conflict among other followers

Third, there is the context. In the context, there is a crisis and instability. Within that context and instability, the leader shows direction.

Fourth, the leader-follower relationship is more than a task relationship. It typically involves projection and transference. The charismatic leader becomes the parent of those who are carrying forward the task.

Fifth, the leader-context relationship is filled with mythmaking, intolerance of the status quo, and identification of opportunities. In other words, in the midst of what everyone else sees as chaos, the charismatic leader sees an opportunity to develop direction.

Sixth, in the follower-context relationship, there is a sense of distress, helplessness, powerlessness, and alienation.

When these six conditions are present, the organization is ready for charismatic leadership. Key to the charismatic leader-follower relationship is the leader's coming forward in the midst of crisis and creating conditions where the followers have a sense that their hopelessness can be eliminated. A relationship of psychological dependency develops.

In the midst of that crisis, the leader articulates a vision, shows a high degree of self-confidence and involvement in the vision, sets a personal example for the followers, and maintains that image in the minds of followers, peers, and superiors. The leader's behaviors are very consistent with the words that the leader speaks. In other words, the charismatic leader "walks the talk," and in doing so, invites the followers to become involved as well.

Conger and Kanungo (1988, p. 52) summarize as follows: "The charismatic relationship has two major dimensions. First is the requisite abilities, interests, and personal traits of the charismatic leader. The charismatic leader needs to express behavior, feel confidence, self-determination, insight, freedom from internal conflict, eloquence, activity, and an energy level that is high. Secondly, the followers' desire and need to identify with the charismatic leader is high. It is a magnetism that is experienced. The followers, consequently, buy in to the charismatic leader."

The charismatic leader is produced out of a context, an environment. Leadership is a function of the individual and the environment. Without significant crisis and chaos, the charismatic leader does not come forward. That is a given that needs to be there in the environment.

## Health Care Leadership: Future Needs

Earlier in this book, we discussed the paradigm shifts going on in health care. What are the implications of these paradigm shifts for health care leadership? The following question then arises: What competencies are needed for twenty-first-century leaders? As health care leaders, what skills do we need to be building? Here are the top six skills identified in one study ("Bridging the leadership gap," 1992, May & June):

1. *Mastering change.* A key competency needed by health

199

care leaders is the ability to help organizations view change as an opportunity for new alternatives. Change now becomes a natural, stated part of the agenda. The expectation, then, is for health care leaders to frame change in such a way that alternatives and opportunities come forth.

2. *Using systems thinking.* A major competency for leaders in the twenty-first century will be to understand inter-relationships and patterns in solving complex problems. Instead of seeing problems in terms of linear cause and effect, they will need to apply a systems perspective and view them as having multiple causes and effects.

3. *Creating shared vision.* Leaders in the twenty-first century will need to be able to craft the collective organizational vision. While on the surface this sounds simple, leaders become the molder of the clay who pull together a multitude of visions of the future from customers, suppliers, employees, physicians, and patients to create a shared vision. This is a major theme of this book—a shared vision means that members of the organization all know what the organization is about, how it is doing it, and why.

4. *Emphasizing continuous quality improvement.* A key competency of the leader is never to be satisfied but constantly to be looking at ways the current system can be improved to increase quality. This fits closely with the previous items. Since those who are closest to work processes are in the best position to create continuous improvement, empowerment of them is a given.

5. *Redefining health care.* The focus moves from dramatic

changes and dramatic breakthroughs to one of a focus on healing, changing life-styles, and a holistic interplay of mind, body, and spirit. Care becomes differentiated from healing.

6. *Building communities.* Health care leaders in the twenty-first century will need to be competent not only at working in health care institutions but also at serving the public and community to weld a social mission to the organization's goals, objectives, and actions.

Take some time to reflect on these competencies for the twenty-first century. As you think of your own leadership, what will you need to shift, change, or reinforce to bridge the leadership gap to the twenty-first century?

## Conclusion

This chapter has been about leadership. Leadership is the midwife of the OPO. Without it, the OPO will go nowhere. There can be no OPO when leadership is absent. The chapter has defined on-purpose leadership as:

- Articulating purpose and vision
- Communicating purpose and vision
- Enrolling people in purpose and vision
- Acting on purpose and vision
- Creating a climate of truth telling, choice, and regard

However, as people define, communicate, enroll, and act on purpose and vision, conflicts will occur. That is a given. We turn to this subject in the next chapter.

201

# CHAPTER SIX

# Harnessing
# the Energy of Conflict

There are things that must cause you to lose your
reason or you will have none to lose. An abnormal
reaction to an abnormal situation is normal behavior.
— Viktor Frankl,
*Man's Search for Meaning*

CONFLICT MANAGEMENT AND conflict resolution are perhaps two
of the most significant topics for health care administrators.
Why? The answer is obvious to most of us in health care. First,
health care organizations depend on a large number of highly
technical people working together to produce an end result:
quality patient care. This happens within organizations that are
heavily value laden. In addition, the physicians who provide
health care organizations with patients may not be part of the
organization. Finally, health care organizations are very diverse.
That in and of itself implies that they are a seedbed of potential conflict. When these internal factors are combined with
a turbulent and changing environment, conflict is inevitable.
Conflict is a given—the only question is how we will choose
to manage it.

Health care professionals must manage conflict on the intrapersonal, interpersonal, interdepartmental, and organizational
levels. It is critical that they manage conflict on all these levels.

Health care professionals need to be able to balance internal (intrapersonal) conflicts. These conflicts within the person arise from conflicting wants. Think about the conflicts that come at budget time. Do we add more FTEs to a department? How do we balance additional FTEs with a conservative position that says hold back? Frequently, these conflicts are the most important to clarify because they cloud other issues.

Interpersonal conflict generally gets the attention. We know that person A and person B disagree, and they are in conflict. They want to use resources differently, they have different values, and they fight it out. Health care professionals need two types of skills. The first type allows them to assist others in working through conflict. This is interpersonal peacemaking. The second type of conflict is conflict directed at the professional. The two types of conflict have their own skills requirements.

Interdepartmental conflict is between departments. It is one thing to be a peacemaker between individuals. It is quite another to be a peacemaker between departments. A different set of skills is needed, skills in getting conflicting departments to work on purpose. Think how dependent departments are on one another to get their jobs done. And, due to the conditions of health care today, such resource conflicts are a given. The decision of who gets the FTEs or dollars is certain to generate conflict. Conflict can make a naturally difficult situation even more difficult.

The health care professional needs one other set of conflict management skills that relate to the conflicts between the organization and the environment. How effective is the health care organization in managing its conflicts with regulatory bodies? Competitors? Suppliers? These are all critical interfaces for the organization.

This chapter begins with an outline of beliefs about conflict. Next, the conflict management cycle is presented in detail. Most frequently, conflict management is crisis oriented. Conflict happens, and we stumble through it rather than learn from it. The conflict management cycle provides a model for viewing conflict that sees it as process to be managed rather than an event to be reacted to. We will use the OPO model as a useful framework for resolving conflict.

A message that you will find throughout this chapter is that conflict resolution is not mere problem solving. Rather, conflict resolution invites birthing something new. It is a process, not an event. When we just view conflict resolution as problem solving, we typically focus on a symptom. We make an adjustment to the situation. If the problem is simple, that may be sufficient. However, when working with problems with nonobvious solutions, conflict resolution needs to be seen as creating something new. We are not just solving problems; we are creating new possibilities. As Fritz (1989, p. 11) says, "We have been trained to think of situations that are inadequate for our aspirations as problems. When we think of them as problems, we try to solve them. When you are solving a problem, you are taking action to have something go away: the problem. When you are creating, you are taking action to have something come into being: the creation. Notice the intentions of these actions are opposite."

The message: any conflict setting invites us to create something new. Phillips and Cheston (1979, p. 76) observe that "conflict is inevitable in organizations. The managerial task is

205

to permit conflict to serve a productive function, focus business issues, to review inconsistencies of work tasks, faulty communication, and other hindrances to organizational effectiveness."

Phillips and Cheston make a very important point. It is not unusual to find managers who believe that if they were really good and really did their job well, there would be no conflict. Nothing could be further from the truth. Conflict is inevitable. In fact, effective managers are surrounded by conflict because they are doing things. The key is how conflicts are managed.

## Beliefs About Conflict

Conflict—the very word brings strong reactions. If we have learned to be comfortable with conflict, we will not be threatened when conflict is happening around us. But if we are uncomfortable with conflict, the very mention of the word may cause us to get nervous. Our reactions to conflict settings are the result of our belief systems about conflict. Remember our discussions on precept language? The intent of this section is to identify fundamental beliefs about conflict.

However, before going into my beliefs about conflict, let us talk about yours.

*If you were writing a book on conflict, what would be the key statements you would make about it? Take time and write down your responses.*

Now compare your thoughts with mine.

*Belief 1: Conflict is a given of life.* It simply *is.* We cannot exist without conflict. Why? Because we have the ability to choose. We have wants. And wants and choices may differ. That means that my wants and desires may be in conflict with your wants and desires. This is true whether those wants are organizational, team, or personal. Within organizations, a multitude of decisions are made. These decisions determine what the organization is, where it is going, and why it is going in that particular way. All of those decisions create potential conditions for conflict. These are the conditions around us that are simply waiting to be discovered.

Problems associated with wants and choices are not only external. We have internal conflicts as well. I want to finish writing this book, but I want to spend time with my family.

Since there is no way to avoid conflict, the only useful question to ask is, how do we effectively manage it so we can use the energy unleashed by it in a creative way?

*Belief 2: Conflict is energy.* If you doubt this, think for a moment about a boring discussion you have been engaged in. A number of candidates probably come to mind for all of us. Suddenly someone says, "I disagree with that." You are alert to a new energy in the room. People begin to sit up straight in their chairs and pay attention. Conflict may bring a revitalizing energy to the meeting. It can also become a destructive force. Either way, conflict is energy. It can be so energizing that you wake up in the middle of the night revisiting the time of conflict.

It is not unusual to find a married couple who stay energized through fighting and conflict. When things are a little boring, they play a game called UpRoar (Berne, 1964). The same is true in many organizations. Especially in health care organizations, it is not unusual to be conflict oriented and work from a crisis management model. In the short term there is energy. In the long term, there is burnout.

207

Figure 6.1. Conflict as Energy.

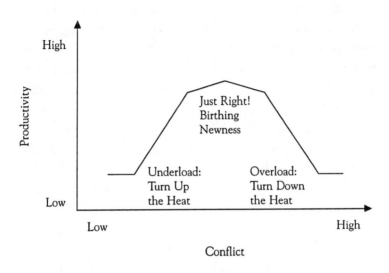

When our level of conflict is too low, the result is low productivity (Figure 6.1). No energy is being expended toward conflict resolution. In the long term, the experience is an endless drain. As the heat is turned up, energies become engaged. The potential is right for greater productivity. There is now energy for responding to the conflict and resolving it. This may mean developing new approaches. It is a time of productivity. However, when we get to an overload setting, our ability to respond may be diminished. The conflict becomes overwhelming.

*Belief 3: Conflict is the potential for birthing something new.* Conflict is a sign that something is not going right. There is a gap between "what I expect" and "what you expect." Conditions are other than what we thought they were. In that sign that something is not going right is the potential for new solutions.

Just as the elevated temperature in an individual indicates that something is wrong, conflict within a work unit or organization lets us know that something is not right. And in that sign is the opportunity for something new. Conflict invites us to stop and ask the question, What is wanted in this situation? Conflict lets us know that an opportunity for change exists.

One of my first jobs was working in fire control with the National Park Service. I was a firefighter. Over and over, I saw examples of a fire coming through and creating conditions for new growth and renewal. That is what conflict invites us to do—to renew.

*Belief 4: The key to conflict management is self-management.* How administrators behave in a conflict setting is based on the belief system that they bring to the setting. Behavior is a response from a set of perceptions about conflict. How an administrator behaves in a conflict setting is a result of learning.

We all learn conflict management skills at an early age. Think back to your family of origin. How was conflict managed in the family? Was it something that was expected and dealt with? Or was it swept under the carpet? Did conflict lead to physical abuse? Verbal abuse? The first place we learn to manage conflict is in our family of origin.

We carry over core learnings on how to manage conflict from our family of origin. And we act them out in the workplace. An exercise that demonstrates this comes from family therapy work.

*Take a few moments and think back to your family of origin. Focus on a time when there was conflict. Now draw a picture of the setting. (Do not let your drive for perfection get in your way.)*

*Draw the room and who was in the room. Beside each person, write what the person was saying, thinking, and feeling.*

*When you finish the family of origin, think back to a recent conflict in your work setting. Again, draw the picture. Who is in it? What are they thinking, feeling, and saying? (Be sure to include yourself!) Now compare the two pictures. What are the commonalities? What are the differences? How much of that early family experience are you carrying into the work setting?*

Typically, this exercise is most useful in pointing out the influence of our early learnings regarding conflict on how we respond to conflict and act it out in the work setting.

Ultimately, conflict management is a function of self-management and awareness. As individuals become aware of dysfunctional behaviors in conflict settings and understand their belief systems, they can make changes. They can relearn how to respond in conflict settings. We can talk until we are blue in the face about how useful conflict is, yet if we behave differently from our spoken words in a conflict setting, those around us will respond to our behavior rather than to our words. Relearning means behavioral learning.

The four beliefs just summarized are the core of the rest of this chapter. Effective conflict management is a vital, reenergizing tool when properly used and addressed in an OPO. When it is not properly used and addressed, it becomes a destructive force. The outcomes depend on our choices for how we will manage conflict.

One quick aside: A story that I like to use in conflict management workshops has to do with a friend of mine who had a very frustrating interaction with another member of her work department. That evening as she went home consumed with frustration and anger, she decided that she would use her artistic creativity to release the conflictual energy. She created a painting entitled "An Ode to Mary." This painting has gone on to win numerous local and statewide art competitions. In fact, it has resulted in significant financial remuneration for my friend. The point: she took the energy from the intense conflict and used that energy to drive her artistic creation. The result: an award-winning work of art.

## Conflict Management Cycle

Conflict is not a neutral word. As noted, the mere mention of it can cause fear and trembling. The purpose of this section is to take the mystery out of conflict and provide a way of thinking about it that implies strategies for management. The model invites you to think of a process for handling conflict.

In doing workshops on conflict management, one of the tools I have found useful is the Grand Canyon Suite, by Ferde Grofé. In this composition, there is a piece known as the "Thunderstorm." The music begins with very light melodies that convey the feeling of a summer afternoon and a cloudless sky. As the storm clouds begin to develop, the suite begins to bring in more and more dramatic tones that indicate the building of clouds. Fairly quickly, the kettledrums and other music instruments begin to convey the sense of the winds swirling and the thunderstorm building, until it reaches a major climactic moment when the thunderstorm (kettledrums) is fully present. The musical sensation is one of being in the midst of a thunderstorm with its flashes of lightning, clapping of thunder, and downpour of rain. Then the music begins to subside, and the thunderstorm

211

moves off into the distance. Finally, there is a return to the quiet and peace of that warm, calm summer afternoon.

This musical score is an effective lead-in to discussing the conflict management cycle, since participants get a distinct sense of the conflict cycle. The conflict cycle appears in Figure 6.2.

Figure 6.2. Conflict Management Cycle.

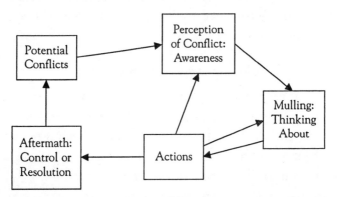

*Source:* Adapted from F. L. Ulschak & S. M. SnowAntle, *Consultation Skills for Health Care Professionals: How to Be an Effective Consultant Within Your Organization,* Figure 23, p. 205. Copyright 1990 by Jossey-Bass Inc., Publishers.

## Stage 1: Potential Conflicts

Potential conflicts exist within organizations for a number of reasons. Status difference is one. Some individuals in the organization will be decision makers. Their decisions impact others. The result of their decision making can be inadvertent conflict. For example, decisions on downsizing may be made by a certain subgroup of individuals within the organization. Other individuals will then implement that downsizing. And others will be directly affected by the decision.

In health care, a specific area of conflict is between physicians and other health care professionals. Physicians have a unique status in health care organizations. They are the ones who supply the patients to the organization. They admit the "customer." At the same time, they may have less investment in the organization then other members of the organization. They may have admitting privileges at several hospitals, which can be a source of conflict. If there is an encounter between the physician and another health care professional, the tendency for administration may be to side with the physician.

Another area of potential conflicts is structural conflict. Structural conflicts occur when various departments in the organization come into conflict because they have (1) mutually overlapping responsibilities, or (2) mutually nonresponsible responsibilities. In the first case, the conflict comes because two departments have responsibilities defined into their "turf." In the second case, there is a question of who will do this—"It's not my job." If responsibility for taking care of the floors has not been defined, both a maintenance department and an environmental services department may be caught in a conflict of who is going to do the job.

Perhaps the most obvious source of conflict in a health care organization is the competition for scarce resources. Whenever resources are scarce—dollars, human resources, space—competition is intensified. That can result in conflict.

One of the classic stories I use as an example of structural conflict involves something that happened when I was part of the senior management team in an organization that was downsizing. In the midst of the downsizing, the CEO walked into the room and announced to the senior team that there would be two new positions added in the coming year. We were told that we should "fight it out among ourselves" as to who should get those new positions. Trust me, we fought it out. Structure can be a significant contributor to conflict.

Another area is that of value differences. Individuals in an organization often have different values. One individual may favor a tight, economically sound organization. Another individual's values may be to create a productive organization in which employees have a satisfying work environment. These values can readily come into conflict. Value differences about the nature of work may lead to conflict between administrators and subordinates. For example, one administrator may believe that people will try to avoid work and consequently will institute tight controls on employees. Another administrator may believe that individuals really do enjoy work and like to do things that matter and make a difference. This person may provide loose controls. The two health care administrators, then, will function quite differently based on their value differences.

Another potential area for conflict—perhaps the major one—involves different expectations. Conflicts happen because individuals expect different things. I may expect you to behave in a certain way, and when you do not behave that way, I find myself becoming perturbed. I may expect you to be at work at 7:30 in the morning, and your expectation is that you will be there at 8:00. Much potential conflict has to do with different expectations that are unknown until tested. Ninety percent of conflict can be understood by understanding how the expectations of the parties involved are different.

Still another area of potential conflict involves misperceptions. Think about a conflict setting you have been in where you realized later that you and the other person did not have any differences after all. You were in full agreement with that person. You were amazed at yourself for being upset. You did not understand that person's viewpoint and thought they were saying something different from what they actually said. Misperception was the problem.

Last is change. While this is a trite statement, I suspect the problem of change is critical for those of us in health care organizations. When we talk about major organizational change, we talk about dramatic change that can impact the whole organization. A case in point is what happened when DRGs came on the scene in the mid 1980s. Change can be organizationwide or it can be unit or department specific. What we know is that health care environments are turbulent, and change takes its place along with taxes and death as one of the givens of life. In the midst of change is conflict at all levels—intrapersonal, interpersonal, work unit, and organizational.

The components of the OPO model provide another framework for viewing sources of potential conflict. The sources of conflict will typically be found in:

Lack of purpose, disagreement with purpose

Role confusion, ambiguity, lack of definition, disagreement

Lack of feedback, nonuseful feedback

Low commitment, overcommitment

Lack of truth telling

Not taking responsibility for choices

Not having regard for self or others

For example, one of the areas of conflict occurs if individuals neither understand nor agree with the purpose of their department or organization. Conflict resulting from a disagreement with or a misunderstanding of purpose is common. Role conflict is a second major type of conflict. Conflict arises when individuals or teams do not know what their role is. And, if they did know, they might disagree with it. This is almost always an issue with conflict. A third area is feedback. Individuals do not get feedback about the impact of their behavior. They do not know if their behavior is on purpose or not. Obviously, this can lead to conflict. Finally, individuals may expect high levels of commitment from each other, only to be disappointed. What I expect from you, you may not choose to give.

Enough said. There are plenty of places for potential conflict. At the moment of experiencing conflict, the conflict moves from being preconscious to conscious. Depending on the severity of the conflict, we now are in our conflict alert mode. Suddenly I am saying, It sounds as if something is not right between me and this other person. Or between these two departments. Or between you and me. The flag now has gone up. Something is not right.

### Stage 2: Perception of Conflict—Awareness

When we experience a conflict, the body physically begins to prepare to fight or to flee. The mind triggers primitive defense mechanisms, and the body goes into action:

1. Stored sugars and fats pour into the bloodstream to provide fuel for quick energy. The body is preparing itself for a fight or a run.
2. The rate of respiration shoots up, providing more oxygen. Red blood cells flood the bloodstream to carry

216

more oxygen into the muscles of the limbs and the brain.

3. The heart speeds up, and blood pressure soars, ensuring sufficient blood supply to needed areas.
4. Blood-clotting mechanisms are activated to protect against injury.
5. Muscles tense in preparation for strenuous action.
6. Digestion ceases, so blood might be diverted to muscles and brain.
7. Perspiration and saliva increase.
8. Triggered by the pituitary gland, the endocrine system steps up hormonal production.
9. The bowel and bladder muscles loosen.
10. Adrenaline pours into the system, as do the hormones epinephrine and norepinephrine.
11. The pupils dilate, allowing more light to enter.
12. All senses are heightened.

The body is preparing itself to fight or flee. When we experience ourselves in a significant conflict, our bodies make preparations. A deep primitive reaction takes place. While it is not quite the same as seeing a saber-toothed tiger standing in front of you, the body begins to prepare to fight or flee the same way it did thousands of years ago. Our senses become heightened so that we can take in information in order to survive.

It is not unusual for individuals to experience these sensations without understanding what is happening to them. They find themselves breathing heavily. Or their heart is racing. Or they are red in the face. Again, at the moment conflict is perceived, the body begins to react and respond to those perceptions.

Conflict can be categorized as first degree, second degree, and third degree. *First-degree conflict* is just a matter of curiosity: "Well, this is interesting. It sounds as if you and I differ . . . " The energy invested is minimal, and the body response to it is minimal. The conflict is not perceived as life threatening. *Second-degree conflict* involves significant investment. People recognize that this can have a crucial impact on them. Perhaps they lean forward in their chair and become intense. In fact, the body does respond in a significant way. *Third-degree conflict* is experienced as threat to survival. Survival conflicts are ones in which people feel fully invested. Now the body responds to the threat of conflict in a major way. Survival conflicts mean that the energy will be totally focused on survival. The key—I sense that my survival is caught up in this conflict.

*Stage 3: Mulling—Thinking About*

Now we have an active conflict. Mulling is a time of letting myself be aware of how I am experiencing the conflict. Conflict is an opportunity for birthing something new. This creates a need for a time for thinking about what might be going on. Mulling may take moments, days, weeks, or even months. What is important is taking time to contemplate and think about what is happening.

A story from a good friend of mine illustrates mulling. In a weekend planning retreat, he found himself becoming very angry with some of the group's members who were dominating the discussion. At first he sat there and steamed about what was going on. Then he began to think about what his frustration was really about. He let himself stay frustrated long enough to realize that the focus of his frustration had nothing to do with those who were dominating the meeting. It had to do with other events going on in his life. That was mulling. He stayed with the conflict long enough to learn what the conflict was saying to him. He then took appropriate actions to respond to the source of the conflict.

Mulling is a time of data collection. It is a time of letting the problem speak to you. It is a time of trying to understand the root cause of the problem (Ulschak, 1978).

*Stage 4: Actions*

We have moved from latent conflicts to the recognition that we have an active "hot conflict." We have assumed that we know the root cause of the problem. Now, we are ready to act. The responses to conflict are numerous. However, we can group them into four categories.

*I Can Do Nothing.* This is a difficult choice for many of us who are action oriented. While many individuals in health care might be concerned about a do-nothing response, the reality is that doing nothing can be a useful tool. Sometimes conflicts are engaged prematurely, and escalation results. Or, if we engage it too quickly, the conflict can be prematurely resolved and then might return. We create a problem for a future day.

A friend of mine has a policy about taking vacations. The idea is that if you are going to take vacation time, take more than five days. By doing so, many of the conflicts that will arise in your first two days away will be resolved. If you do not stay away long enough, these conflicts will hang around and wait for you.

*Confront.* You identify a conflict and move to correct it immediately by confronting it. This is a straightforward strategy that

219

"snowplows" through the conflict to resolution. If the choice is to confront, important preparations should be made.

When confrontation is the key, numerous questions can be answered for setting up the actual confrontation. Do you want to include a mediator? If both parties involved feel that there is a deadlock, a mediator might be important. What is the best place for the confrontation to take place? Does a neutral place need to be selected? What about confidentiality? How confidential do both parties agree that this confrontation is going to be? Do other supporters need to be there? Within a conflict setting, the individuals involved might want to have unbiased, neutral parties there for support.

Other considerations regarding confrontation include the following:

*Timing.* Are the parties involved ready to work out the conflict? Are they committed to working it out?

*Purpose.* Do the parties agree on the purpose of the confrontation? Are both interested in correcting the situation?

*Roles.* Do the parties agree on the roles and ground rules for the time?

*Commitment.* Are the parties committed to working the issue through?

*Truth telling.* Are the parties committed to truth telling?

*Choice.* Are the parties willing to accept responsibility for choices they make?

*Regard.* Is there a baseline of regard for one another? At some level, do the parties have respect for one another?

These are useful tips when designing individual confrontations.

Jones and Kurtz (1973) discuss criteria for deciding if confrontation will be useful.

1. The confronter starts by evaluating the relationship with the confrontee. If the relationship is weak, steps to strengthen it may be needed before the confrontation takes place.

2. The confronter needs to answer the following question: Can I accept the confrontee as a person? This is a question of mutual regard. If the answer is no, the confronter should not proceed with the confrontation.

3. The confrontation needs to be seen as a time for suggestions, not demands. This means listening and paying attention to possible solutions.

4. Comments are directed toward behavior, not the individual. This gets back to respecting the individual. The confronter may disagree with the confrontee's behaviors but still endorse the confrontee as a human being.

5. Positive confrontations should be the target. Positive confrontations are when mutual wins are involved. Both parties have a sense that they have benefited.

6. Represent facts as facts and feelings as feelings. One area that can get confusing is talking about our feelings as "facts," when really we are talking about feelings. Feelings are data, not facts.

Confrontation involves at least two people. So far, we have talked about guidelines for the confronter. What about the confrontee? For the confrontee, helpful conditions include:

1. Accept the invitation to explore self. Accept the fact that confrontation can be extremely useful in helping you better understand yourself.

2. Be prepared for the openness of confrontation to give

you more information about how you are experienced by others.

3. Be willing to tolerate temporary disorganization. As you get feedback from that individual, you may find that you are going to mull over that feedback. You may find yourself somewhat disorganized for a while.

The discussion so far has focused on one-to-one conflicts. One more tool is useful.

Walton (1969), in an early work on interpersonal peacemaking, provides an excellent tool for responding to conflict settings. The tool is called the *confrontation meeting*, during which, he suggests, there should be presession work. Presession work involves defining the purpose of the meeting and the roles of the individuals involved. The participants' definitions of the problem are identified. What do they see as the problem? Is it a solvable problem? Are they interested in solving it?

The actual session starts with ground rules, which are the structure for the meeting. The basic ground rule is that whoever is leading the meeting controls its structure. The others control the content. Participants establish boundaries that define acceptable and unacceptable behaviors. A typical ground rule is the need for participants to use active listening.

Once ground rules are established and agreed to, the meeting moves to a discussion of what is seen as the problem (conflict). The discussion then moves to what the parties want from each other.

*Compromise with the Others.* Through compromise, each of the parties involved recognizes that each loses something and gains something. Neither party has a total win. Both will get part of what is desired but not all.

In many management settings, managers attempt to control for this by overbudgeting. However, in a situation of compromise, they know that not all of what they would like will be accepted.

The matrix in Figure 6.3 is useful in thinking about compromise.

Figure 6.3. Want Matrix.

My Wants . . .

|  | Wants Met | Wants Not Met |
|---|---|---|
| Wants Met |  |  |
| Wants Not Met |  |  |

Your Wants . . .

*Collaborate with the Other Parties.* The goal is to come up with a solution that allows both parties to win and get their needs met. This is the most difficult approach because it involves creating something new. It is also the most creative strategy.

One useful model for viewing collaboration was developed at the Moffitt Cancer Center (Figure 6.4). According to the model,

- Trust needs to happen between individuals, work units, and the organization.
- Accountability for actions is across the organization.
- Focus is on the purpose of the work unit and the organization.

Figure 6.4. Collaboration Model: Moffitt Cancer Center.

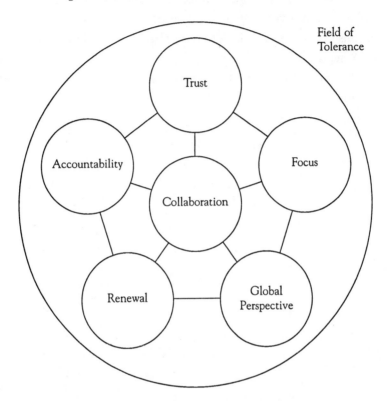

- A global perspective is taken; emphasis is placed on looking to the broader impact of solutions on the organization.
- Renewal is constant and ongoing.

The core of the model is collaboration. Around that core is a field of tolerance. The behaviors of individuals and work units must fall within that field of tolerance.

*Stage 5: Aftermath—Control or Resolution*

The last phase of the conflict management cycle is damage control. This is really evaluation. Did the action that took place in the last step intensify the conflict, lessen the conflict, or resolve the conflict?

Sometimes conflict management results in an escalation of the conflict. Especially if the conflict is in an early stage or if time was not taken to find a root cause, it is not unusual for the resolution not to be forthcoming. The result of the intensification can mean that the conflict recycles to the perception-of-conflict stage. The conflict is perceived in a new and different kind of a way. Different actions are now tried. On the other hand, if the conflict has been partially resolved, it is important to know what parts have been resolved and what parts still need to be addressed.

Finally, if the conflict has been resolved, this is a time of celebration. And we move on to another conflict to be resolved.

## Suggested Strategies

This section is built on the assumption that conflict can be understood as a difference of expectations. These can be expectations for self, others, or organization. The goal of conflict management strategies is to identify the specific gap in expectations and then to answer the question, How can the gap be managed or closed?

Some gaps in expectations are easy to identify. The manager wants a larger office—the organization does not have more offices. If the conflict stems from a gap in values, it may be more difficult to resolve. In other words, a conflict of values may result

225

in an irresistible force meeting an unmovable object. The CFO may favor a reduction in force strategy to get expenses down. Another executive may favor a participative approach to controlling expenses. Behind the gap lies a basic value difference.

This section proposes identifying the gap in expectations and the actions that will close or manage that gap. This is all that is required.

### Setting the Stage

Conflict management is easy. We simply identify the gap between what is and what is desired. However, to identify the gap, we need valid data. All conflict management and resolution processes depend on having accurate data. That is where conflict management becomes a challenge—identifying the data that indicate the nature of the gap.

The key stage setting in any conflict management process means the individuals involved have a desire to resolve the conflict, are willing to be truthful about their view of the world, and have a fundamental respect for themselves and others. While this may sound trite, it is not.

### Intrapersonal Conflict Management

In conflict settings, the first order of business is understanding what is happening within myself. When conflict occurs, the first question is, What are my internal expectations that are not being met? This self-understanding is a key to successful conflict management. What are my own wants that are in conflict? For example, my daughter asks me to take her to a rock concert. I feel divided. One want is to spend a quiet evening at home. The other want is to be a good father and take my daughter to the rock concert. The beginning of my conflict management is understanding how these two wants are pulling me in different directions. The next step is to make a choice based on my awareness of the wants.

One good technique for understanding differing internal wants and expectations is the internal dialogue. This can take many forms. In its simplest form it is the "On the one hand . . . " discussion. Begin a discussion with yourself by standing in front of a mirror and looking into it. Start by saying, "On the one hand . . . " Carry the thought through to completion and let yourself be aware of feelings that come with your statements. Then, say "On the other hand . . . " and carry this thought through to completion. Again, be aware of feelings that you have as you go through the discussion. Pause for a few moments and let yourself become fully aware of these reactions. Now ask yourself, "Given the two wants, how can I meet them?" Then make your choice. The goal is to turn the fuzzy internal conflict into a choice of options.

Another technique is to think about a conflict setting that you are in. Now, create an internal dialogue on paper. Write about how the conflict is important for you. Write about its key features. Now reflect on the conflict and make a choice.

One last technique. For those who are into imagery, do this. Sit down in a quiet place. Remember a wise person. Maybe it is a parent, a grandparent, or an aunt or uncle. Imagine that you consult them with your conflict. What advice would they give you regarding it?

Self-awareness is key. Without it, we readily end up blindsided in conflict settings. Why? Because if we are internally unclear, the external conflict will be exacerbated. Remember, the start of conflict management is understanding what is happening within.

### Individual Conflict Management

The first question that needs to be asked in individual conflict management is the following: Is this a hot conflict right now? If the conflict is full-blown at this moment, it may be important to give the individuals involved a cooling down time or a time out. This can be done in a number of ways. One is by doing the classic "count to ten." Another way is by taking a walk. Still another is holding off the discussion for a period of time. The goal is to give the people involved a break from the immediate heat of the conflict. If this is not done, the conflict may readily escalate.

The conflict was hot, and the individuals have now cooled down. They have talked about why it is important to resolve the conflict. They are committed to telling "their truth." Now is the time for the next step. The most effective conflict management tool is to engage the individuals in active listening. The goal of active listening is to have each individual understand the other person's view of the world and to accurately identify the gaps in expectations. The other individual involved listens reflectively and demonstrates an active understanding of what the first person is saying before responding. This invites individuals to understand each other. The goal is to help the two individuals involved understand each other's position and to understand the gap in expectations.

Most of the time needs to be spent understanding the gaps and the differences. When that is done, the actions for managing are easy to come by. Once understsnding is there, the next question is, What is the best way to manage or resolve the gap that was discovered? The individuals should recognize that there are some settings in which they will not resolve conflict but will need to manage it.

A variant of active listening is structured discussion. The participants identify (1) what it is that they want for themselves, (2) what they want from the other individual, and (3) what the other individual wants from them. Each individual takes time to respond to three questions: "What I Want for Me," "What I Want from You," and "Here is What I Think You Want from Me."

Completing that matrix gives the individuals a basis for identifying the gap. The ground rule for the discussion is active listening.

*Team Conflict Management*

The first section looked at conflict within and the second at conflict between individuals. This section looks at conflict in a team. One strategy for dealing with conflict in a team is outlined below.

*Step 1: Contracting about the team conflict resolution process.* This is a time of discussion with the team about the process we will be going through and why. The goal is to provide a road map and sanction for the process. When a spotlight has been focused on the conflict, it can sometimes become more intense.

*Step 2: Collecting Data.* Data collection is the critical dimension of resolving team conflict. We need to identify the current conditions and what aspects of the current condition are the root causes of the conflict. Questionnaires and interviews

229

are used to discover the team members' views of the conflict and any suggestions for resolving it. They are asked their ideas on the source of the conflict and what they see as corrective actions.

Typical questions include:

Is conflict management a problem for this team?

If so, how extensive is it?

How do you know it is a problem?

What are the behaviors?

What are the causes?

What would correct the situation?

What needs to happen in this work unit?

If nothing is done, what will happen?

*Step 3: Holding a team meeting.* Once the initial information has been collected and analyzed, the information is presented back to the team for verification and recommendations on next steps. This is a sensitive step. When the result of the data collection focuses the problem on a person or persons, the data need to be presented tactfully. If the "problem" individual happens to be the manager of that particular team, prior to the presentation, time will be spent coaching this individual on how to respond to the information.

Once the material has been presented back to the team for discussion and verification, the next step is action.

*Step 4: Forming an action plan.* The action plan defines the key areas of the conflict and develops a specific strategy for corrective action. Normally, this is a who, what, when approach.

The purpose of this step is to develop a plan for action that identifies the specific measures the team can take to correct the conflict.

One useful tool is the *nominal group* (Ulschak, Nathanson, & Gillan, 1981), which is readily used to identify next steps and prioritize them.

*Step 5: Monitoring.* Points to monitor need to be identified so the team can assess the impact of the action plan on the resolution of the conflict. The question is, how we will know if the plan is working?

The monitor questions are:

What will we monitor?

When will we monitor?

Whom will we have monitor?

The goal with team conflict management is to identify conflicts, bring them to the team, have the team identify ways they can respond to the conflict, and then establish monitors to provide information on the resolution. The process presented in Chapter Eight is an excellent tool to use with a team in resolving conflict.

*Organizational Conflict*

One of the most effective organizational conflict tools is the confrontational meeting. The *confrontational meeting* is a positive organizational conflict approach that allows various conflicted departments to come together in a retreat to identify sources of conflicts and develop action plans for corrective action. Prior to the retreat, the participants are informed about the nature of the retreat (purpose), their role at the retreat, and the hoped-for outcomes. Ground rules for the retreat (acceptable behaviors) may be identified at this time or in an opening exercise at the retreat.

The retreat is structured as follows:

1. Initially, departments meet as cohesive units. The cohesive units are asked to respond to the following questions: How do we see ourselves? How do we view the other departments? How do we think those other departments view us?

2. Each department then presents to the total group their response to the questions. After the presentations are complete, discussion takes place between the departments, with the active-listening rule as the guideline for the discussion. The goal: to identify the gaps in expectations.

3. The next phase of the confrontational meeting involves mixed groups—that is, groups composed of a cross section of individuals from the departments involved. They discuss what needs to happen in the organization to bridge the perceptual gaps. These cross-functional teams then present their views on what they see as important actions for the organization to take.

4. The final phase is action planning. Cross-functional teams are formed to address what appear to be the high-priority items that have grown out of the discussions of the cross-functional teams. The action plan then is implemented, along with a plan to monitor the action plan.

There can be many variations on the theme, but the goal in all three cases is to identify the differences in expectations, to clarify them, and to develop plans for managing or address-ing them.

A final note: good data are essential for conflict manage-ment. Truthful communication is implicit in all the strategies discussed. If truthful communication is not taking place, good data are not generated. This means that the stage needs to be set early on to incorporate truthful communications. The as-sessment begins with management emphasizing the importance of truthful communication by words and actions.

## Conclusion

This chapter has defined and discussed the conflict management cycle. Conflict management strategies have also been identified.

The four concepts of truth telling, choice, regard and renewal are vital ingredients in successful conflict management. Truth telling is being willing to share our view of the world. Without truth telling, which leads to good data, resolving conflict be-comes dubious.

Choice making recognizes that we are part of the decision-making process. According to this concept, each of us is respon-sible for the choices we make. This attitude is extremely useful in the conflict management process. Instead of blaming others, I look at my role in the conflict as well. We are constantly mak-ing choices; the question is whether we will take responsibility for them. When we enter a conflict setting with these three elements in place, there is a high probability that the conflict setting will work itself through effectively.

Regard is the degree to which we see ourselves and others

233

as valuable human beings. Think about that when you go into a conflict setting. When I have regard for myself and others, the probability of success increases dramatically.

Renewal provides us with ongoing improvement. It means that philosophically and practically, we are evaluating ways to continually improve on what we are doing.

If the foundation of truth telling, choice, regard, and renewal is in place and the individuals involved are sensitive to the conflict management cycle, the choices they make have a high probability of leading to successful conflict resolution.

# CHAPTER SEVEN

# Managing Change

Age differences are pressed into service to bestow one
kind of order on all societies. A man and a woman of
the same age who had lost their memories and were
isolated on a desert island would have no notion of
the life cycle. They would imagine they could live
forever. The changes in their bodies as they grew older
could be continuously astonishing, and death even
more so. They would not fear what they did not
expect, although as they neared death they might be
filled with even more foreboding than if they had
known what was going to happen. But surround them
with their parents and children and other people of
different ages on the same island, as they are in every
society, and the couple would at once realize what
they had been and what they would become. They
would be surrounded by the tutors, young and old.
                                    —Michael Young,
                                    *Metronomic Society*

IN THE WORLD OF HEALTH CARE organizations, perhaps no greater
skill exists than the ability to manage change and crisis effectively. Change is rampant. Think about your setting. What are
some of the important changes you have experienced in recent
years? What key changes are you encountering now? What key
changes do you see on the health care horizon?

When did change begin to impact health care in its current magnitude? Probably in the mid 1980s. Before 1983, health care financing was based on cost reimbursement. Since 1983, it has been prospective pricing. The world of health care has become a topsy-turvy world. Prior to that time, health care had a high degree of predictability. You could have annual budgets and actually live them out. For the bold and daring, five-year plans were realized. However, with shifting reimbursement came significant change. Predictability dropped off. Hospitals moved into major cost containment programs. Hospitals became competitive. Hospitals went out of business. All of this happened along with major changes in technology, demographic shifts, and so on.

Today's health care world has become one of almost continual turbulence punctuated with occasional calm. The management challenge in the midst of change is to learn how to manage in rough waters rather than under easy, predictable conditions. That is the theme of this chapter.

The objectives of the chapter are:

1. To identify and discuss individual patterns of response to change
2. To present a model for understanding and planning for organizational change
3. To identify hints for managing change

The challenge for us as health care professionals is to understand how to manage when the water is rough. The logical starting point is our own beliefs and actions when we face turbulent conditions.

## Beliefs Regarding Change Management

As we look at the topic of managing change and crisis effectively, we might recall the point borrowed from Fritz (1989) in Chapter Six. He noted that problem solving and creating are two different things. With problem solving, we are trying to eliminate something (the problem). But with creating, we are trying to bring something into being (the creation).

Most of us have been raised in a tradition of problem solving and have had little to no exposure to the creative process. In times of crisis and turbulent change, we can become locked into managing existing problems rather than creating our own direction. The most important thing we can do is to take that innovative step. This is not a new theme. It has been stressed a number of times in this book.

Over the years, I have been part of many organizational change efforts. These change efforts have included:

- Mergers
- Downsizing
- Start-ups
- Ordinary change efforts

I have been part of change at a macro level. I have introduced new computer systems and performance review plans, moved people to off-site locations, introduced continuous quality improvement (CQI) programs, and so on. Perhaps my most challenging experience with change (aside from raising teenagers) was being responsible for space allocation. That is change! As a result of these experiences, I have developed several beliefs regarding change management.

1. Change is a given, and it is revolutionary. In the past, change was slower. It was more evolutionary. Health care organizations were good places for people who could not deal with fast-paced change. Change was not too noticeable. But there has been a trend away from steady, staid organizations with a high degree of predictability toward organizations that are unpredictable, with rapidly changing markets and technology that can change from moment to moment. Computers are a tremendous example of change. What is new today is slow and outdated tomorrow. Change is a given in health care organizations, and it is dramatic.

2. The most important tool we can bring to organizational change is our own management of change. We are the most important tool when it comes to change management. Our assumptions, beliefs, and responses directly impact our ability to lead and facilitate others through the change process.

This understanding is critical for those of us in administrative or management positions in health care. How we facilitate the process of change management will have a direct impact on those around us. If we find ourselves overwhelmed and unable to cope with the change, that will affect those who work with us. All the pert charts, gantt charts, and change management models mean nothing if senior management panics in the midst of the change process. But if we find ourselves approaching change as a positive part of our environment, those who work with us will have a different attitude toward change.

3. Our ability to manage time can be a major asset and ally in change management. Crisis equals inadequacy of time. Think about that for a moment. Any crisis, given time, becomes a noncrisis. An example is the basic crisis in an emergency room,

a trauma. If the trauma team has time, the crisis can be minimized. The implication of this belief is that when we are in a crisis setting, the number one resource that we need to explore is how we are managing time. It means, again, that those of us in management and administrative positions need to critically look at how we manage time in change and crisis situations.

A corollary to this is that if we manage time badly in noncrisis settings, we set the stage for crisis. Think about managers you have worked for who create crises by not responding to potential crises. If we are managing a significant organizational change poorly, we are going to create crisis.

4. Change will bring resistance. It is a given that whether the participants desire change or it is forced on them, there will be resistance to it. Even in oppressive situations, resistance exists. At least the oppressive situation provides us with predictability.

We need to expect and welcome the resistance to change. We need to see it—like conflict—as a friend we can learn from as we proceed through the change process. The goal for us in administrative and management roles is to manage the resistance to change.

The change cycle demonstrates an important principle that change is a process, not an event. Frequently, we look at it as an event: "Tomorrow we will move to a new building." When we do that, we miss the point that change is a process that extends on either side of the event. It begins when those involved begin to hear a rumor about the change through the grapevine. And it ends long after the specific event has taken place.

5. In the change process, we need to recognize that all feelings are legitimate. Some individuals may find change relatively easy to deal with, and they will handle it effectively. Others may

have great difficulty in changing. In either case, we need to recognize the feelings as legitimate. Feelings will vary from person to person. For one person, the feeling might be anger. For another, it might be sadness. For another, it might be "so what?"

The grief model is useful to think about in change. People who are involved in change (and organizations and work units) will go through many of the same stages of denial, anger, and acceptance as the grief model demonstrates. Change is a grieving process. It represents the death of a known and the introduction of an unknown. As with other grieving processes, the individuals involved will go through a roller coaster ride of feelings regarding it. Management needs to legitimize the feelings that come with the change process.

While all feelings are legitimate, not all behaviors are. If individuals begin to act on feelings and the resulting behaviors get in the way of the change process, management has a responsibility to confront the behaviors. The individual may not like a change. That is a feeling. If this behavior actively blocks the change, that is unacceptable behavior.

6. Enjoy! In the midst of planned change activities, recognize that you are creating. The best laid plans of mice and men do not necessarily work out like we had so arduously planned. Therefore, in planning for change, keep a sense of humor and perspective on what is happening.

Change is a given. Our only option is to learn how best to manage it.

## The Starting Point: Understanding Yourself and Change

Ever experience ambiguity? Thomas (1984, p. 13) points out that "computers can make errors, of course, and do so all the time in small, irritating ways, but the mistakes can be fixed and nearly always are. In this respect, they are fundamentally in-human, and there is the relaxing thought: Computers will not take over the world, they cannot replace us, because they are not designed, as we are, for ambiguity." We are designed for ambiguity! A point stressed in the previous section was that the most important tool brought to a change setting is self-awareness. I might expand that to include our ability to manage ambiguity. Some doubting Thomases reading this might dis-agree. Take a few moments and work through the following questions.

*Imagine yourself in a past setting where you were experiencing significant change. Describe the setting. Who was there? What was the context? What associations come with it for you? Complete the following:*

1. *I think . . .*
2. *I feel . . .*
3. *I respond . . .*
4. *When I am faced with change, I . . .*
5. *I cope with my responses to change by . . .*

A key message of this chapter is that the most important tool we have is understanding and managing our reaction to change. That is why exercises such as the preceding one are so important. They allow us to better understand our own responses, and in doing so, they give us more leeway for manag-ing change and crisis.

Ackerman (1985) suggests six common approaches to han-dling change.

1. *Experiencing regression or denial.* "Let's go back to the way

it was." Even in settings where the change is desirable, individuals may have a tendency to say, "Let's go back. Let's do it the way it was. Even though it wasn't all that great, it was better than what we have now."

In one setting, the change being implemented was a conversion to a new computer system. Prior to the conversion, individuals were saying, "We definitely want to become automated." However, after the conversion and the automation, they began to say, "This just does not work. Let's go back to the way it used to be." They were practicing regression or denial. This is a natural part of the process of going through change. However, if it calcifies, it can involve major resistance to change.

2. *Maintaining the status quo.* "If it's not broke, don't fix it." Let's keep things the way they are. Let's not be proactive. Let's simply wait." The status quo response is akin to the ostrich sticking its head in the sand and ignoring what is going on. Things are okay, so let's keep on going as we are.

3. *Taking baby steps.* The incredibly timid theme might be, "Let's take very small, very carefully planned out steps. Let's not move too fast. Let's not rock the boat. Let's do this perfectly." The key is *perfectly.* Generally, when we set out to do something perfectly, we do not do anything at all. When we are in a time of attempting to manage change, we are unlikely to be successful if we use the incredibly timid approach. Change will pass us by.

4. *Acting like John Wayne.* As John Wayne would say, "Come hell or high water, we are going to do it. Who cares. Let's just crash forward and do it." This approach does not look at the costs or casualties. It does not try to weigh the side effects of the change. Like the proverbial bull in a china shop, it just says, "Get it done." And get it done at all costs.

5. *Taking a laissez-faire approach.* "Don't push it; let it happen. Don't push the river. As the change needs to happen, it will happen. Let's not anticipate it; let's not plan for it. When it's here, it will be here." This approach lets the change unfold at its own rate. The change emerges.

6. *Being a navigational facilitator.* This approach to change says, "Let's be strategic about change. Let's plan where we want to go and then proceed to go there." This approach is the most promising in terms of successful management of change and crisis, because it allows us to keep an eye on a target as opposed to being randomly tossed around in the whitewater. Even in the midst of the turbulence, we can be looking ahead and seeing if we are moving toward that specific target.

Each of these approaches to change has advantages and disadvantages. Regression and denial may be useful when change is on overload. Or if change was not thought out and there is an increase rather than a decrease in problems. There may be pieces of the "way things were" that need to be recaptured.

The status quo approach is useful when the environment is overloaded. Keeping things the way they are for now may be a useful strategy. We may deliberately keep one part of the organization stable while changes take place in another part. We would not make changes that will not yield an important gain.

Taking baby steps is useful as a way of managing certain types of change. Perhaps the change needs to happen, but it does not need to happen right now. Or the movement is toward an unknown where each baby step needs to be taken slowly and carefully. The feedback from the step is evaluated before the next step to be taken.

The John Wayne scenario might be most appropriate when

the organization has remained stuck and has not moved off base. Recently, I was part of a project team that took a John Wayne approach. We have been talking about establishing a screening center for five years. We now said, "We are going to do it." In the words of a song, "It's now or never . . . "

The laissez-faire attitude is useful when you are not sure of next steps. In exploring conflict management, we discussed letting the problem do the talking. By letting the problem further define itself, we are able to target our actions more effectively. This is a way to let the change gradually appear before you take direct action.

The navigational facilitator is useful in planned change efforts. This may be the person with the computer using project management programs to produce resource charts, pert charts, gantt charts, and so on. This individual can tell you exactly what the sequence of steps needs to be and the best strategies for moving ahead.

Each approach has positive and negative aspects. Take a moment to review your responses to the exercise at the beginning of this chapter. Think about which of these common approaches is your preferred approach to handling change and crisis. If you find yourself answering, "But I use all of them at one time or another," say, "That's right, and the one that I find fitting me most of the time is . . . " After you have spent some time reviewing which of these approaches you find most congenial, think about the effectiveness of that approach for you. Are you satisfied with it? Does it get done what you want?

Finally, think about a change that you are about to make or are currently experiencing. What do you think is the most effective way to approach this change?

Another tool in exploring how you manage change is looking at your management profile. Think about the instrument in Exhibit 7.1.

Exhibit 7.1. Themes for Managing Change: Your Profile.

---

*Consider your approach to change. Mark an X on each continuum for where you currently are. Mark an O for where you would like to be. Remember, your responses may change over time and may be different for different situations.*

1. I am reactive. ⟵————————————⟶ I am proactive.

2. I act out of habit. ⟵————————⟶ I act consciously.

3. I feel victimized by change. ⟵————⟶ I take responsibility.

4. I use the routine. ⟵————————⟶ I am creative; I take risks.

5. I am problem focused. ⟵————⟶ I am opportunity focused.

6. I act as an administrative manager. ⟵————⟶ I act as a leader.

7. I allow mediocrity. ⟵——————⟶ I pursue excellence.

*To summarize for yourself, when you are in the midst of change, how does this profile help you deal more effectively with it?*

---

*Source:* Adapted from Ackerman, 1985, p. I-11.

## The Change Process

Change is a given in life. Seasons change. Organizations change. People change. Tillich (1963, p. 122) puts it this way:

It is our destiny and the destiny of everything in our world that we must come to an end. Every end that we experience in nature and mankind speaks to us with a loud voice: You also will come to an end! It

245

may reveal itself in the farewell to a place where we have lived for a long time, the separation from the fellowship of intimate associates, the death of someone near to us, or it may become apparent to us in the failure of a work that gave meaning to us, the end of a whole period of life, the approach of old age, or even the melancholy side of nature, visible in autumn. All this tells us: You will also come to an end.

So far in this chapter, the premise being discussed is that we are the key tool in the management of change. In this section, we begin to look at the change process as an organizational process.

The classic model for managing change is that of Kurt Lewin (1935); it involves three steps.

1. Unfreezing
2. Changing behavior
3. Refreezing

The OPO model is a useful framework for understanding these three stages of the change process. To begin with, unfreezing may be of purpose, roles, feedback systems, or levels of commitment. For example, unfreezing purpose means that the originally agreed-on purpose for a particular project or a department no longer is agreed on. Purpose has changed. Or perhaps roles have become confused. Instead of being effective, they are no longer understood. Or feedback systems are unfrozen. The current benefit package is exchanged for another benefit package. Or levels of commitment are eroded. Whatever the case, unfreezing means that those things that were taken for

granted—that is, purpose, roles, feedback, and commitment—
are now up for grabs. We are now in a time of transition.

The good news about unfreezing is that in the midst of transition, new clarification and agreement regarding purpose, roles,
feedback, and commitment can take place. For example, it is
not unusual for a crisis setting to be rich in opportunities to
evaluate what is not working and to create new conditions. It
can be a time of transformation and renewal.

Unfreezing has occurred. Now there is behavior change. If
we have been alert to changes, this is the time to intentionally
decide new behaviors. Otherwise, habit will take over.

Refreezing is taking the new behaviors or systems and making them routine, so that they become habits. Think of the
standard stimulus-response paradigm of behavioral science. Essentially what we are saying is that we are now locking in a
new set of responses to the previous stimulus. If the refreezing
is accepted, the new behaviors will become invisible to the members of the organization. They will be taken for granted. They
will be expected and predictable.

The change process in today's world is much more complex
and rapid than Lewin's model allows for. His model emphasizes
linear definition. However, the speed of change is such that
this linear approach needs to be reconsidered. For example, instead of unfreeze-transition-refreeze, the rapid and dramatic pace
of change today in health care means than unfreezing is happening at the same time as transitioning; transitioning is happening
at the same time as refreezing; and refreezing is happening at
the same time as unfreezing. In other words, in very few changes
can we talk about isolated unfreezing or changing a behavior,
going through a transition period, then refreezing into a new

behavior. Instead of the linear model, we have a rapidly changing, manic state.

Beckhardt and Harris (1977) talk about three states of change. The three stages build on the Lewin model. One is the existing stage, two is the transition time, and three is the new state. The existing time of change means that we are involved in the old way of doing things. We understand purpose. We may even have forgotten purpose. Or we take it for granted. An example is an organization that does not have a mission statement. The question of mission statement never was raised because there really was no change of mission within the organization. Or if there was change, it was minute. The old ways of doing things prevail. Within those old ways, there are familiar roles. They are expected and predictable. The world feels in control because of the high degree of predictability.

Transition means letting go of the old work habits and roles. It means moving toward new ways of relating. The world of physician-administration relationships and physician practices is rich with examples of letting go of the old and moving toward the new. The roles have seen significant shifts in the last few years. Transitions have impacted purpose, roles, feedback systems, and commitment.

During this time of transition, there can be a significant sense of loss. It is a time of preparing for something new that is yet to be. It is like breaking in a new pair of shoes. The new ones do not quite feel as good as the old ones. There are pinches and rubs that have to get worked out. This is the "advent" state of change.

Finally, there is the new state. The purpose, roles, feedback systems, and commitment are renewed. While there is a degree of unknown and risk involved, we have grown familiar with the new way of doing things. We have new habits. The shoes fit.

The advantage of Beckhardt and Harris's model is that it demonstrates the movement from the existing to the new state. Schutz (1979, p. 98) talks about movement and change in terms of energy cycles:

> Human behavior may be perceived as a series of energy cycles. The cycle begins with some type of imbalance, a discomfort, desire, anxiety, wonder. Something that serves to motivate me to change my state so as to satisfy the imbalance, either by reducing the discomfort or anxiety or by satisfying the desire. I then mobilize my resources to reduce the imbalance or prepare myself to do something by thinking, planning, and preparing my body for some kind of movement. . . . This charge comes next, expressing in action the behavior which I have prepared. . . . Action leads to rebalance or feeling determined by how close the action came to satisfying the motivating imbalance.

The challenge for us as managers is to manage the transition time so that we prevent a crisis from developing. We know we are moving from "what is" to a new state.

How can we who are in the midst of rapid change move through the change process in a relatively stable way? Note the phrase "relatively stable." There will be chaos in any significant change. However, we can try to minimize the turbulence.

Remember the primary tool? It is ourselves and our comfort level with change. Along with our self-awareness, an understanding of what the organization will go through as it makes transitions is important. This leads to hints for managing change. The following hints are organized in terms of the three stages of transition. We begin with the *current state:*

1. The rationale for change needs to be clearly defined and communicated. We need to understand why we are proposing the change. This means assessing the current conditions and the readiness for change. Once we understand that, we can communicate it to others. The initial step is for us to understand the rationale for change—to think in terms of purpose.

2. We need to create a vision of the desired state. This is a vision that is practical and workable. In our role as managers of change, we should paint a realistic picture. We need to say, "Yes, you will be going through a disruptive time, but the outcome is this." "This renovation project is tearing down a wall in your area, but in another month, you will have a new work setting." It is important to help people understand what is on the other side of the change. Remember the story of the three bricklayers? When asked what they were doing, the first said, "I am laying as many bricks as I can each day." The second replied, "I am building a building." The third stated, "I am building a cathedral that will provide people with a place to praise God." Each had a view of the change they were producing. Which bricklayer would you want working on your building?

3. Identify what needs to be changed or created. Instead of being problem focused, we need to focus on what we

are creating and let that vision lead people ahead. This is one of the most powerful tools we have.

The following need to be done during the *transition time*:

1. Identify and monitor impacts.
2. Make midcourse corrections. This means that somewhere in the change process we will have identified the vision we are working toward and key milestones or checkpoints.
3. Supply information. Good information is essential.

The *new state* should be marked by these developments:

1. Celebrate. The state that was envisioned has probably not been fully achieved. The planned version will have been bumped around and knocked and bruised through the process of change, but hopefully what was accomplished will be close to the desired state. There needs to be celebration.
2. Reestablish stability. Going back to the Lewin model, this means refreezing.
3. Establish new systems to reward the new behaviors. If you want the new behaviors to continue, you need to make sure you are rewarding the new behaviors. For example, if you are encouraging people to become "risk takers" and make decisions, you will want to make sure you have a system of rewards that support those behaviors. Without the new rewards, the old behaviors will persist.
4. Monitors for measuring the impact of change are needed. This is called *maintaining the gain*. Any organiza-

251

tion will have a tendency to revert to the previous conditions. Inertia is built into all organizations, and this invites the previous behaviors to return. Maintaining the gain involves identifying monitors to see that we continue to maintain the desired change.

The previous hints have discussed the change process in general. Here are some additional hints that are important to managing the ongoing, rapid change that exists in health care organizations.

1. The reaction to change begins when awareness of it first dawns on someone. The importance of this cannot be overstated. Many times, individuals think reactions to change happen when the change occurs. This is fallacy of "event thinking." Change happens when the idea of the change is introduced in the mind. If you come into my office and indicate to me that in three weeks, I will be moved, impact begins at that moment. It is not at the point of moving. This is critical for us to understand as we think about managing change. Once the word is spoken, reactions and processes begin.

2. In the change process, it is impossible for us to communicate too much. People can be overloaded with paper and data. However, we need to continually communicate what is going to be changed in the existing condition, how that change will be managed, and how people will be impacted.

There is a common syndrome regarding communication. Those who have been working on a project know it well. They have spent countless hours making sense of the project. When they come to communicate it, they forget that they have put hundreds of hours into it but the people they are communicating with have put mere moments into thinking about it. The error is in assuming that others have put in as much time thinking about it as you have!

3. In the absence of data, we tend to make up data. If we begin to hear rumors of change but get little information or data about those changes, we will probably make up our own data. Frequently making up our own data is much scarier than the actual event. This means going back to the first two points: Change begins at the moment of awareness, and it is impossible to communicate too much.

4. The most important resource we bring is ourselves. The individuals who work with us and for us will closely watch how we perceive and manage change. They will see how we "walk the talk." As Schein (1985, p. 230) says, "When an organization faces a crisis, the manner in which leaders and others deal with it creates new norms, values, and working procedures and reveals important underlying assumptions. Crises also are significant in culture creation and transmission, partly because the heightened emotional involvement during such periods increases the intensity of learning. If people share intense emotional experiences and collectively learn how to deal with very emotionally involving situations, they are more likely to remember what they have learned."

A second aspect of this is our need to be caretakers for ourselves. In the midst of change, we should remember to be solicitous of our own welfare. It can be easy in the midst of crises, long hours, full in-baskets, and so on to forget that we need to take care of ourselves. We know for certain that becoming overstressed will not facilitate the change we desire.

5. Change is a constant process. The goal is to constantly

keep focused on the end result and the current reality. Fritz (1989) calls this *structural tension*. In times of crisis and change, we need to keep the tension between vision (the result we want to create) and current reality (what we have right now). When we maintain that tension, the tension of the gap seeks resolution. By knowing the desired end result and the current reality, we are able to plot our course, moment by moment, hour by hour, week by week.

6. The management role during the change process (unfreezing-transition-refreezing) is to provide continual clarification of purpose (what is the purpose we are about, what is the end result), roles (who will be monitoring, who will be seeing that people are taken care of in the process, who is minding the shop, and so on), and feedback mechanisms. What feedback mechanisms are in place to provide information on progress?

7. Those impacted by the change should have some level of decision-making power. They should be given choice points. A choice point might be how the furniture goes in a room. Maybe it is the color of the walls. Maybe it is the date that they will move. Whenever possible, they should have opportunities to make decisions.

Finally, a story. A number of years ago, I was vacationing with my family in the north woods of Minnesota. While we were there, being the fine fisherman that I am, I went out daily in our canoe and fished. In the lake, there were a number of speedboats. As the speedboats came by, they created wakes, and the canoe would bob up and down. Well, I became known as a person not to be in a canoe with unless you wanted to get wet.

Now, my daughter had two wants. One want was to go fishing, and the other want was to keep dry. The problem was that as she saw me fishing, that want came into conflict with the other want to stay dry. She saw the number of times the canoe turned over. Finally, the want to go fishing became the dominant want. So Heather and I went out in the canoe. True to form, as we were sitting out in the canoe fishing, a speedboat came by and a wave hit the canoe. The canoe began to "rock and roll." When I looked at Heather, I saw her grasping the sides of the canoe. She was mumbling to herself, "Fear, courage, fear, courage, fear, courage." Intrigued, I asked her what that meant. She said that while she was afraid, she would not let her fear of getting wet get in the way of her desire to fish. Now, that is a fisherperson!

Translated into health care organizations today, it sounds like this. There are plenty of times in the midst of change when we fear change and the unknown. But fear itself is not a sufficient condition for not going ahead. That is where courage comes in.

So, the next time that you find yourself in the midst of managing change and crisis, remember the canoe and think about fear, courage, fear, courage.

## Taking Care of Self

We have talked much in this book about the importance of administrators' and managers' own understanding and self-awareness. It is also critical to incorporate the concept of self-care. We have used the analogy of turbulent water. Health care organizations have moved from their stable and calm environments to the turbulent white water. Today, health care is not just riding the rapids—it is riding the rapids and going over the falls. Health care organizations are collapsing and evolving into new types of health care organizations. How can we, as members

255

of the health care profession, take care of ourselves in the midst of this very turbulent environment?

A starting point is to identify typical traps that we as caregivers have.

## Traps of Caregivers

Think for a moment about why you chose to be a health care professional. What were the attractions of this field? What personal values of yours make the health care profession appealing?

When these questions are asked of health care professionals, the predominant response has to do with helping others. People in the health care field have a "helping quality." There is a quality of "I became a nurse and later an administrator because I am interested in working in an organization that contributes to the well-being of others."

Within this desire to reach out and be helpful exist some traps for caregivers (who can include administrators, management, and direct patient caregivers, as well as those in the non–patient care areas of the health care facility).

*Trap 1: The Drama Triangle.* If a lecture were being given on how not to take care of yourself, a good place to begin would be with the creative use of the drama triangle. The *drama triangle* is a tool that has come out of the transactional analysis school. If you think about a typical drama, you will notice that the audience remains interested in the play because there is a shifting of roles. The drama triangle is concerned with identifying these roles. The three primary roles in any drama are those of rescuer, persecutor, and victim (see Figure 7.1).

First is the role of rescuer. In the rescuer role, someone in

Figure 7.1. Drama Triangle.

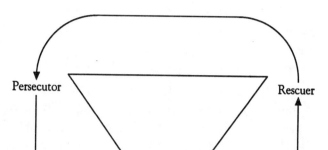

Source: from *Transactional Analysis After Eric Berne: Teachings and Practices of 3 TA Schools*, by Graham Barnes. Copyright © 1977 by Graham Barnes. Reprinted by permission of HarperCollins Publishers, Inc.

the play is trying to be helpful to another person. The rescuer rushes in where angels fear to tread but often oversteps the boundaries of the relationship. As a result, problem solving may be blocked, and the stage is set for a role shift in the drama triangle.

Second is the role of the persecutor. The persecutor is a someone who is either physically or mentally abusing someone else in the drama. The persecutor generally is the villain of the play. Persecutors get hisses and boos as they come out on the stage or the screen.

Third is the victim. The victim is the individual in the drama to whom something is being done. Victims appear helpless. The world is out of control, and the only problem is that they just happen to be in the wrong place. Rescuers rush in to save them.

The essence of the drama triangle and the source of the play's excitement is the shifting of roles. At one moment, an individual is a rescuer coming in to save a victim and intercede between the victim and the persecutor. However, in the next scene, that same person may become a victim. Now the former victim is looking at the rescuer and saying, "Who invited you?" The former victim persecutes the rescuer—or possibly the original persecutor—and so the tables are turned. The cycle goes around and around.

The important dynamic of the drama triangle is that people tend to move from position to position on the triangle. Problems are not solved. The only things that change are the roles in the drama. When an organization of caregivers gets caught up in a drama triangle, there is much activity but little is accomplished. The organization may appear to be exciting, but results will be minimal.

The way to break out of the drama triangle is to ask two questions: What needs to happen? Who needs to do it?

*Trap 2: Avoidance of Deliberate Choice.* Another trap for caregivers is to live in a gray area of not making deliberate choices. This is a key way in which the drama triangle we just discussed is fed and kept going. Being in an area of grayness when it comes to choices means statements such as the following: "Well, I suppose, if . . . but I certainly don't have a say . . . " and "Well, maybe, yes, but all I can do is go along with . . . "

There is ambivalence. Instead of making a clear decision— "Yes, this is the direction we are going to go," or "Yes, we will provide this individual with service"—we find ourselves avoiding deliberate choices.

When we choose not to make choices, we are making choices. If we make the choice to let things ride, we will find that they will move to where they want to go. The important point: To choose not to make choices is a choice. It is a trap of caregivers.

*Trap 3: Low Self-Regard.* There is no way to address the issue of self-care without looking at self-regard. How do we regard ourselves? Like avoidance of choices, low self-regard feeds the drama triangle. Our tendency will be to distrust our intuition and our ability to think through a problem. The views of others become overwhelmingly important; ours do not matter. The result can be a tug between many different people with different ideas.

Low self-regard leads to giving up the ability to choose.

As an aside, I might mention the well-known Biblical injunction to love your neighbor as you love yourself. Translated: If I have low-self regard, I have low regard for others as well. And if I have high self-regard, I will regard others highly as well.

*Trap 4: Lack of Self-Honesty.* The classic Shakespearean line from *Hamlet* "To thine own self be true, and it must follow, as the night the day, thou canst not then be false to any man" is relevant here. Lack of self-honesty fuels low self-esteem. Not being honest with myself about my thoughts and feelings builds on low self-regard. My ability to make informed, deliberate choices is impaired, because without self-honesty, I have poor data about current conditions. Lack of self-honesty also means that I do not appreciate and understand when I have hit my boundaries. The result is overextension and burnout in myself and others.

A solid foundation of self-honesty is critical to self-care. Ultimately, it is from that foundation that self-regard and choices grow.

*Trap 5: Focus on Others and Not Self.* Focusing on others is generally appropriate, but focusing on others without looking at self means possibly being caught up in a whirlwind of avoidance. Focusing on others first means that I have not taken time to focus on what I believe to be important. As a result, I miss the views and feelings of a very important person—myself.

We have identified a handful of traps. What do we need to do to avoid these traps? The next section provides some answers.

## Golden Rules of Self-Care

There are four golden rules, or keys, to self-care in today's turbulent health care environment:

- Truth telling
- Choice
- Regard
- Renewal

*Golden Rule 1: Truth Telling.* Truth telling is the great simplifier of personal and interpersonal difficulties, since it is the central building block of self-knowledge, relationships, and organizations. Within organizations, a high level of truth telling allows us to have Total Quality Management programs. It allows us to identify our strengths and weaknesses. Without truth telling among the members of the organization and the customers they serve, the organization goes astray. If I am part of a work unit that is a "truth-telling work unit," I do not have to guess what is going on in other people's minds—they will tell me.

Within relationships, truth telling has a tendency to release energy. Think about this for a moment. Think about a relationship that you have had that was built on a lack of truth telling. What happened at the point that truth was finally told? It resulted in the release of significant energy. And energy is the source of individual, relational, and organizational achievement.

Truth telling also allows us to monitor our own health in a very significant way. If I am unwilling to let myself be aware of when I am stressing myself out, it becomes easy to burn out. Truth telling allows me to be aware that I am not sleeping properly. Or that I am drinking too much. Or that I am over-extended in certain areas of my life.

If you are interested in finding out how much impact truth telling can have, do the following exercise:

*Take a few moments and talk to the person next to you in what might be known as a cocktail-hour mode. Talk about the weather, show pictures of your kids, and so on. For three or four minutes, carry on that type of discussion. Then pause, turn to the person, and talk to that person in a truthful way about something meaningful to you. Notice the difference.*

The first truth option is self-honesty—letting myself be aware of feelings and thoughts. This is internal truth telling. External truth telling means that I am telling others what my view of the world is. Whether it is internal or external, I have a number of options with regard to truth telling.

One alternative is that I can choose to be honest. When I am honest, I share thoughts and feelings with myself and with others.

The second truth option is to withhold. When I am withholding information, I am aware of something that I am not telling the other person. This is the classic deception or lie. Significant energy can be tied up in withholding.

Another truth option is what Schutz (1979) refers to as the "sincere politician." The sincere politician is not aware of self-truth. This person talks a great deal but is unaware of what is going on within. In organizations, we frequently talk about these individuals as being shallow. They are people who we perceive to be doing a lot of talking, but we do not pay much attention to them.

A last truth option is a "blind spot." This is that part of ourselves that we are not aware of but that others may be aware of. The only way that we understand the blind spot is through direct, honest input from others. Perhaps there is no greater gift we can give one another than the gift of truth telling. It also cuts the other way. The tendency is that when I share my truth with you, you are invited to do the same. And the relationship builds.

Schutz has defined levels of truth telling:

Level 0 is simply silence. It is a time of withholding.

Level 1 is typically what we refer to when we say, "If I tell them the truth, I will level them." Truth telling is akin to attacking.

Level 2 begins with the statement of "about you I feel . . ." This is deeper truth. The focus is on my feelings.

Level 3 involves making a statement: "Because of . . . , I . . ." This is a time of connections. I connect something that I feel with something you do.

Level 4 is identifying my own defenses to you in the statement. This may go something like, "When you make those kinds of statements, I begin to feel under attack."

Level 5 is the deepest level of truth telling. In level 5, I make statements that identify that I am clearly aware of my self-truth. I am saying things like, "About me, I fear that I . . . "

Many times, people say: "If I tell the truth, bad things will happen to me. If I tell the truth in this organization, I will be killed. If I tell the truth in this organization, no one will pay attention to me anymore. If I tell the truth in this organization . . . " Typically, they are referring to level 1 truth telling. If level 5 truth telling is going on, the response is generally quite different.

In short, truth telling is vital to self-care in an organization.

*Golden Rule 2: Choice.* Empowerment comes through self-responsibility. Think about that for a moment. Do you agree? When I operate out of a premise of choice, I move from self-blame and blaming others to the recognition of myself as a creative decision maker. Instead of being in a victim role, I find myself in a position of empowerment.

Innovation Associates (1988) have identified five primary choices in life. The first is the choice to be *loving and lovable.* Notice the two parts of this choice. To be loving means that we choose to reach out in compassionate ways to others. We can be nurturing of another person. A powerful thing happens when I am nurturing another person—I am also nurturing myself.

The second part is being lovable. We do things that invite others to express love toward us. This can be summarized by saying that it is an ability to reach out to others and to be reached by others. Others do not have to go through a major battlefield to get to us. Nor do we need to go through major battlefields to reach out to others.

The second primary choice is to be *competent*. This is a question of mastery. Being competent has to do with having skills. But even more so, it has to do with the ability to cope. Competence is a feeling of adaptability. Whatever life "throws at me," I can handle.

The third primary choice is to be *true to self.* This was discussed at great length earlier in this chapter. Self-honesty is a choice.

The fourth primary choice is to be *healthy—physically, emotionally, psychologically, and spiritually.* This means decisions with regard to exercise, diet, and sleep patterns that keep me fit. It means that I also look at the environments in which I work and live and look at how those environments support me emotionally, psychologically, and spiritually. We do know that some organizations have toxic environments. If I experience that in my organization, I need to recognize that I am at a choice point.

The fifth primary choice is to be the *primary creative force of my life.* Think about this for a moment. To be the primary creative force for myself, I need to have self-truth. If I am not letting myself know what is important to me, if I am not letting myself learn from myself and others, I will not be able to make informed choices. Being the primary creative force in my life means that I am an enlightened decision maker.

*Take a moment and think about those five choices. With each choice, say: I choose to be loving and lovable. I choose to be competent. I choose to be true to self. I choose to be healthy. I choose to be the primary creative force in my life.*

Let this become a daily litany for you. The five primary

choices reflect that very popular recruitment phrase, "Be all that you can be." If I adhere to these five choices and choose to live life according to them, I will be all that I can be.

*Golden Rule 3: Regard.* Think about the following statement and your level of agreement with it: The ultimate basis for my personal, professional success is for me to understand, respect, and like myself. Think about a ten-point scale, with ten being "I very much agree" and one being "I disagree." Where are you on that ten-point scale?

Ultimately, self-regard is built on a foundation of self-truth and choice-fullness. It is the recognition that I am making choices, that I am that primary creator in my life, that I am giving to myself the information I need in order to make wise decisions. Self-regard provides me with the ability to be a dynamic, energetic part of my organization. Self-regard is the bottom line of self-care. If I like and respect myself, I will care for myself. Self-care will not be a problem for me.

One exercise I have found useful in looking at self-regard is a vision of greatness for self. I invite people to do the following:

*Take a few moments and think about yourself and your relationships. And then think about greatness in relationship and what that means for you. Imagine that you are living in your fullness. What do you see in that fullness and uniqueness? What are you doing? What are you feeling? Who is there with you in that fullness and greatness?*

*Second, think about how you see yourself relating to others. When you see yourself in relationship to others, imagine that you are living in your fullness and in your uniqueness. What do you see happening in that relationship? What do you see yourself doing? Who is there?*

*Now form a visual image and let yourself in your mind's eye see yourself in your greatness.*

Golden Rule 4: Renewal. Renewal is the last key to self-care. How do you renew yourself when you are drained out? What do you do to prevent being drained out?

Self-renewal is important for us all. It is continuous quality improvement focused on the individual level. We can look at improvements in self, relationships, and our professions.

*Take a moment and think about the following questions: What is an area of your life that you are feeling a need for renewal in? How might you get renewal in that area? What are the first two steps you could take?*

There is a story about an eagle that was taken from its nest as a baby and raised by a farmer with his chickens. Each morning the eagle got up and found itself in a chicken coop. It went out and ate chicken food and spent time with the chickens doing chicken things. Well, things went well until the eagle grew up. Obviously, the other chickens made fun of it. Its beak was curved. It couldn't eat as well as the chickens. It couldn't sit as well on the roost. It had a tendency to hit its head going in and out of the coop. It was an oddity. Then, one day a naturalist was in the area. As he drove by the farm, he saw that eagle out there with the chickens, and he marveled at the sight. He went to the farmer and asked: "Why do you have that eagle with those chickens?" The farmer said, "Well, it's really no longer an eagle. It's an eagle that thinks it's a chicken."

The naturalist said, "This is such a shame. I would like to return it to the wild." The farmer replied, "Look, if you can do it, fine, but remember this eagle thinks he's a chicken."

The first day, the naturalist went over to the eagle and picked it up, looked it in the eye, and said, "You are an eagle. You belong with eagles, flying and soaring." He threw the eagle up in the air, but the eagle dropped to the ground with a thud and waddled back to the chicken coop. The farmer laughed, and the naturalist said, "Well, I am going to have to give it another try."

The next day, he took the eagle out of the chicken coop and went up the mountain. He picked up the eagle up and said, "You are an eagle. You belong with eagles doing eagle things. You must soar." He threw the eagle up in the air, and one wing started flapping, then the other. Gradually, the eagle began to fly just high enough to see the chicken coop and then went back down to the coop. Again, the farmer laughed. But the naturalist said, "One more time."

The naturalist got up bright and early and took the eagle out to a mountain top. Just as the sun was coming up over the mountains, he pointed the eagle toward the sunrise and said, "That's where you belong. You belong up there soaring, doing eagle things." The eagle began to flap its wings. Then the eagle caught a current and floated off into the sunrise, discovering its "eagleness."

The importance of that story for self-care is that we need to recognize the eagleness within us. We need to tell ourselves the truth about who we are and what we are. We need to make conscious choices.

## Conclusion

This chapter has been about change. One thing in life is a given—there will be change! And in health care organizations, this is especially true. We all know the turbulence of our environment. We also know that when the environment is turbulent, that is exactly the time we need to be sensitive to how we take care of ourselves. Three major keys for self-care have been provided. The first key is truth. Truth in regard to self builds a foundation for truth with others. The second key is choice. I recognize that things do not simply happen to me. I make choices. I have the ability to choose my response to those things that happen to me. The third key is self-regard. The ultimate gift that I give an organization is a gift of valuing myself. Self-care organizations have high levels of truth, choice, and self-regard within them. They will be organizations positioned for the white water of the 1990s.

Management of change begins with you and your approach to management. This chapter has been designed to give you a model for understanding change, steps for managing the change process, and hints for the change process.

# CHAPTER EIGHT

# Solving Problems

The greatest leaders and statesmen in history have
not been problem solvers. They have been builders.
They have been creators. Even in times of great
conflict, such as war and depression, they have taken
action to bring into being the society they envisioned. Two shining examples of statesmen-creators
were Winston Churchill and Franklin Delano
Roosevelt. They did not simply try to bring relief to
their constituencies. They were able to use the times
they lived in as a foundation for building a future
they wanted.

—Robert Fritz,
*The Path of Least Resistance*

SOLVING PROBLEMS USUALLY INVOLVES identification of a "gap."
The gap is the difference between what is happening now and
what is desired. Whether the reference is to leadership, conflict,
or marketing, the same four questions are raised:

1. What is the current situation?
2. What is the desired situation?
3. What is the gap?
4. How does the gap get narrowed?

This chapter provides a method of gap analysis. It is based
on several assumptions.

The first assumption is that gap analysis is *data driven*. This means that while opinions may be one part of gap analysis, the goal is to get "hard data"—numbers and statistics.

The second assumption is that gap analysis involves *truth telling*. Truth telling is stating "my view of the world." Truth telling means that individuals are willing to say, "Here is what I believe to be true about this situation." A second aspect of truth telling is that "my truth is challenged and molded by what you believe to be true about the world." Truth telling leads to good data. And good data is vital to gap analysis.

The third assumption of gap analysis involves *respect for ourselves and others*. Gap analysis mandates that we have respect for others and ourselves in the process of identifying problems and corrective actions. This means that the process is collegial. Whenever we begin to move into adversarial relationships, our ability to do effective gap analysis is diminished significantly. Collegial relationships, which are defined and built on mutual respect, allow us to express our "truth of the world" and, consequently, they provide a setting for good data.

The fourth assumption of gap analysis is that the *spirit of inquiry* is crucial. Inquiry means that we agree to meet together to find out why we have a gap. We inquire into the nature of the gap. Inquiry is built on systems thinking that invites us to consider the context of the gap. Does the resolution of this problem result in the creation of problems in other areas? How do we know that our "theory of the problem" is on target? Inquiry demands that we look at the context of the problem and at our current models of thinking regarding the problem.

These are the four assumptions on which gap analysis rests. The rest of this chapter defines a specific process for problem solving: *4Cs+1*. This process can be used by an individual or a group. It was developed by Sharon SnowAntle and myself at the H. Lee Moffitt Cancer Center. I will discuss it in the context of a team.

## Problem-Solving Process

The problem-solving process discussed in this chapter involves four basic steps:

1. Contracting
2. Causation
3. Corrective actions
4. Controlling

These four steps are built on a foundation of collaboration. Collaboration is the pillar on which the four steps rest. We will discuss each of these factors in detail.

The model is depicted in Figure 8.1.

### Step 1: Contracting

Contracting is a time of deciding on our gap analysis—a time when we agree to put the spotlight on a particular problem to be resolved. Contracting moves the problem from being an irritation in back of the mind to a point where we say, "It is important for us to focus on this issue."

During a contracting time, we discuss two important conditions. The first is the current situation. Typically, we begin by sharing opinions: "Here is a problem. Here is how we see it as a problem. Here are what we think are solutions to the problems." However, a key part of the contracting time is to move from opinions to actual data about the current condi-

Figure 8.1. 4Cs+1 Model.

Contracting
1. Identify the process to be improved
2. Collect data to develop a graph (visual)
3. Obtain the organization sanction
4. Develop the team mission statement

Causation
1. Define current situation
2. Develop high-level flowchart
3. Identify key characteristics of problem
4. Stratify to get to "vital few"
5. Use cause-and-effect diagram
6. Develop "theory of cause"
7. Test theory

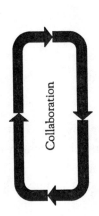

Collaboration

Control
1. Check performance—"Are we getting the desired result?"
2. Standardize process
3. Decide when and how to monitor "maintaining the gain"
4. Flowchart process

Corrective Action
1. Identify alternative solutions
2. Select high-probability solution
3. Plan for managing resistance to change
4. Develop action plan—Who? What? When?
5. Implement

tion. This is why we encourage data collection during the contracting phase. We need to determine what data to collect to show that we do indeed have a problem.

Contracting involves collecting enough initial data to say, "This is a problem that we need to pursue. It is significant enough for us as an organization or as a team within the organization to spend time and resources to resolve." This means prework is done. The prework usually involves key parties to the problem area. These key parties begin the preliminary analysis regarding the scope and nature of the problem. A guideline we like to use is to collect enough information so that we can produce at least one graph of the problem. The production of a graph generally means that we have quantitative data.

Second, this is a time for obtaining the organization's sanction to carry out the problem-solving process. If the problem is of any consequence, there needs to be an organizational sanction. This may be as simple as obtaining approval from the next level of the hierarchy to proceed. Or it may be approval of the executive team. However it happens, it is important that the organization formally approve the problem to be resolved.

Assuming that we have done the preliminary work and that we are satisfied that this is a problem we want to commit organizational resources to, we now move to the establishment of a problem-solving team. What is a problem-solving team? It is a team brought together to solve a problem or to improve the way we are currently carrying out an activity. It is a team formed to provide a solution to a problem waiting to be solved.

The nature of the problem itself determines the composition and size of the team. The goal is to involve people who have immediate ownership and responsibilities within the problem area. We want people who are closest to the problem to be a part of the team. Usually a senior management group will have many opinions about a problem and how it might be addressed. However, opinions are different from having team members who actually are involved in the day-to-day working of a team. The same can be said of size. If the problem is unique to one person's work process, the team size may be one. However, if the problem crosses several work units, the size might be quite large.

Roles of the team members are as follows:

1. *Team leader.* The team leader is the individual who has management responsibility for the "problem area." The team leader could be a department head, an administrative person, or a first-line supervisor. The important point is that this person has organizational ownership and responsibility for the problem area. The team leader has an ability to commit resources to the team project.

2. *Team members.* As noted earlier, the team members need to be people who are tied closely to the actual problem. There may be six to eight team members. They are the brain trust of the team. The team has been formed because one individual does not have adequate information to solve the problem.

3. *Team facilitator.* Based on work with teams and the quality improvement processes, it is important to have someone on the team who monitors how the team is working and helps the team identify and overcome blocks in the process. This is the role of the facilitator. The facilitator is an objective third party for the team. This person has little ownership in the actual problem area. The facilitator establishes a climate of truth telling that allows people to be comfortable in stating their views.

4. *Historian/recorder for the team.* One of the functions of this person is to record the progress of the team and create the "team's story." This is an area that frequently can be overlooked. In cases involving significant systemic problems, meetings may occur over a series of weeks, months, and at times even years. The "historian" plays a key role in recording this history and process of the team.

One goal of contracting is to create a team and establish the team's mission. At the initial team start-up meeting, it is important to have the team leader present the team's sanction: "Here is the organizational charge for this team."

Step 1, then, involves the start-up work necessary to get a team up to speed to address a particular problem. Questions to be answered during this time include:

What is the problem that we are focusing on?

How do we know this is a problem? What data can we collect to verify that it is a problem?

How do we get the organization's sanction to form a team to take this problem on?

Who do we need to be part of the team?

What is the mission statement we have for the team?

## Step 2: Causation

A team is now formed. The problem has been identified. At least the initial problem has been identified. It is not at all unusual to have a team begin to delve into the problem only to find that the initial problem is just a symptom of an underlying problem.

The tendency in most organizations is to move quickly to solutions. This is especially true for health care organizations. However, this urge needs to be resisted. The causation step is a time for exploring possible causes of the problem and arriving at a root cause.

The first task of the team and, in many cases, the most challenging, has to do with identifying the cause. Remember our guidelines: We are looking for data. Opinions are useful places to start; however, quantitative data need to be identified as the basis for decision making. In identifying the cause, the team goes through several steps.

The current situation first has to be defined. This may be done in numerous ways. One way is for the team to flowchart the work process where the particular problem appears. This provides the team with a view of what currently happens that results in the problem situation. This provides a context for the problem.

Next, key characteristics of the problem are identified. The question is, What are the key pieces of the flowchart that define a beginning and end point that cause a problem to be a problem? The team is developing a "theory of cause." Flowcharts help the team identify where they might most productively spend their time and energy.

The flowchart also provides useful information about where more data need to be collected. The collection of data using the flowchart as a skeleton to work from provides the basis for a pareto chart. A pareto chart allows us to look at the "vital few" causes that contribute most to the problem. Pareto is the 80/20 principle—that is, 80 percent of the "problem" is caused by 20 percent of the possible causes. It is a way of reducing long lists of possible causes to get to the "vital few." For example, there may be thirty reasons why blood specimens get rejected. However, of these thirty, only three or four are responsible for 80 percent of the rejections. Pareto is a powerful tool and philosophy.

Now the team is ready to take the problem and look at it in greater detail. The pareto chart has reduced a multitude of causes to a vital few. A very useful tool now is the cause-and-effect diagram. Given this effect—that is, a problem—what are the key causes that lead to that effect? The goal of the cause-and-effect diagram is to develop a picture of what contributes to the "effect." What are the people contributions? Material contributions? Process contributions? Equipment contributions? And so on.

During the causation time, the team develops a theory of cause. Now the team tests the theory. This might be a small experiment designed to see if the theory of cause can be substantiated. The goal is to get to the root cause of the problem.

A problem has been identified, the organization's sanction has been received, and now a theory of cause has been uncovered. Next step: corrective actions.

Questions to be answered during this time include:

What is the current situation?

What is the work process that the problem is embedded in?

What are the key characteristics of the problem?

What are the vital few features of the problem that have the biggest impact on it?

What does a cause-and-effect diagram suggest for primary contributors to the problem?

What is our theory of cause?

How can we test it?

*Step 3: Corrective Actions*

During the corrective action phase, the team identifies alternative solutions. The target of the solutions is the root cause from the causation stage. A number of tools can be used to identify the alternative solutions. Two examples are nominal group and brainstorming. The goal of both is to identify actions that have a high probability of resolving the problem. Much has been written elsewhere about these processes (Ulschak, Nathanson, and Gillan, 1981).

Once a variety of possible solutions have been identified, the team focuses on selecting the high-probability solution. A decision matrix can be used to rank the potential solutions according to a set of criteria. The end result is that the "high-probability action" rises to the surface. When this happens, the team moves to developing an action plan (who, what, when) for the correction action. One part of the action plan addresses resistance to change. Since most corrective actions will involve someone's changing, there will be resistance. The question is, How to manage resistance to the solution?

The team has done various things. It has identified potential solutions. It has discussed how resistance might be managed. It is now time to test the proposed solution. The goal is to pilot test the solution to allow the team to gather information about the effectiveness of the corrective action. When the action is implemented, will it resolve the problem?

278

If the pilot test produces the desired result, the team now proceeds to implement it across the organization.

Questions to be answered during this time include:

What are the alternative solutions for the root cause?

What criteria do we want to measure the solutions by?

Which solution has the highest probability of success?

How will we manage the resistance to the change?

Who will do what and when?

*Step 4: Controlling*

The team has now gone through the problem-solving process. However, the question is, How do we control for the continued resolution of the problem? In other words, how will we know if the problem begins to become a problem again? The tendency is for problems to return. This means the team needs to identify monitors to indicate that the problem has been resolved and the gains are being maintained. They need to identify checkpoints to measure whether they are getting the desired result and if they are continuing to get the desired result. In other words, they want to maintain the gain.

Monitors are decided on and put into place. At various times, they are checked to see that they are still maintaining the gain. As a last step in this, the team may, in fact, create a flowchart that looks at the improved process.

Questions to be answered during this time include:

Are we getting the desired result?

How do we know that?

What do we need to be measuring?

When do we need to measure?

Who needs to be doing the measuring?

How will we know if we begin to lose the gain?

### Collaboration

The first four are "meat-and-potatoes" steps of the problem-solving process. However, we mentioned a fifth C, which is collaboration. We mentioned that collaboration is the foundation on which the rest of the model stands. Collaboration involves several components. The first is trust. The individuals in the team need to trust that it is okay to share their views—that is, to be truth tellers. In the team, there is a sense of regard for self and others.

In order to be effective, a problem-solving team needs to have good information. This can only happen when people in the team feel comfortable that their ideas will be listened to and acknowledged. In the work of a team, we need to follow ecological principles: All ideas will be carefully listened to and evaluated. We have brought a team together because an individual has not come up with an effective solution. The ecology of ideas says that we need to pay special attention to each and every idea so we are able to design the best solution.

Second, collaboration involves focus. There are on-purpose behaviors that happen in a collaborative process. The members of the team recognize that there is a greater purpose than that of their individual department. Their behaviors become focused on the broader issue of resolving a particular problem.

Third is accountability. A team uses organizational resources and is responsible for outcomes. Team members need to be accountable for the use of these resources.

Fourth is global focus. Collaboration means that individual fiefdoms become secondary to the overall organization. Members look at a global perspective rather than at an individual enhancement perspective.

Fifth and last is renewal. Collaboration suggests that the renewal process is constant. This means continuous improvement. There is a constant opportunity for us to look at what we are doing and develop schemes for how we might do better.

## Conclusion

This chapter has been an introduction to a process for doing gap analysis. Problem solving is simply identifying the current situation, a desired future situation, and the gap between the two. Problem resolution involves moving from where we are to the desired future condition.

Three resources follow this chapter. Resource A describes the development of the OPO model and gives a brief history of organizational behavior theories that influenced the model's development. Resource B is a tool kit whose purpose is to guide individuals or groups in their thinking about the OPO model as it relates to the organization, work unit, and individual. Resource C contains a workbook for the 4Cs+1 approach.

# Benchmarks of the OPO

IN THIS RESOURCE, I first describe how I developed the OPO model, then I provide a brief history of theories of organizational behavior that have influenced my thinking.

## Origins of the OPO Model

Any trip to a bookstore will demonstrate that many management and organizational behavior books are available. Some are complex and mystical. Others are simple. The continuum is from hugely academic books that leave readers pondering their practical applications to simplistic books that trivialize the concepts discussed. Each book presents its author's journey.

The intent of this resource is to identify benchmarks and individuals who have impacted the development of the model. How is this useful to you? It provides you not only with the end result with but the process of arriving at it as well. In other words, this gives you another layer of insight into the concepts outlined in this book. Not only do you have the concepts themselves, but you have the ground in which they were grown. This section is similar to what happens as you find out more information about friends. By knowing their background and key moments in their lives, you grow in your ability to understand what they are currently thinking and feeling.

This book grows out of my experience and reading in the subject matter of organizational behavior and organizational development over the last eighteen years. Those eighteen years include fifteen years of teaching at the graduate and undergraduate level, consulting, and writing. The topic is approached through the eyes of an organizational development person who has spent the last twelve years in "organizational labs." Those labs have been the health care organizations that have graciously allowed me to work with them.

During those years—as my bookshelves and résumé attest—I have sifted through numerous books and studies in an effort to make sense of how best to live and work in an organization. I have been part of a variety of organizational transitions—downsizing, merging, start-up, and even simple maintenance of organizations. I have had the privilege of participating in all phases of organizational life cycles.

My starting point for understanding organizational behavior was on an Indian reservation in northern North Dakota in the early 1970s. During that time, I was the executive director of an organization known as the North Dakota Institute for Community Understanding. The mission of this organization was to promote understanding and communications between the Indian community and the non-Indian community in the Dakotas. Needless to say, this was a formidable task—not unlike trying to solve "world sin." As a result of the work being done, I was asked to be part of the negotiating team that responded to the crisis at Wounded Knee in South Dakota in the 1970s. This was a formative experience for me in working in a very intense, armed crisis. In the midst of it, I began to find that the counseling skills that I had been trained in did not suffice. A new set of skills was required.

The next step for me was to identify the skills that were needed. Those mainly fell in group process and organizational development. That led me to study with the Southeast Institute for Group and Family Therapy. There I was introduced to a wide variety of group process skills. This was a valuable time for me in working with issues of individual and group change. This was also my first encounter with systems theory and systems thinking.

About this time, I was beginning to notice the second gap in my understanding and skills. That was in the area of organizational development and behavior. On several occasions, I would do a consultation with a group, only to find that the individual modality or the group process skills did not get at another level—the organization. The organizational culture limited the group's effectiveness. This was brought home to me in work I was doing in a state hospital setting. The group work with staff members was effective. However, within a short time, the old practices and divisions returned. The organizational culture was influencing the work we were doing in ways that undermined the creative conflict management. The organization was able to bring back in line the "deviant." The lesson I learned was the power of organizational culture.

This was a time of decision. As usually happens in life, a door was opened, and I met one of the most unique persons in my life, Gustave Rath. Gus, a professor in industrial engineering at Northwestern University, became my mentor in organizational behavior and organizational development. He introduced me to organizational systems thinking and provided me with opportunities to learn about organizations in both theory and practice. He "walked the talk"—and I learned much from him.

I vividly remember my first weeks as one of fifteen of Gus's Ph.D. students. I kept trying to figure out how best to learn from this man. One day, it came to me. Gus consulted once a week with a Veterans Administration hospital outside of Chicago. I volunteered to drive him so that he could prepare en route. It worked! Over the next few months, I was able to see Gus at work firsthand. I began to find that I now had a foundation that allowed me to work at three important levels in the organization—individual, group, and organizationwide. Perhaps, even more important, I found in Gus a person who modeled how those three levels interact and how effective interventions at all three levels were needed to bring about effective organizational change. This was a crucial find. It is fundamental to the OPO model.

Later, work with the University Associates and their models of group and organizational work added experiences and concepts that filled my organization bag full of tools and models. A major influence in my life at that time (as well as today) was the work of John Jones, one of the cofounders of University Associates. John's model of the organizational universe was one of the first practical models of viewing organizations that I discovered. He also taught me about passion for the study of groups and organizations. And he showed me how to play. Organizational behavior was fun as well as "heavy work."

Much of my work life up to this time was spent in academic settings. I taught organizational behavior and management theory, with occasional consulting. Now came a moment of truth. I was offered the opportunity to leave full-time academic pursuits and work as an internal consultant with a health care organization. I remember this time well. A good friend of mine who was working with the Sisters of Mercy turned to me one day and asked when I would decide to move from the academic world to the "real world." Some months later, I decided to take her up on the offer and to leave academics for a short time. Alas, I still have not returned!

This decision represents a major turning point for me. At the time, I was settled into an academic setting, teaching at the graduate and undergraduate level, consulting, and writing. However, I wanted the adventure of the "living lab." I wanted to test ideas and thoughts that I had been teaching. I wanted to apply them in organizational settings and evaluate their effectiveness. It was one thing to consult regarding leadership or team building and quite another to be the person responsible for team building or leading. This was where the "tire hits the pavement." The organizations I have been associated with have allowed me to walk the line of an academic practitioner—that is, a person who is basically an academic but who chooses to live in an environment where practice is key.

What happened for me with this decision was that I moved from a world where ideas were discussed and talked about to one where results mattered—did we get done what needed to get done? I found that many of my ideas and thoughts were now put to the test. Some of them passed with flying colors and others did not. My work world became a lab setting for a multitude of organizational issues. This is where I began to develop the OPO model in detail.

About this time, I became interested in the work of Will Schutz and the Human Element. Specifically, Will's work on truth, choice, and self-regard in organizations has had a profound impact on me. In fact, the OPO model rests on these three pillars.

My involvement with the American Hospital Society and the American Society for Healthcare Education and Training (ASHET) began about this time as well. This has been a very important part of my journey for a number of reasons. First, as a result of my involvement with ASHET, I have had the opportunity to travel nationwide and meet with hundreds of different health care professionals in a multitude of settings. By being able to do workshops and consulting in these settings, I have had my horizons expanded regarding health care organizations. I have had the privilege of witnessing health care management practices in numerous settings. Second, as a result of this experience, I have published a number of books and articles related to health care organizations. This publishing is where early work with OPO can be found.

One of the major opportunities in my professional life came in the invitation to join the senior management team of a new start-up health care organization. Much of my synthesis of the OPO came from working in an organization that has strong "on-purpose" behaviors.

The OPO model is a result of this journey. It reflects my work with individuals, work units, and the organization in total. The model focuses on four major areas that I find constantly in need of definition and clarity. These are purpose, roles, feedback, and commitment, four components built on the pillars of truth telling, choice, and self-regard.

The OPO model did not come easily. It has gone through many stages of development. As a result of discussions and experience, it has grown and changed. And it will continue to grow and change. This book presents the model in its current form. It provides tools for developing the "common bond"— that is, constancy of purpose in the organization.

## Benchmarks of the OPO

Models of organizational behavior do not just appear. They are generally built around the experiences of an individual, who then begins to generalize them. This section is a small aside. It is a "trip down memory lane." I want to discuss in a brief form some of the history of organizational behavior.

The key questions addressed in this section are the following:

1. Where does the history of present-day organizational behavior begin?
2. How does this history help us understand current organizational behavior theories?

This book began with the image of questing. This is an important section because it identifies some of those early pioneers in the work of organizational behavior. Also, those early pioneers in organizational behavior still influence us today. This means that we are not only looking at past history, but we are looking at history as it is currently informing us in doing our organizational work. This section is not meant to be an in-depth history of organizational behavior. It simply is intended to be a series of snapshots about benchmarks in the history of organizational behavior.

Asking the first question—When does the history of present-day organizational behavior begin?—is like asking when humankind began. One often-mentioned starting point of management is the work of Moses in the Old Testament. At one point, Moses is complaining to God because of the amount of work he personally needs to supervise and the disorganization of the Exodus. As a result of that discussion, the word comes down to "delegate," and the first management structure appears with divisions of ten.

The Moses story is fun. But it does not represent the beginning of management history. Management has been with us since the beginning of time. Management has been present ever since two or more people needed to work together to accomplish some mutual goal. The answer to the first question, then, is that organizational behavior dates from the very beginning of the human experience. The second question demands that we first identify key schools of organizational behavior.

*Frederick Taylor and Scientific Management*

The first of several snapshots is that of scientific management. Scientific management came about from the work of Frederick Taylor in the early 1900s. Previously, managers literally functioned by the seat of their pants, making decisions on the spot. In the midst of that scene, Frederick Taylor appeared, working mainly in steel mills. As he watched people perform tasks, he began to formulate task analysis. He developed time-motion studies. This involved looking at the time it took individuals to do the various motions to accomplish tasks. His contribution is actual measurement of what is happening.

In his personal life, he was also a deliberate man. When he played croquet, he would plot the angles for the croquet ball, count the strokes, count the steps, and so on so that his shots were scientific. Task analysis had no boundaries.

Taylor made a number of basic assumptions that he incorporated in the theory of scientific management. One was that management and workers were tied together for maximum prosperity. Taylor was not antiworker and pro-management.

He believed that both elements needed to work together to arrive at a maximum outcome. This was an early definition of a "win-win" situation.

Taylor believed that workers' basic drive was economic. He believed that various obstacles prevented management and workers from cooperating to achieve this maximum prosperity:

1. If you, in fact, achieve maximum productivity in work, you put people out of business. Consequently, being highly productive can be self-defeating.
2. Soldiering—which occurs when everyone works at the same pace and gets paid in the same way—can be another problem. Taken to its negative extreme, soldiering happens when overachievers are politely or not-so-politely informed by others that overachieving will not be tolerated.
3. Ineffective or "fly-by-the-seat-of-the-pants" management, which was the standard in Taylor's day, is another obstacle to maximum prosperity.

In scientific management, then, maximum prosperity became the key guide. According to Taylor, both management and workers held the key to achieving maximum prosperity. Taylor's approach is illustrated by the following classic passage from his book *The Principles of Scientific Management* (1967, p. 43), in which he talks to a hypothetical worker named Schmidt.

The place was Bethlehem Steel. The time was the Spanish-American War. The task was loading 80,000 tons of steel onto railroad cars. In a typical work shift, seventy-five men would load the railroad cars. Each load would be ninety-two pounds.

The target was twelve and a half tons per day. Taylor looked at this and formulated a plan requiring each worker to load forty-eight tons per day. This was approximately four times what they were doing at the time. That is the setting in which the following discussion with Schmidt took place:

> We selected one from among the four as the most likely man to start with. He was a little Pennsylvania Dutch man who had been observed to trot back home for a mile or so after his work in the evening about as fresh as he was when he came trotting down to work in the morning. We found that upon wages of $1.15 a day he had succeeded in buying a small plot of ground, and that he was engaged in putting up the walls of a little house for himself in the morning before starting to work and at night after leaving. He also had the reputation of being exceedingly "close," that is, of placing a very high value on a dollar. . . . The task before us, then, narrowed itself down to getting Schmidt to handle 47 tons of pig iron per day and making him glad to do it. This was done as follows. Schmidt was called out from among the gang of pig-iron handlers and talked to somewhat in this way:
>
> "Schmidt, are you a high-priced man?"
>
> "Vell, I don't know vat you mean."
>
> "Oh, come now, you answer my questions. What I want to find out is whether you are a high-priced man or one of these cheap fellows here. What I want

to find out is whether you want to earn $1.85 a day
or whether you are satisfied with $1.15, just the same
as all those cheap fellows are getting" [pp. 43–44].

The discussion about being a high-priced man continued.
In the end, Schmidt was told that the way to become a high-
priced man was to do exactly as he was told by his supervisor.
When the supervisor said "sit," he was to sit. When the supervisor said "work," he was to work. Schmidt did it and became
a high-priced man.

This portrayal of Schmidt would obviously raise the hackles
of working men and women. However, in certain respects Taylor's work helped protect working people, because he introduced
various scientific techniques for analyzing tasks and making them
more efficient. Prior to Taylor, management of "initiative and
incentive" prevailed, according to which any problems that occurred lay with the worker. With scientific management, at least
half the problem belonged to management.

Scientific management informs the OPO model in a basic
way. A core of the OPO model is the assumption that decisions should be based on data. Taylor was influential in bringing data to the workplace in an effort to move away from ar-
bitrary management practices.

*Therbligs*

The next snapshot we will look at is that of Lillian and Frank
Gilbreth. The Gilbreths were also very much a part of the
scientific management movement in the early 1900s. They are
best known for their time-motion studies. These studies looked
at the amount of time and motion it took to produce goods.

Detailed photographs would be taken of the motions needed to accomplish a specific task. From those detailed photographs, more effective motions would be identified.

One of the classic stories about the Gilbreths involves how they bathed their children. There was no wasted motion. As with Frederick Taylor, the shortest distance between two points was identified so that there would be no wasted soap and no wasted motion.

The Gilbreths, then, identified the units of motion, which they called *therbligs*. *Therblig* resembles their name spelled backward.

Both the Gilbreths and Taylor were critical contributors to scientific management. The connection with the OPO is in the use of data and structure.

*Elton Mayo: Founder of Human Relations Theory*

Elton Mayo worked in the early twentieth century. The time of a famous experiment called the *Hawthorne experiment* was 1927. The place was the Western Electric plant. The objective of the study was to look at fatigue in women workers in the plant. The scenario went something like this.

Women were selected into separate work groups. They were working forty-eight hours per week with no rest periods. Mayo and his colleagues designed the following intervention. First, they gave the women two five-minute rest periods a day. They found that productivity went up as a result. Second, they added four more rest periods. The result was that productivity again went up. Then they added one fifteen-minute rest period in the morning and a ten-minute rest period in the afternoon. Productivity again increased. Then they eliminated the Saturday work. Once again, they found that productivity went up. They proceeded to take away all of the rest periods, and again productivity increased. The question emerged, What was causing these women to increase productivity?

One explanation was that it was a social phenomenon. The women were, in fact, forming a social unit. As a result of the social unit, several things were happening. One was that the women felt important. They had been selected to be part of this experiment. Second, they were helping to solve problems. Third, they had been asked to work together in a cooperative way. Fourth, they were consulted before changes were made, and someone listened to their reactions. Finally, they were allowed to talk during work. All of this created a social unit that caused an increase in productivity. As Mayo said,

Viewed from the standpoint of social science, society is composed of individuals organized in individual groups, each group fulfilling some function for the society. Taking this fact into account, psychology—the science of human nature and human consciousness—is able to make at least one general assertion as to the form a given society must take if it is to persist as a society. It must be possible for the individual as he works (to see) that his work is socially necessary; he must be able to see beyond his group to the society. Failure in this respect will make disintegration inevitable.

The working man is still conceived of (by the employers) as a mere item in the cost of production rather than as a citizen fulfilling a social function. No increase in wages or improvement of working conditions can atone for the loss of real autonomy and of all sense of social function [1970, p. 130].

With Mayo, the focus moved from scientific management to the nature of human relationships. The social relationships at work were recognized as having a direct impact on productivity.

Taylor and Mayo had similarities. First of all, both were concerned with the production process and with increasing productivity. Second, both paid attention to the worker and to the manager. Third, both saw the manager's role as crucial. Fourth, both believed that the worker, unaided by management, could not increase productivity.

They were also different. Taylor focused on the individual. Mayo focused on the work group. Taylor focused on higher wages as the basic incentive. Mayo focused on human relations incentives. Taylor focused on physical changes that led to increased productivity. Mayo's work focused on the social relationships. Taylor tried to overcome informal contacts that were going on between workers. Mayo recommended the use of informal contacts. In fact, Mayo's focus was really the grounding for looking at the informal organization. His basic message: social satisfaction will lead to increased productivity.

The human relations approach is seen in the OPO model in the emphasis on commitment, choice, and regard. Also, the OPO model emphasizes the role of the work unit.

The next snapshot will deal with Henry Fayol, the father of administrative science.

*Henry Fayol: Founder of Administrative Science*

Henry Fayol also appeared on the scene in the early 1900s. His background and work were in mining and engineering operations. The general approach at that time, as is still often the case, was that individuals who were highly competent as miners or engineers were then promoted to management and administrative activities. Fayol's major contribution was to identify management skills as a separate set of competencies.

The six key functions Fayol identified for organizations included:

1. Technical (production)
2. Commercial (buying and selling)
3. Financial (funding, development, capital)
4. Security (securing of the products)
5. Accounting (management of the books)
6. Managerial

Fayol also looked at management functions that helped the organization get those six functions done. He identified the relevant management functions as being planning, organizing, staffing, directing, coordinating, reporting, and budgeting. In this way, he identified management as a set of competencies independent of the competencies of the particular task.

Fayol's definition of administrative roles has had an impact on the OPO model.

### Mary Parker Follett and the Law of the Situation

So far, we have talked about Frederick Taylor and scientific management. We have discussed the Gilbreths and time-motion studies. We have talked about Mayo and human relations. Finally, we have considered Fayol and management functions. All these individuals were concerned with managing conflict between individuals and tasks within the organization.

Mary Parker Follett's contribution as a *situationalist* was the integration of conflicts, which was her key concept. Managers do not depend on one threat or opportunity but on the *law of the situation*.

Her time frame was the 1920s. As she looked around at organizations and organizational issues, she recognized that the key issue was how conflicts could be integrated. Her basic message was this: Obedience and problem solving need to occur. However, the focus of obedience and problem solving should be the situation. Therefore, she advocated the law of the situation. Instead of two individuals being locked in a personality conflict, they need to look at what the situation demands of them. What is the greatest good for the organization?

Follett emphasized informal cooperation on problems, face-to-face meetings, free expression of thoughts and ideas, recognition of different views, recognition of different interests, and reconciliation of those different interests.

Follett (p. 161) outlined her thinking as follows:

My solution is to depersonalize the giving of orders, to unite all concerned in a study of the situation, to discover the law of the situation, and to obey that. Until we do this, I do not think we will have the most successful business administration. This is what does take place, what has to take place, when there is a question between two men in positions of equal authority. The head of the sales department does not give orders to the head of production, or vice versa. Each studies the market, and the final decision is made as the market demands. This is ideally what should take place between foremen and rank and file, between any head and his subordinate. One person should not give orders to another person, but both should agree to take their orders from the situation. If orders are simply part of the situation, the question of someone giving and someone receiving does not come up. Both accept the orders given by the situation, employers accept the orders given by the situation. . . . Our job is not how to get people to obey orders, but how to devise methods by which we can best discover the order integral to a particular situation. When this is found, the employee can issue it to the employer, as well as the employer to the employee. This often happens easily and naturally. My cook or my stenographer points out the law of the situation, and I, if I recognize it as such, accept it, even though it may reverse some order I have given. . . . If those in supervisory positions should depersonalize orders, then there would be no overbearing authority on the one hand, nor on the other, that dangerous blasé-aller, which comes from the fear of exercising authority. Of course, we should exercise authority, but always the authority of the situation [1970, p. 161].

Follett's contribution, the law of the situation, lets the specific situation guide the participants.

The link to the OPO model is purpose. When conflicts and disagreements arise, the question is, What is the purpose of the organization? Given that purpose, what is the law of the situation? Purpose is the higher good that is appealed to.

## Joan Woodward: Technology

A more recent contribution in management history is a focus on technology. Joan Woodward, working in the 1950s, studied three types of technology. The first was the unit or small-batch technology. This is the least standardized. It is the small-shop operation—the mom-and-pop grocery store or the woodworker who turns out unique wood carvings. The second is mass production. We all are familiar with mass production as it manufactures our automobile, household appliances, and so on. The third is continual process, which is automatic processes. We would include things here such as a nuclear power plant. The process itself is mainly automated.

The key learning from Woodward's study of technology is that we need to fit the technology to the structure and the structure to the technology of the organization. If we do not, we will miss what needs to be seen within the organization. Also, the best way to organize is to organize within each technological grouping.

The major lesson we get from Woodward is the importance of technology in deciding structure. Within the OPO model, this relates to purpose and roles.

In this section, we have looked at six different snapshots. The key learning from these snapshots is that in today's organizational world, the views of all of these theorists are alive and well. Effective organizational work involves task analysis, human relations, carrying out management functions, stepping back from personality conflicts and looking at what the system is doing, and constantly looking at the question of how the technology of what we are about is influencing the work. Essentially, what we are talking about, then, are sociotechnical approaches to the organization. This means looking at the total organizational system. Table A.1 shows how these views come together in today's health care world.

Table A.1. Sociotechnical Approaches to the Organization.

| School of Thought | Sample of Behavior |
|---|---|
| Scientific management | Management engineering studies. Work process studies. |
| Therbligs | Time-motion studies. Looking at the exact motions that go into getting a job done. |
| Human relations | Evaluating how social needs are met at work and how work units meet the social as well as employment needs. |
| Administrative science | Identifying key characteristics of administration regardless of the nature of the business. Administration has its own unique skills and competencies. |
| Law of situation | Asking the questions, What does this situation demand of us? What is the greater good that needs to be addressed? |
| Technology | What is the impact of technology on the work process? How does it impact the nature of our work? How does it impact the way we structure our organization? |

As an outgrowth of the complex and insightful intellectual tradition just sketched, the OPO model can enhance the functioning of an organization by calling on the full organizational system.

# The OPO Toolkit

THIS WORKBOOK IS DESIGNED to be used either by an individual or by a group. Its purpose is to guide you through thinking about the OPO model as it relates to the organization, work unit, and individual. Completing the workbook should be an ongoing process; it needs to be revisited and reaffirmed frequently. Many of the exercises in earlier chapters can be useful as you think through these questions. You may also want to discuss your responses with others.

## The Organization

This section asks you to think about your organization in terms of the four major components of the OPO.

*Purpose*

1. What is the key reason your organization exists?
2. As you reflect on the purpose of your organization, what core values come to mind? What are some of the features of that purpose that are very important to you?
3. What is your vision for the future? Where do you want to take this organization? Articulate as clearly as pos-

sible where you want to be at some future time with
regard to:
Customers
Services and products
Relations among employees
Community

*Roles*

1. Who are your key external customers?
2. What are their requirements of you?
3. How do you know these are their requirements?
4. What role do you want to play with regard to the following business features:
   Market share
   Products and services
5. What role do you want to play in your community?
   What role does the community want you to play?

*Feedback*

1. What feedback will you need in order to know that you
   are achieving purpose? What will be your indicators of
   success?
2. What feedback will you need in order to know that you
   are being effective in your role? What will be your indicators?
3. What feedback do you need from employees?
4. What feedback do you need from physicians?

*Commitment*

1. What level of commitment do you expect from your
   employees?

2. What is your level of commitment to your employees?
3. What is your level of commitment to the community?
4. What is your level of commitment to your organization's external customers?
5. What is your level of organizational pride? How do you know it?

As you review your responses to the above questions, where do the gaps appear? What questions were not easy to answer? Which answer did not satisfy you?

For each gap you identified, identify action steps you can take to respond to the gap.

## The Work Unit

This section focuses on your work unit.

*Purpose*

1. What is the purpose of your work unit? How does it fit in with the organizational purpose?
2. What are the key values—that is, those things that are really important to you—of your work unit?
3. What is your work-unit vision with regard to:
   Services and products you produce
   "Customers" you serve
   Relations within the work unit

*Roles*

1. Who are the people who depend on your products and services?
2. What are their requirements of you? How do you know those requirements?

3. Who do you depend on for services and products in order to do your job? Have you communicated your requirements to them?
4. What is your key role in the organization?
5. How well known is that role to your co-workers and others with whom you work closely?
6. How effective are you in the role? How do you know?

## Feedback

1. What feedback do you need from the organization to know that you are on purpose? Do you get this feedback?
2. What feedback do you need from your customers? How do you get it? How often do you get it?
3. What feedback do you need regarding your work processes and relationships? How often do you get it?

## Commitment

1. What level of commitment does the organization expect of your work unit? Do you provide it? How do you know you do?
2. What level of commitment do your "customers"—that is, those you provide goods and services to—expect of you? Do you provide it? How do you know?
3. What level of commitment is expected in your work unit? Is it provided? How do you know?

Take time to review your responses. Are there gaps in the responses that you would like to address? If so, what are they?

What can you do about them? (Chapter Eight might be useful for you as you identify gaps.)

## *The Individual*

This section provides you with a guide in reviewing the individual application of the OPO model.

### *Purpose*

1. Imagine that you know the purpose of your life. What is it?
2. When you think of things that are important to you, what comes to mind? How do you know they are important to you?
3. What is your vision for yourself? As you think of a future time, what would you like to see yourself doing? Who are you with?
4. How does being part of this work unit help you in moving to that vision?

### *Roles*

1. What are your key roles in the work unit? What is expected of you?
2. How effective are you in those roles? How do you know?
3. What do you need to do or have in order to be more effective?

### *Feedback*

1. What are your indicators that you are on target with being on purpose? How often do you get that information?

2. What are your indicators that you are effective in your role? How often do you get that information? From whom?
3. What information would you like to have regarding your work effectiveness?

*Commitment*

1. What is your current level of commitment to the work unit? The organization?
2. How effective is that current level of commitment? Why do you say that?
3. What do the work unit and the organization do to enhance your commitment? Get in the way of it?

Take time to reflect on your comments. What are the gaps? What steps do you need to take to diminish the gaps? Chapter Eight has useful hints on problem solving that may be helpful.

RESOURCE C

# 4Cs + 1 Workbook

*developed by*
Francis L. Ulschak
Sharon SnowAntle

*under the auspices of*
H. LEE MOFFITT
CANCER CENTER
& RESEARCH INSTITUTE
*at the University of South Florida*

Welcome to the 4Cs + 1 Workbook. This is a problem-solving workbook. By following along in the workbook, you will be able to follow a step-by-step procedure in problem solving. Please note: This is a guide. You may find yourself recycling parts of steps.

---

**I. CONTRACTING:** Goal is to define the research question and
identify the plan for action.

---

**A. Situation Description**

1. Describe the current situation. How do you know a problem exists?

   _____
   _____
   _____
   _____

2. How is the current situation a problem for you? How important is it?

   _____
   _____
   _____
   _____

3. For what other persons is the current situation a problem? How is
   it a problem for them?

   _____
   _____
   _____
   _____

4. Who needs to be involved in resolving the current problem?

   **Who**                    **Relation to Problem**

   _____              _____
   _____              _____
   _____              _____

5. How will the resolution of this problem be useful for you? For others?

   _____
   _____
   _____
   _____

6.  Identify one key indicator you can use to determine the success of your project. Use the chart below to graph that indicator.

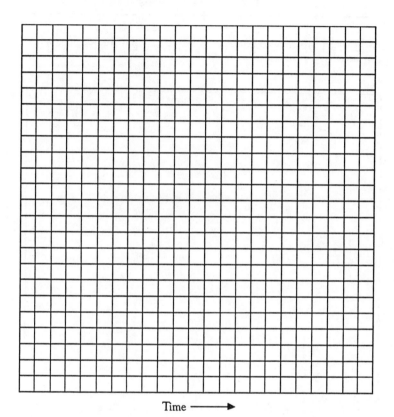

Time ⟶

B.  **Research Question**

Statement of problem as a research question:

_____

_____

_____

_____

II. CAUSATION: Goal is to identify "root cause" and to test
theory of cause.

A. Develop a high-level flowchart of the process you are studying. What
are the key parts of the process?

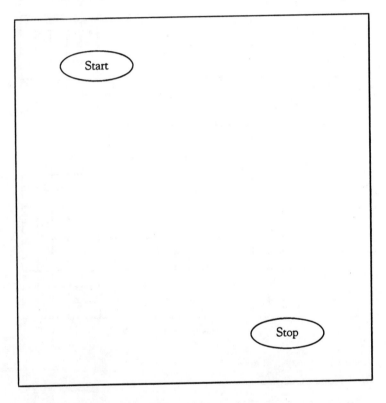

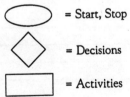 = Start, Stop

= Decisions

= Activities

B. What data do we need to collect to identify possible causes?

_____

_____

_____

_____

C. Develop a pareto chart

1. What are the "vital few"?

_____

_____

_____

2. Which of the "vital few" would you initially target? (Vital Few Target)

_____

_____

_____

D. Cause-and-effect thinking

    1. Using the cause-effect diagram, identify causes for the Vital Few Target (II. C. 2.).

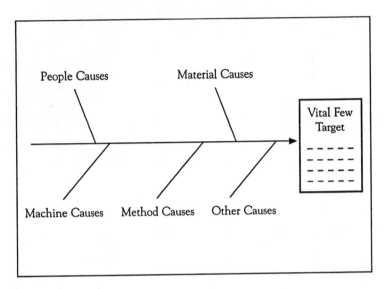

    2. Based on your analysis, what is your "theory of cause"—that is, the root cause?

_____

_____

    3. What is the one way to test that this is the "root cause"?

_____

_____

---

**III. CORRECTIVE ACTION:** Goal is to identify corrective action steps and implement them.

---

A. Given the "root cause," what possible corrective actions could be taken? List them below.

Root Cause

Possible corrective actions

1. _____
2. _____
3. _____
4. _____
5. _____

B. As you think about a corrective action, what criteria for correction do you need to keep in mind?

Key criteria

1. _____
2. _____
3. _____
4. _____

C. Decision matrix

List your possible corrective actions down the left side of the matrix. Across the top, list key criteria. Use a 1–5 scale.

(5=fully meets criteria; 1=does not meet criteria)

| Possible Corrective Actions | Criteria _____ | Criteria _____ | Criteria _____ | Criteria _____ |
|---|---|---|---|---|
| 1. | | | | |
| 2. | | | | |
| 3. | | | | |
| 4. | | | | |
| 5. | | | | |

D. Based on your analysis, what corrective action should be implemented?

_____

_____

_____

_____

E. For the corrective action to be taken, what are the key steps to take, who needs to take them, and when?

| What Steps? | Who? | When? |
|---|---|---|
|  |  |  |
|  |  |  |
|  |  |  |
|  |  |  |
|  |  |  |
|  |  |  |

---

**IV. CONTROL:** Goal is to maintain results from corrective actions.

---

A. What will we monitor?

_____

_____

B. When will we monitor?

_____

_____

C. Who will monitor and report back to us?

_____

_____

*Congratulations! You have taken a major step toward making the problem history.*

# References

Ackerman, L. (1985). *Managing complex change.* McLean, VA: Organizational Consulting.

Autry, J. (1991). *Love and profit: The art of caring relationships.* New York: William Morrow.

Beckhardt, R., & Harris, R. (1977). *Organizational transitions.* Reading, MA: Addison-Wesley.

Bennis, W., & Nanus, B. (1985). *Leaders: The strategies for making change.* New York: HarperCollins.

Berne, E. (1964). *Games people play.* Secaucus, NJ: Castle Books.

Blanchard, K., & Peale, N. V. (1988). *The power of ethical management.* Escondido, CA: Blanchard Training and Development.

Block, P. (1987). *The empowered manager: Positive political skills at work.* San Francisco: Jossey-Bass.

*Bridging the leadership gap in healthcare.* (1992, May/June) *Healthcare Forum.* Handout.

Buckley, W. (1968). *Modern systems research for the behavioral scientist.* Hawthorne, NY: Aldine.

Burns, J. McG. (1978). *Leadership.* New York: HarperCollins.

Campbell, J. (1988). *The power of myth.* New York: Doubleday.

Carnevale, A. P. (1983). *Human capital: A high yield corporate investment.* Washington, DC: American Society for Training and Development.

Churchman, C. W. (1968). *The systems approach.* New York: Delta Books.

Conger, J. A., Kanungo, R. N., & Associates. (1988). *Charismatic leadership: The elusive factor in organizational effectiveness.* San Francisco: Jossey-Bass.

Davis, K., Frederick, W., & Blomstrom, R. (1980). *Business and society*. New York: McGraw-Hill.

Deming, W. E. (1986). *Out of crisis*. Boston: MIT Center for Advanced Engineering Study.

Drucker, P. (1974). *Management*. New York: HarperCollins.

Egan, G. (1988). *Change agent skills*. San Diego, CA: University Associates.

Farr, J. (1984). Greensboro, NC: Farr Associates. Workshop handout.

Follett, M. P. (1970). The illusion of final authority. In E. Dale (Ed.), *Readings in management: Landmarks and new frontiers*. New York: McGraw-Hill.

Frankl, V. (1963). *Man's search for meaning*. New York: Washington Square Press.

Fritz, R. (1989). *The path of least resistance*. New York: Fawcett.

Fromm, E. (1973). *The anatomy of human destructiveness*. Troy, Mo.: Holt, Rinehart & Winston.

Goldberg, A., & Buttaro, R. (1990). *Hospital departmental profiles*. (3rd ed.) Chicago: American Hospital Publishing.

Goldberg, P. (1978). *Executive health*. New York: McGraw-Hill.

Greenleaf, R. (1973). *Leader as servant*. Cambridge, MA: Center for Applied Studies.

Grinder, J., & Bandler, R. (1975). *Structure of magic II*. Palo Alto, CA: Science and Behavior Books.

Healing Linn County. (1992). *Healing Healthcare*. Newsletter, pp. 5–6.

Herman, S., & Korenich, M. (1977). *Authentic management*. Reading, MA: Addison-Wesley.

Innovation Associates. (1988). *Leadership and mastery*. Framingham, MA: Author.

Johnson, C. (1986). *The creative imperative*. Berkeley, CA: Celestial Arts.

Johnson, R. (Speaker). (1989). *He: Understanding masculine psychology*. Los Angeles: Audio Renaissance Tapes.

Jones, J., & Bearley, W. (1986). *Organizational change*. Bryn Mawr, PA: Organizational Design and Development.

Jones, J., & Becker, D. (n.d.) *Principles of purpose*. Unpublished manuscript from Organizational Universe Systems, San Diego, CA.

Jones, J., & Kurtz, R. (1973). Confrontation: Types, conditions, and outcomes. In J. Jones & W. Pfeiffer (Eds.), *The 1973 annual handbook for group facilitators.* San Diego, CA: University Associates.

Lauderdale, M. (1982). *Burnout.* San Diego, CA: University Associates.

Lewin, K. (1935). *A dynamic theory of personality.* New York: McGraw-Hill.

Luft, J. (1984). *Group processes: An introduction to group dynamics.* Mountain View, CA: Mayfield.

Maehr, M., & Braskamp, L. (1986). *The motivation factor.* Lexington, MA: Lexington Books.

Marks, L. (1989). *Living with vision.* Indianapolis, IN: Knowledge Systems.

Marrow, A. (1969). *The practical theorist: The life and work of Kurt Lewin.* New York: Basic Books.

Maslow, A. (1954). *Motivation and personality.* New York: HarperCollins.

Mayo, E. (1970). Social growth and social disintegration. In E. Dale (Ed.), *Readings in management: Landmarks and new frontiers.* New York: McGraw-Hill.

Moore, R., & Gillette, D. (1990). *King, warrior, magician, lover.* San Francisco: HarperCollins.

Moore, T. (1992). *Care of the soul.* New York: HarperCollins.

Pareek, U. (1980). Dimensions of role efficacy. In J. Jones & W. Pfeiffer (Eds.), *The 1980 annual handbook for group facilitators.* San Diego, CA: University Associates.

Pascarella, P., & Frohman, M. A. (1989). *The purpose-driven organization: Unleashing the power of direction and commitment.* San Francisco: Jossey-Bass.

Paulson, P., Brown, S., & Wolfe, J. (1988). *Living on purpose.* New York: Fireside Books.

Pfeiffer, J. (1981). *Power in organizations.* Marshfield, MA: Pittman.

Phillips, E., & Cheston, R. (1979). Conflict resolution: What works? *California Management Review,* Summer, pp. 76–83.

Phillips, S., & Elledge, R. (1989). *Team building source book.* San Diego, CA: University Associates.

Reddy, W. B., & Jamison, K. (1988). *Team building blueprints for productivity and satisfaction.* Alexandria, VA: National Training Labs.

Reisman, J. (1979). *Anatomy of friendship.* New York: Irvington.

Schael, A. W., & Fassel, D. (1988). *The addictive organization.* San Francisco: HarperCollins.

Schein, E. (1985). *Organizational culture and leadership.* San Francisco: Jossey-Bass.

Scherer, J. (1975). In J. J. Sherwood & J. J. Scherer (Eds.), *A model for couples: How two can grow together.* Journal for Small Group Behavior, February, 1975.

Scholtes, P. (1989). *The team handbook.* Madison, WI: Joiner Associates.

Schutz, W. (1979). *Profound simplicity.* New York: Bantam Books.

Schutz, W. (1984). *The truth option.* Berkeley, CA: Ten Speed Press.

Senge, P. (1990). *The fifth discipline.* New York: Doubleday.

Taylor, F. (1967). *The principles of scientific management.* New York: Norton.

Thomas, L. (1984). *Late night thoughts on listening to Mahler's Ninth Symphony.* New York: Bantam Books.

Thomas, M., & Thomas, T. (1990). *Getting commitment at work.* Chapel Hill, NC.: Commitment Press.

Tillich, P. (1963). *The eternal now.* New York: Charles Scribner's Sons.

Twain, M. (1981). *The adventures of Tom Sawyer.* New York: Bantam Books. (Original work published 1876)

Ulschak, F. (1978). Letting the problem do the talking: A systems framework. *Transactional Analysis Journal, 8*(2), 148–153.

Ulschak, F. (1988a). *Creating the future of health and education.* Chicago: American Hospital Publishing.

Ulschak, F. (1988b). Your most important management tool? You! *OR Focus.* (Newsletter published by Baxter Healthcare, Chicago)

Ulschak, F. (1989). Corporate culture: The impact on productivity and performance. In M. McDougall, R. P. Cobert, & V. B. Matton (Eds.), *Productivity and performance management in health care institutions.* Chicago: American Hospital Publishing.

Ulschak, F., Nathanson, L., & Gillan, P. (1981). *Small group problem solving: An aid to organizational effectiveness.* Reading, MA: Addison-Wesley.

Ulschak, F., & SnowAntle, S. (1990). *Consultation skills for health care professionals: How to be an effective consultant within your organization.* San Francisco: Jossey-Bass.

Ulschak, F., & SnowAntle, S. (1992). *Managing employee turnover: A guide for healthcare executives.* Chicago: American Hospital Publishing.

Vaill, P. B. (1989). *Managing as a performing art: New ideas for a world of chaotic change.* San Francisco: Jossey-Bass.

Walton, R. E. (1969). *Interpersonal peacemaking-confrontations and third-party consultation.* Reading, MA: Addison-Wesley.

Weisbord, M. R. (1987). *Productive workplaces: Organizing and managing for dignity, meaning, and community.* San Francisco: Jossey-Bass.

Whyte, L. L., Wilson, A., & Wilson, D. (1969). *Hierarchical structures.* New York: American Elsevier.

Woodward, J. (1958). *Management and technology.* London: Her Majesty's Stationary.

Young, M. (1988). *Metronomic society: Natural rhythms and timetables.* Cambridge, MA: Harvard University Press.

# Index

## A

Accomplishment/competence
 needs, and commitment,
 173–174
Ackerman, L., 241, 245n
Alignment: and purpose, 14–15;
 in work units, 122–128
American Hospital Association,
 89
American Hospital Society, 287
American Society for Healthcare
 Education and Training, 287
Apple Computer, and playfulness,
 175
Autry, J., 87

## B

Bandler, R., 133–134
Barnes, G., 257n
Bearley, W., 27–28
Becker, D., 14
Beckhardt, R., 248–249
Behavior: model of, 132; and per-
 ceptions, 133–140; and pur-
 pose, 146–147
Bennis, W., 74–75, 180, 186
Berne, E., 207
Bethlehem Steel, 290–292
Black Elk, 151
Blanchard, K., 82
Block, P., 99

Blostrom, R., 80
Board of directors, and purpose,
 65–66
Braskamp, L., 105, 116
Brown, S., 144–145
Burns, J. M., 187, 189, 190,
 192–193, 195
Buttaro, R., 89

## C

Campbell, J., 131, 144
Caregivers: golden rules for,
 260–267; traps for, 256–260
Carnevale, A. P., 6–7
Causation: in problem solving,
 275–278; in workbook,
 310–312
Change: approaches to, 241–243;
 aspects of, 235–268; beliefs
 about, 237–240; of commitment, 177; conclusion on,
 267–268; and conflict, 215; of
 culture, 56, 60–61; and energy
 cycles, 249; as given, 238;
 guidelines for, 250–255; in
 health care organizations,
 235–236, 252–255; and leadership, 199–200; and management profile, 245; and OPO
 model, 246–247, 254, 260–267;
 and perceptions, 139–140;
 process of, 245–255; resistance

Drama triangle, roles in, 256–258
Drucker, P., 61, 77

# E

Egan, G., 19
Elledge, R., 18, 167
Employee agreements, and commitment, 119–120
Employees, new, commitment for,
118–121
Empowerment: and choice, 263;
and purpose, 15–16
Energy: from conflict, 207–208;
cycles of, and change, 249; and
truth telling, 261
Environment: of commitment, 38;
and leadership, 182–183,
188–189
Ethical issues: and commitment,
78–83; principles for, 82–83
Ethics, defined, 79

# F

Farr, J., 1, 4, 69
Fassel, D., 29
Fayol, H., 295–296
Feedback: aspects of, 23–26,
41–42; collecting points for,
76; disadvantages of, 25–26;
environments of, 38; and followers, 194; functions of, 25;
for individuals, 115, 162–169;
and leaders, 196; for organizations, 74–77; sources for,
113–114; suggestions for,
167–169; systems for, 75; in
work units, 111–116; in workbook, 302, 304, 305–306
Flowcharting, for work-unit roles,
108–109
Follett, M. P., 296–298
Followers, and leadership,
193–195, 198

Francis's Principle, and roles, 162
Frankl, V., 15, 33–34, 203
Frederick, W., 80
Fritz, R., 34–35, 205, 237, 254,
269
Frohman, M. A., 13, 16, 102

# G

Gap analysis, for problem solving,
269–281
Gidewell, J., 156n
Gilbreth, F., 292–293
Gilbreth, L., 292–293
Gillan, P., 231, 278
Gillette, D., 191
Goals and objectives, and purpose,
14
Goldberg, A., 89
Greenleaf, R., 63, 100
Grief model, and change, 240
Grinder, J., 133–134
Grofé, F., 211

# H

Harris, R., 248–249
Hawthorne experiment, 293–294
Headband exercise, and informal
roles, 20
Health care organizations: change
in, 235–236, 252–255; human
capital in, 8–10; interdependence in, 9–10; leadership
needs in, 199–201
Health needs, and commitment,
176
Herman, S., 153
Human capital, managing, 5–10

# I

Individuals: aspects of, 131–178;
background on, 131–133; commitment for, 169–177; conclu-

323

111–116; formal structures
of, 90–94; functional types of,
91–92; informal structures
of, 94–96; level of, 50–51,
89–90; matrix type of, 93; and
OPO model, 96–122; purpose of,

97–104; rationales for, 90–91;
roles of, 105–111; structures of,
90–96; workbook on, 303–305

## Y

Young, M., 23, 235